I0841252

The Psychology of Depression

DEVELOPMENTAL, ATTITUDINAL & LIFESTYLE FACTORS

G. A. MOHR, PhD

WORLD HONS MULT.
CEO, TRI
(TRANSWORLD RESEARCH & INNOVATION)

The Psychology of Depression

Developmental, Attitudinal & Lifestyle Factors

G. A. Mohr, PhD

World Hons Mult.
CEO, TRI
(Transworld Research & Innovation)

© G. A. Mohr 2018

All rights reserved. No part of this publication may be reproduced, stored in a retrieval system, or transmitted in any form or by any means, electronic, mechanical, photocopying, recording, or otherwise, without the prior written permission of both the author and publisher.

G. A. Mohr
The Psychology of Depression
Developmental, attitudinal & lifestyle factors

TRI

Transworld Research & Innovation
9 Hampstead Drive
Hoppers Crossing VIC 3029
AUSTRALIA

ALSO BY G. A. MOHR

Finite Elements for Solids, Fluids, and Optimization

A Microcomputer Introduction to the Finite Element Method

The Pretentious Persuaders:
A Brief History & Science of Mass Persuasion

Curing Cancer & Heart Disease,
Proven Ways to Combat Aging, Atherosclerosis & Cancer

The Variant Virus, Introducing Secret Agent Simon Sinclair

The Doomsday Calculation: The End Of The Human Race

The War of the Sexes: Women Are Getting On Top

Heart Disease, Cancer, & Ageing:
Proven Neutraceutical & Lifestyle Solutions

2045: A Remote Town Survives Global Holocaust

The History & Psychology of Human Conflict

Elementary Thinking for Modern Management

The 8-Week+ Program to Reverse Cardiovascular Disease

The Scientific MBA;   Mohr's Law of Hierarchies

The DIY Cardiovascular Cure,
A Comprehensive Program to Reverse Atherosclerosis

Combating Cancer, Proven Neutraceutical & Lifestyle Remedies

ALSO WITH R.S. MOHR/RICHARD SINCLAIR & P.E. MOHR/EDWIN FEAR

The Evolving Universe: Relativity, Redshift and Life from Space

World Religions: The History, Psychology, Issues & Truth

World War 3, When & How Will It End?

The Brainwashed, From Consumer Zombies to Islamic Jihad

Human Intelligence, Learning & Behaviour

New Theories of The Universe, Evolution, and Relativity

The Population Explosion

World Religions: From to Animism to Mohronism

Human Conflict: An Attitudinal Psychology Model

Brainwashed Zombies: Religious, Political & Consumer Persuasion

The Psychology of Hope;   The Psychology of Success

The Psychology of Life: A practical introduction to psychology

ALSO BY G. A. MOHR

Finite Elements for Solids, Fluids, and Optimization

A Microcomputer Introduction to the Finite Element Method

The Pretentious Persuaders:
A Brief History & Science of Mass Persuasion

Curing Cancer & Heart Disease,
Proven Ways to Combat Aging, Atherosclerosis & Cancer

The Variant Virus, Introducing Secret Agent Simon Sinclair

The Doomsday Calculation: The End Of The Human Race

The War of the Sexes: Women Are Getting On Top

Heart Disease, Cancer, & Ageing:
Proven Neutraceutical & Lifestyle Solutions

2045: A Remote Town Survives Global Holocaust

The History & Psychology of Human Conflict

Elementary Thinking for Modern Management

The 8-Week+ Program to Reverse Cardiovascular Disease

The Scientific MBA;   Mohr's Law of Hierarchies

The DIY Cardiovascular Cure,
A Comprehensive Program to Reverse Atherosclerosis

Combating Cancer, Proven Neutraceutical & Lifestyle Remedies

ALSO WITH R.S. MOHR/RICHARD SINCLAIR & P.E. MOHR/EDWIN FEAR

The Evolving Universe: Relativity, Redshift and Life from Space

World Religions: The History, Psychology, Issues & Truth

World War 3, When & How Will It End?

The Brainwashed, From Consumer Zombies to Islamic Jihad

Human Intelligence, Learning & Behaviour

New Theories of The Universe, Evolution, and Relativity

The Population Explosion

World Religions: From to Animism to Mohronism

Human Conflict: An Attitudinal Psychology Model

Brainwashed Zombies: Religious, Political & Consumer Persuasion

The Psychology of Hope;   The Psychology of Success

The Psychology of Life: A practical introduction to psychology

Contents

PREFACE

*The term clinical depression finds its way into too many
conversations these days. One has a sense that
a catastrophe has occurred in the psychic landscape.*
Leonard Cohen, *International Herald Tribune*, Paris, 4 Nov. 1988.

We are, strictly speaking, simply one of many kinds of animals, but what sets us apart from other species is the enlarged cerebral cortex required to store the semantic memory needed for our advanced and complex languages. Thus Part I, Childhood and Education, briefly discusses the evolution of the human brain, language and learning, how memories are stored, various stages of education, and 'Real IQ'.

Part II, Developing Attitudes and Habits, discusses the psychology of attitudes, how the media and advertising influence and persuade us, the psychology of habits, and the important of self-confidence and hope in life.

Two chapters are devoted to hope, self-confidence and optimism, and how these attributes can greatly improve our lives, and reduce both the likelihood of depression, and, should it occur, as it usually will at some point in life, how these attributes help one cope with depression.

Part III, Adult Life, discusses how we interact in the workplace, negative aspects of hierarchical organizations, finding a 'life partner', family, life, social life, and retirement and old age.

These subjects are, of course, relevant to depression, for example, being too low in a hierarchy, living alone, or having few friends and little or no social life often being major factors in people suffering from depression.

Part IV, Psychology and Psychiatry, discusses the most common mental illnesses, theories of personality, the psychology of sex, the psychology of conflict, and assessment and treatment of mental illnesses.

Two chapters are devoted solely to depression, the second of these to 'manic depression' or bipolar disorder.

Part V, Conclusions, discusses how we can improve our lives and plan for success and draws some bottom lines

Appendix A presents the Mohr Psychological Inventory (MPI), and Appendix B case studies of a few men and women with depression, and in some cases other mental health issues as well.

Finally, once again I am grateful to the publishers for yet again doing an excellent job of promptly publishing this book.

Geoff Mohr, Melbourne, 2018

PART I
CHILDHOOD

Chapter 1

THE HUMAN BRAIN

We must, however, acknowledge, as it seems to me,
that man with all his noble qualities . . . still bears in his bodily
frame the indelible stamp of his lowly origin.
Charles Darwin, *The Descent of Man* (1871), ch. 23.

Evolution of the human brain

Bacteria were the first organic life form on the planet. There are two theories as to how they first appeared:

(a) Nitrogenous rains formed the first organic compounds in warm vents at the bottom of the ocean, these developing into bacteria.

(b) Dormant bacteria came to the Earth on meteorites, springing to life in these warm vents. The author favours this theory in the recent book *The Evolving Universe* (Mohr, Sinclair & Fear, 2014, retitled 2nd edn 2018a).

Next plants developed in these hot springs, eventually making their way to the land. Around this time fungi developed, presumably from bacteria (there seems no other possibility), some scientists believing that bacteria can also transform into viruses (Cantwell, 1990).

Then bacteria merged somehow to form larger organisms in the sea, this process of evolution continuing to produce larger and larger creatures in the sea, brains developing in such creatures as fish to allow them to control their bodily functions.

Then the fins of some fish species developed in such a way as to allow them to move onto the land, beginning the evolution of land-based animals.

The remarkable process of evolution continued to allow birds to take to the air, their two-legged nature placing them on the same early branch of the tree of evolution as man.

With the evolution of apes came chimpanzees, with which we share 96% of the same genes and somewhat similar social and other behaviours such as that of alpha males and tribal conflicts.

Comparisons of blood proteins and the DNA of the African great apes with that of humans indicates that the line leading to modern people did not split off from that of chimpanzees and gorillas until comparatively late in evolution, perhaps 6 million to 8 million years ago.

Fossils of the first *hominines,* the *australopithecines*, have been discovered dating to 5 million years ago. This genus seems to have become extinct about 1.5 million years ago, but before doing so one of seven species of australopithecines, *Australopithecus africanus*, evolved into the genus *Homo* between 1.5 and 2 million years ago.

The earliest evidence of stone tools comes from sites in Africa dated to about 2.5 million years ago. These tools have not been found in association with a particular hominine species.

Around 1.7 to 1.9 million years ago two new species of large brained, small-toothed hominines emerged, *Homo ergaster* in Africa and *Homo erectus* in Asia. Later *H. erectus* skulls possess brain sizes in the range of 1100 to 1300 cc (67.1 to 79.3 cu in), within the size variation of *Homo sapiens*.

A number of archaeological sites dating from the time of *Homo erectus* reveal a greater sophistication in tool making than was found at the earlier sites. Evidence found at the cave site of "Peking Man" in northern China, suggests that *H. erectus* used fire.

The remains of the foundations of an oval structure built by a *Homo erectus* group were found at the Terra-Amata site in France, and within this structure there was a fireplace (Weiss & Mann, 1978).

The *Homo* species spread widely and by 350,000 years ago planned hunting, fire making, wearing of clothes, and probably burial rituals, were well established.

Between 200,000 and 300,000 years ago, *Homo sapiens* evolved.

The Neanderthals or *Homo sapiens neanderthalensis* had similar DNA to modern man and occupied parts of Europe and the Middle East as early as 120,000 years ago. They lived only in family groups, the men being hunter-gatherers to feed the family.

The Neanderthals left cave paintings which were an important evolutionary advance. These often depicted a simple activity, perhaps a precursor to the highly pictorial hieroglyphic script of the ancient Egyptians (Egerton Eastwick, 1896).

Though Neanderthals had 10% larger brains than modern man, there is some evidence that the part of the cerebral cortex devoted to language and thinking in modern man was underdeveloped in Neanderthal man, casting some doubt on whether Neanderthal man was capable of modern spoken language. Thought by some to be a different evolutionary branch, the Neanderthals disappeared from the fossil record about 30,000 years ago.

Differing in appearance, modern humans or *Homo sapiens sapiens* evolved in southern Africa or the Middle East perhaps 90,000 to 200,000 years ago and 70,000 years ago began to spread to all parts of the world, reaching Europe about 40,000 years ago, soon outnumbering, perhaps interbreeding with, and finally supplanting the local, earlier *Homo sapiens* populations.

Like chimpanzees, homo sapiens sapiens formed tribes and there is evidence of religion, recorded events and art dating from 30,000 to 40,000 years ago implying the advanced language and ethics required for the ordering of social groups.

The structure of the human brain

In the human brain the upper layer, the cerebrum, is the largest part of the brain and its external layer is called the cerebral cortex. The outer portion is grey because it contains billions of nerve cell bodies, and the inner portion is white from the tangle of axons coated in myelin sheaths.

The cerebral cortex makes up 76% of the human brain and provides the information processing necessary for language, reason and creative thought. It is the larger frontal cortex of man that gives him greater intelligence and far more complex language than other animals.

There are only two main types of cells in nerve tissue:

[1] The actual nerve cell is the neuron, the 'conducting' cell that transmits impulses and is the structural unit of the nervous system.

[2] Neuroglia, or glia for short, the word 'neuroglia' meaning 'nerve glue'. These are nonconductive and maintain homeostasis, form myelin, and provide support and protection for neurons in the central and peripheral nervous systems. Homeostasis is the metabolic equilibrium actively maintained by several complex biological mechanisms that operate via the autonomic nervous system to offset disrupting changes.

The human brain has circa 10 billion neurons and circa 50 trillion neuroglia. Each neuron has three basic parts: the cell body (soma), one or more dendrites, and a single axon. The soma is from 10 to 25 micrometres in diameter and is often not much larger than its nucleus.

Neurons are complex and very numerous, and are the core components of the brain and spinal cord of the central nervous system (CNS), and of the peripheral nervous system (PNS).

Dendrites branch many times into a complex 'dendritic tree' with thousands of 'spines'. An axon, also called a nerve fibre when myelinated, may branch hundreds of times. Axons and dendrites in the CNS are about one micrometer thick and sensory neurons can have axons that run from the toes to the posterior column of the spinal cord, or more than 1.5 metres in adults.

In the brain messages are transferred from the axon terminals of one neuron to the dendrites of another via connections called synapses, memories being stored in the dendritic spines.

Neuron structure and size varies considerably, for example unipolar neurons having a single 'tree' for the axon and dendrites, whereas multipolar neurons have several tree-like structures to accommodate the axon and numerous dendrites.

Neurons can also be classified by function:

(a) Afferent neurons or *sensory neurons* transmit information from tissues and organs to the CNS.
(b) Efferent neurons or *motor neurons* transmit signals from the CNS via nerve fibres to the effector cells of muscles or glands to stimulates contraction or secretion.
(c) Interneurons connect neurons in different regions of the CNS.

The nervous system

Figure 1.1 shows the structure of the nervous system (Sweeney, 2009). The central nervous system consists of the brain and the spinal cord and it interprets sensations and issues commands in the form of motor responses, which are based on current sensations, reflexes, and experiences.

The peripheral nervous system comprises the axons that branch from the spinal cord and carry nerve impulses to and from the brain.

The autonomic or 'involuntary' nervous system is based in the midbrain's pons and medulla and it regulates the functions essential for life, such as heart function and breathing.

The sympathetic branch puts the body on alert and supplies it with energy in response to fear or excitement. The parasympathetic branch relaxes the body, lowering heart rate, breathing rate, and blood pressure.

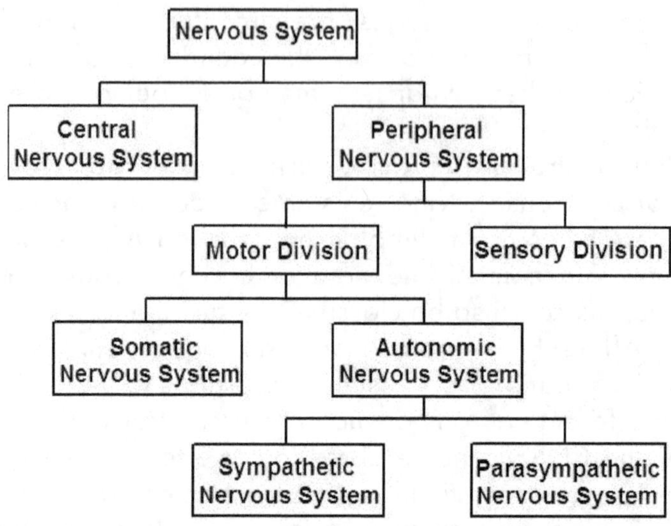

Figure 1.1. Divisions of the nervous system.
Each division is responsible for the collection of and
response to different stimuli.

Chemical effects

Neurons release neurotransmitters that bind to chemical receptors of which there are three types:
[1] Excitatory, causing an increase in firing rate.
[2] Inhibitory, causing a decrease in firing rate.
[3] Modulatory, causing long-term effects unrelated to firing rate.
Table 1.1 shows the key neurotransmitters, their location, and function.

The cell membrane of the axon and soma contain voltage-gated ion channels that allow neurons to generate and propagate an electrical signal or 'action potential'. These signals are generated and propagated by charge-carrying ions including sodium (Na^+), potassium (K^+), chloride (Cl^-), and calcium (Ca^{2+}). Several types of stimuli can activate a neuron by causing ion-specific channels to open, allowing ions to flow through the cell membrane and change its potential.

Table 1.1. Neurotransmitters.

Neurotransmitter	Location	Function
Acetylcholine	Nervous system parts associated with motion, including the brain's motor cortex	Makes muscles contract. Also plays a role in attention, memory, and sleep.
Dopamine	Brain and the peripheral nervous system	Body motion and reward experiences, including pleasure.
Endorphins	Brain, pituitary gland, and spinal cord	Powerful, natural opiates, that block pain
Gamma-aminobutyric acid (GABA)	Retina, spinal cord, hypothalamus, and cerebellum	Commonest neuro-transmitter – quiets neurons.
Glutamate	Brain and spinal cord	Activates cells for learning and memory.
Norepinephrine	Brain and peripheral nervous system	Regulates moods, blood pressure, heartbeat and arousal
Seretonin	Brain stem, cerebellum, pineal gland, and spinal cord	Crucial for sleep and appetite. Linked to depression and anxiety.

Thicker axons carry action potential more rapidly, many of them having myelin insulating sheaths to increase the efficiency and effectiveness of impulse transmission (Sweeney, 2009).

Conduction of nerve impulses in on an 'all or none' basis, that is, if a neuron responds at all, it must respond completely. Thus greater intensity of stimulation doesn't produce a stronger signal but can produce a higher frequency of firing.

Many drugs, besides pharmaceutical ones, affect the brain, for example (Sweeney, 2009):

[1] LSD "binds so tightly to serotonin receptors" that very small amounts greatly affect the brain, causing hallucinations and sometimes psychosis.

[2] Marijuana's active ingredient, delta-9-tetrahydro-cannabinol (THC) inhibits the release of glutamate and GABA, reducing communication between certain neural networks. In contrast, caffeine has the opposite effect, slightly raising cognitive function.

[3] Morphine affects the cerebral cortex without affecting the lower parts of the brain.

[4] Cocaine stimulates the whole brain, but particularly its emotional centres.

Storage capacity of the human brain

Each of circa 10 billion (10×10^9) neurons in the brain can have from 1,000 to 10,000 dendritic spines, so that, assuming 1,000 spines, there are about 10 trillion (10×10^{12}) spines. Assuming each spine can store 1 byte of information, the total brain capacity is 10 Terabytes (10×10^{12} bytes).

Because of the level of 'noise' in the brain, however, each bit of information must be stored redundantly in as many as 100 spines, so if the average 'redundancy' is 10 spines, the effective capacity of the brain is 100 Gigabytes (100×10^9 bytes).

The brain must have 'spare capacity', however, so that only part of the brain is used, so a conservative estimate of 'effective' brain capacity might be about 50 GB.

Note, however, that some estimates of the number of neurons in the brain are as high as 100 billion, giving an effective brain capacity of 500 GB.

This we might compare with a fairly good, but not top of the range, PC which today would have at least 5 GB of RAM (random access memory), and a hard disk storage capacity of at least 500 GB.

The number of neurons in the brain varies greatly between species, the nematode worm having only 302 neurons, whereas the fruit fly has circa 100,000 neurons.

As might be expected, some studies have found a correlation of 0.40 or more between brain size (measured by MRI or CAT) and IQ, the correlation being higher in adults than in children (Mackintosh, 2011).

It is generally assumed that the humans have evolved with relatively large brains in order to provide the large amount of semantic memory required for our advanced languages. Animals, of course, rely largely on 'visual memory', and one might expect that visual memory requires more storage capacity than language. We learn and remember language, however, in a largely visual fashion, thus recognizing both letters of the alphabet and words or 'word parts' in visual fashion, so that, indeed, a substantially larger brain is required for the semantic memory required to store language.

The memory system

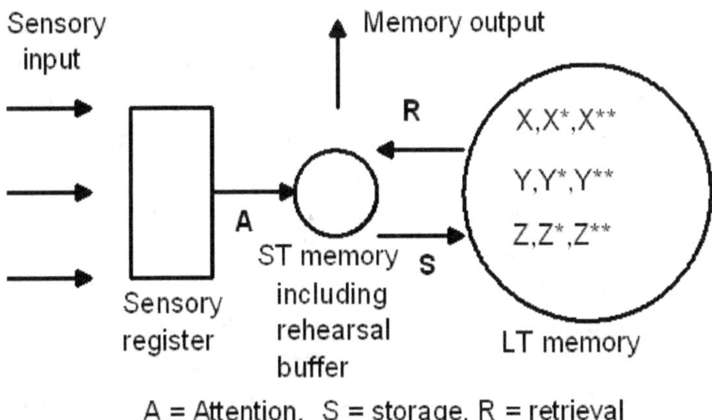

Figure 1.2. Information processing model of memory.

Figure 1.2 shows the multi-store or Atkinson-Shiffrin information processing model of memory (Atkinson & Shiffrin, 1968). In this, the *sensory register*, located in a part of the brain called the thalamus, processes information from sensory channels associated with vision, hearing and other senses.

The visual sensory register can hold 10 - 20 bits of information for only about 1 second, whereas the auditory sensory register can hold information for up to 4 or 5 seconds.

Of the up to 20 bits of information that our visual registers can accommodate with a brief glance, for example an array of letters of the alphabet, we can only remember four or five of them, this number being called the *span of apprehension.*

As a consequence most information in the sensory registers is lost but that to which sufficient attention is paid is transferred to the *short-term-memory* (STM), located in a part of the brain called the hippocampus. Here it is held for about 20 - 30 seconds and some of it is processed by being rehearsed in the *rehearsal buffer*, the rest being lost.

This model fits everyday life fairly well. For example, when somebody tells you a phone number and you are interrupted while dialing it you are likely to forget it because it will be lost from STM. This is because the STM holds only about 5 - 9 items and, under certain conditions, as few as two or three.

Sternberg (1998) conducted an experiment that illustrates how memory, in this case STM, works. He showed a group of people sets of from 1 to 6 digits and seconds later asked them if the set contained a particular digit. Response times were closely proportional to the number of digits shown, demonstrating that the coding of the set in STM was searched serially or one digit at a time.

In the rehearsal buffer such processes as repetition of the information link it to information already stored in memory and then pass it to *long-term-memory* (LTM) where it remains for periods of days up to a lifetime. In LTM information is *consolidated*, a process that may take from half an hour up to months. If consolidation is somehow interrupted some memory loss occurs.

An important part of the process of LTM processing is *long-term potentiation* (LTP) in which chemical 'dosing' strengthens neural connections.

Thus the strength of a memory depends upon the type or amount of attention paid to the stimuli. Attention to physical characteristics is encoded less than the sounds of words, whilst emotional content enhances encoding, sometimes leading to 'flashbulb' memories which may include minute details of extremely emotional moments.

Similarly, memories that in LTM that have recently been accessed are 'dosed' chemically so that they are easier to recall again in the near term, whereas memories that have not been accessed for a long time are difficult to recall, taking from a few minutes up to several hours to recall.

Most LTM information is stored in the cerebral cortex, the 'thinking' part of the brain which is much more developed in humans than in other species.

Simple passive repetition of information, or *maintenance rehearsal,* is not sufficient to ensure that items are passed to LTM. The active process of e*laborative rehearsal,* involving reorganization of the material and attaching meaning to it is more likely to pass information to LTM.

There are four types of LTM:

[1] *Procedural memory* or implicit memory is 'knowing how' to perform some skill, often learnt by procedural or implicit learning.

[2] *Declarative memory* is 'knowing that' or memory of data or facts and events.

[3] *Episodic memory* of prior life experiences is a type of declarative memory. 'Flashbulb' memories are clear episodic memories of unique and highly emotional events, an example being the movie footage of the 'twin towers' collapsing after the 9/11 attacks.

[4] *Semantic memory* such as words and language rules is another type of declarative memory which involves more 'preprocessing' in STM than episodic memory.

In such processing, even inherently organized material is *subjectively organized* by the learner into categories. Up to a point, it is found that the more categories used the better the material can be recalled.

Semantic memory uses *constructive processes* to store information in an organized manner, often into a hierarchical structure of categories and sub-categories.

Recall of the information then occurs by *reconstructive processes.* With these speed of recall depends upon the hierarchical level at which information is recalled, more general 'heading' information being recalled more rapidly than specific information.

Thus, when we have difficulty remembering a person's name, for example, we often can only remember one or more names similar in some respect such as their first letter and then finally remember the required name anything from seconds to days later.

Memory processing also makes much use of images and *concrete* images are easily formed for words like 'cat' whilst *abstract* images for words like 'mercy' are more difficult to form.

Australian aborigine elders, for example, remember centuries of tribal history by associating important events with environmental features and recall and pass on this history by 'walking through' these places.

Information stored in LTM is easier to recall if it is stored with *retrieval cues* which are associated with 'blocks' of information. Individual items within these blocks are then stored with 'tags'.

How easily information is recalled later depends much upon how well it has been associated with images, categorized and provided with cues.

An example of how images affect information recall from LTM occurs if witnesses who saw a speeding car crash are asked:

"How fast do you think the car was going when it _ _ _ _ _?"

with the final verb having such variations as *contacted, hit,* and *crashed.*

Speed estimates will increase in the order of these three verbs by as much as 25% because the new information in the wording of the question conflicts or *interferes* with the memory and associated images of the event in LTM.

Information that has been stored in a well-organized fashion can sometimes be recalled by *redintegration*, the process by which some event such as a 'leading question' unlocks a rapid sequence of memories that may be connected by a chain of associations.

This is the ideal situation when we read an exam question. One or more words in the question quickly trigger recall of a stream of relevant information. If the exam is the usual written answer one we tend to forget part of the answer before we can write it down.

Conclusion

Humans make a wide array of tools, we cook food, we build houses, roads and bridges, we heat and cool our buildings, we build ships, cars and aircraft, and man has walked on the moon. It is advanced language, in particular, that sets us apart from other animals and allows us to do these things, communicating our ideas to successive generations so that our knowledge and skills have advanced for many thousands of years. Language and learning, therefore, are discussed in the following chapter.

In the foregoing chapter the basic structure of the human brain was discussed, showing that our senses transfer and store information in the dendritic spines of the neurons, perhaps in the synapses at the ends of these spines.

It was estimated that our brain capacity was comparable to that of a modern PC, though some writers estimate human brain capacity to be an order greater than this, if not more.

☺☺☹☺☺☹☺☺☹☺☺☹☺☺☹

1. The Human Brain

Chapter 2

LANGUAGE AND LEARNING

> *Some people have argued that language is what makes the human species different from other species.*
> Roger Bell & Ralph Hall, *Impacts: Contemporary Issues & Global Problems*, The Jacaranda Press, Milton QLD, 1991.
>
> *Language is the autobiography of the human mind.*
> Friedrich Max Müller,
> Quoted in *Scholar Extraordinary* (Nirad Chaudhuri, 1974).

The development of language

Despite his larger brain size, there is some doubt whether Neanderthal man had developed language. Doubtless the roots of language lie in the 30 different vocal sounds made by vervet monkeys (Insight, 1982), no doubt related to *lallation* or meaningless mumbling in infants. Given some encouragement they are then ready to learn such 'baby talk' as

da da, ma ma, wee wee
gee gee, puff puff, bow wow

The messages in any language are built up from a small catalogue of elementary speech sounds which are combined to form words from which sentences are built up.

Generally, these words are *arbitrary* and do not sound like or have any other relationship with the things they represent but there are a few exceptions such as some of the words for animal noises, a phenomenon called *onomatopoeia* (using words that imitate the sound they denote).

Language involves a *duality of patterning* (Foss & Hakes, 1978) in which it relates two different forms of representation: an external *phonological system* for sound and an internal *semantic system* for meaning. These two systems are related by a language's *syntactic system.*

We understand a sentence spoken to us because our brain stores it temporarily in our short-term-memory (STM) and compares it to the word and language rules stored as *semantic memory* in our long-term-memory (LTM). If we *rehearse* the message in STM it may be stored in LTM.

How we understand language

The way in which text is remembered provides an insight into why key words are important in the memory process. It is believed that text is not stored in memory literally but as a number of *propositions*, each of which has a *relational term* for which there are *arguments* (using the latter word in the same way it is used in connection with mathematical functions, especially when they are used in computer programs).

The sentence "Tom hit Jack", for example, is remembered as

(HIT, TOM, JACK)

If later "Tom apologized for hitting Jack" this is stored as

((APOLOGIZE, TOM), (HIT, TOM, JACK))

with the simple proposition of the original memory embedded in a complex one. Here the 'strong' word HIT acts as a key word and it is linked directly to the word TOM in long-term memory.

There is no doubt that a deer can remember events such as, "Lion killed deer" as a visual memory stored in *episodic memory*. As a result the *declarative memory* 'danger' would be added to the neuron in LTM storing the image of a lion, or perhaps to a newly formed adjacent neuron.

Some clue to how humans developed language is found by observing that howler monkeys have massively developed larynxes and hyoid bones (the bone that supports the tongue) so that their spectacular howls can be heard for miles.

Somehow, somewhere, humans gradually evolved with the physical attributes required to produce a variety of sounds and began to associate these with objects, passing this knowledge on to following generations.

As noted in the penultimate section of the present chapter, Krech's remarkable environmental enrichment experiments with rats demonstrated vividly that the gradually growth in the development of human language was undoubtedly largely responsible for the evolution of the large cerebral cortex that distinguishes modern man from other species.

The spread of language

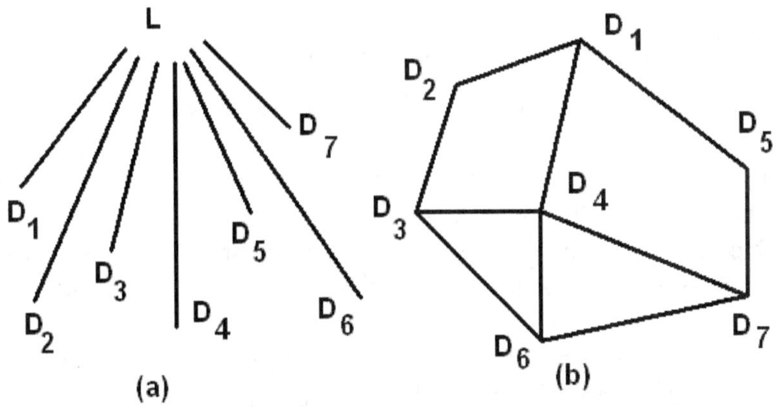

Figure 2.1. Language and dialects: (a) according to the notion of pure language; (b) a more accurate representation.

Somehow language spread with the migration of early humans, perhaps during the Agricultural Revolution, so that some languages have similar words, for example for father:

pater (Latin), *padre* (Italian), *pere* (French)
vater (German), *father* (English)

Just as European languages are rooted in Greek and Latin, oriental languages have roots in ancient Chinese and languages in the Middle East have roots in the ancient Babylonian and Egyptian languages.

There are now, of course, many languages and many more dialects. As a rule of thumb, two people speak the same language if they are mutually intelligible. Two exceptions are the Chinese dialects Mandarin and Cantonese which are not mutually intelligible. Another is that Norwegians can usually be understood by Swedes.

Language, however, is not a 'pure' thing such that any variation from it is impure or substandard, as depicted in Fig. 2.1(a). From the point of view of modern linguistics Fig. 2.1(b) is the more nearly correct picture and it avoids linguistic chauvinism, a notion that has often led to one group of people trying to impose their language on another. This view also corresponds to way in which language spread globally.

Language development in infants

At birth the human brain is relatively large compared to the body. Almost all the neural cells that will ever be available are present but only a basic network of the *axons* and *dendrites* that connect *neurons* together exists. At the outset these connections develop as the infant learns basic perception and motor skills, the long *axons* that extend from the brain cells then receiving signals from *receptor cells,* such as the small hair cells in the inner ear, or sending signals to *effector cells* in the muscles.

This development in the bulk of the brain parallels that in all animal species and is that necessary for basic functioning and survival.

What sets humans apart, however, is the considerable development of the *cerebral cortex*, the envelope of brain cells that covers the brain. This is where our thinking and storage of abstract memory information such as language occurs.

Development of the articulatory mechanisms required for controlled speech and the cortical mechanisms that control them is a slow maturational process that occurs in *Broca's area* of the frontal cortex. It has been suggested that babbling, however, is a sub cortical process.

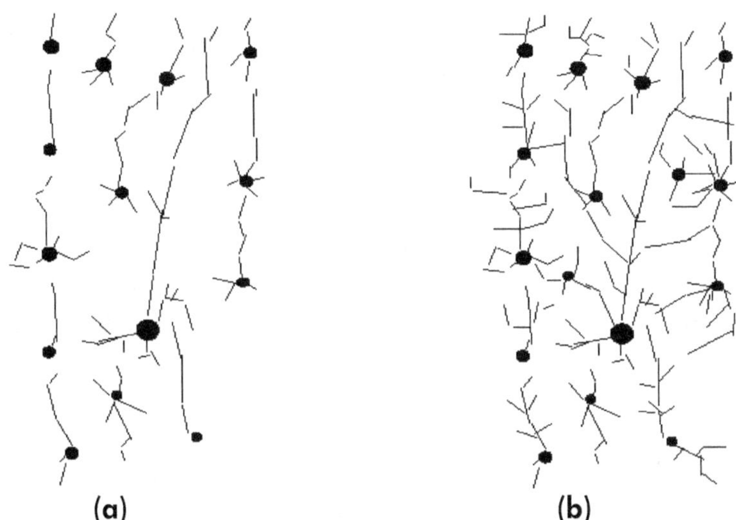

Figure 2.2. Postnatal development of the human cerebral cortex around Broca's Area (language related): (a) newborn; (b) 1 month.

Semantic memory of language is stored in *Wernicke's area* of the temporal lobe of the cerebral cortex.

Figure 2.2(a) shows a small part of the cerebral cortex of a newborn child in which long *axons* extend from the neurons and form branches. Fine *terminal arbors* at the end of these branches connect at *synapses* to the short *dendrites* surrounding other neurons. Figure 2.2(b) shows considerably more dendrites and branching of the axons at the age of one month (Foss & Hakes, 1978). At the age of 24 months the neural network is a good deal denser.

The network continues to develop in following years and the neurons, while not increasing in number, do increase in size.

In addition, the motor nerve pathways that control such activities as speech production must gradually develop sheaths of the protein *myelin* that prevent 'short-circuiting' of impulses between nerve tracts.

As a result of this gradual brain development each human characteristic is developed at a different rate.

Eye coordination, for example, develops much more rapidly than speech. Nevertheless, for the first few months the infant may smile at any moving object such as a dummy head whereas later it may be upset by the faces of strangers.

Packard (1978) cites an example of the importance of timing in which two Harvard researchers studied the way kittens learnt to recognize shapes and patterns, a physiological ability that develops in the fourth week. If the kittens were blindfolded for this week they effectively became blind for life. Thus there appear to be periods when the infant's brain is highly receptive so that it is easiest to change a child's intelligence for better or worse before the age of four.

Imprinting

Imprinting is an important part of the early learning process in higher animals that plays a significant part in brain development.

Konrad Lorentz, an Austrian ethologist, demonstrated this by being the first moving object seen by ducklings after hatching. He waddled in a squatting position and quacked and soon the ducklings assumed him to be their mother and followed him about and flew to him when he quacked.

In other famous experiments baby monkeys have been persuaded to accept a foam-rubber dummy monkey complete with feeding bottle as their mother and kittens have been imprinted to accept as fellow kittens rats placed in their cage.

It has been suggested that the most critical period for imprinting in humans is from six weeks to six months and in this period the human infant develops attachments, particularly to its mother.

As the experiment of blindfolding four week-old kittens demonstrated, neural links in the brain close at certain ages for every function. Similarly, it is difficult to become a top musician if you start late.

Imprinting occurs, at least to some extent, in the learning of languages, so that becoming truly bilingual gets more difficult as one gets older. When older it is well nigh impossible to master a second language with the same ease, fluency and accent as the first.

Much of our language learning is stored as *semantic memory*, one of four basic long-term-memory types discussed earlier in this chapter. Semantic memory is very stable so that the meanings of words or the rules for their use may never be forgotten.

Some experiments have shown that semantic memory stores information in logical hierarchies which go from general categories to specific ones, so that clusters of words with related meanings are stored in the same location in the brain.

Much of this stable memory base for language and other knowledge is founded by imprinting at a very early age and it is important to take advantage of this in educating young children.

Modeling

According to some experts the critical period in a child's intellectual, social and emotional development is between eight and eighteen months.

During this period, in particular, much of a child's learning is by *modeling* or *imitative learning,* also referred to as *learning by observation.*

It is desirable, therefore, for parents and others to use controlled modeling with infants in order to give them a head start in learning language and other skills.

After only four weeks babies begin to mimic the mother's mouth movements in speech and babbling begins at about two months, followed by laughter at about three months.

At six months *lallation* begins, that is, the baby utters repeated sounds such as 'ma ma' or 'ba ba'. At 10 months the baby begins to try to copy sounds made by the parents and by the end of the first year it may have learnt one or two real words.

In the first years much of the effort in training children is directed at development of survival skills such as eating, learning to walk and potty training. Modeling plays an important part in this, for example in the process of learning to walk, where the infant has had plenty of opportunity to watch the actions of adults.

Learning in a child's first year could be much advanced, therefore, by conscious and careful use of modeling, that is, demonstration of skills to be developed such as development of effective and clear speech.

In these early efforts use could be made of pictures and objects with which to associate the baby's first word efforts, for example the mother pointing to herself when vocalizing ma-ma.

Much of the time we also instinctively use *conditioning*, that is, repetitive presentation of items associated with simple skills to be learnt, often followed by praise when satisfactory progress is made.

At this early stage the cot can become the infant's first learning centre and objects that might be helpful to its learning can be placed within the infant's field of view, for example a picture of a dog in order to teach the word 'bow-wow'.

Here advantage might usefully be made of a TV set to play tapes or DVDs of simple movies, for example involving objects the words for which are to be learnt, perhaps including the numbers 1 to 4.

Demonstrating the possibilities for abstract learning at an early age, chimpanzees have been found better able to recognize the symbols for the numbers 1 to 4 than groups of objects up to four in number.

The important point, however, is that a good deal of patience is needed in the education process, particularly at the outset. Time is taken for memories to develop and fix and it is perhaps best to be a month or two ahead of the child's expected capabilities in trying to inculcate knowledge and skills for, as we all know, in later life it can be years after getting a certain idea that we actually get around to acting on it.

What is certain, however, that the sooner a mother begins to talk to her baby the better and, to a lesser extent perhaps, the same no doubt applies to many other areas of early learning.

Group modeling

At around the third month the baby recognizes the mother and smiles at her. Before this point it will be amused by many objects, including strangers, but now attachments have been formed by imprinting and it may be upset by strangers.

Within the first year, therefore, it would make good sense to involve the infant in *play groups* involving small groups of mothers and infants. In these early efforts at group activities can be attempted and the child can begin its social development.

Packard (1978) raised the interesting possibility of the use of professional people to teach by modeling.

These people would be trained to know the periods during which learning of various areas of knowledge areas can best be commenced and in how best to use modeling techniques to initiate that learning. Such people would then visit the home or attend play group sessions.

Packard cited an experiment with a form of group modeling was undertaken at New York Medical College. This began with twenty pairs of mothers and babies when the babies were only four weeks old and lasted three years at the end of which the children were compared with those of a control group. The children in the experimental group were a good deal more advanced in language and other skills than the control group.

Indeed, some experts doubt the competence of the modern family for child rearing and believe that more professional efforts are essential to help develop emotional stability and intellectual development in infants.

Vocabulary growth in early childhood

When children reach the age of one the pace at which learning can take place greatly increases.

Much of what has already been learnt will have been learnt by modeling, for example the ability for form words. Other skills like that of standing upright and then walking will have been learnt in part by conditioning and the associated reinforcement of praise as progress towards the objective is made.

Now learning can be accomplished with a host of aids such as pictures, simple books and educational toys.

In addition, more formal processes such as those of rote learning of words can be used. At the outset the words to be learnt should carefully chosen, for example objects within the child's everyday environment to allow associative processes to help fix the words in long term semantic memory.

By this formative age the child has been out and about a good deal and optimistic attempts have been made to teach it many words of which it will have learnt only a few.

Table 2.1. Words learnt with age.

Age (years)	Words learnt
1	3-5
1.25	15
1.5	25
1.75	100
2	250
2.5	450
3	900
4	1550
4.5	1900
5	2100
5.5	2300
6	2550

As shown in Table 2.1, however, word learning occurs at a quite rapid rate from here on, to the point at which a basic command of language has been obtained at age five.

Whilst the first year is instrumental in learning to begin to talk, in the second year a comparatively massive growth in vocabulary occurs. Thereafter the rate of increase is approximately linear but slows down as the child comes to grip with a widening range of subjects at school.

By the time they have learnt to read a little, however, children are able to learn things by *cognitive* learning which *processes* and stores *abstract* information.

Latent learning occurs when subjects are exposed to a body of information, rather than in small parts, and they then apply that information later on, perhaps in a test.

A laboratory example of this is that an experimental group of rats allowed to roam a maze will then do better in learning to get through it for a reward than a control group with no prior experience of the maze.

At school children are taught by presenting them with visual and verbal information to learn subjects in discrete 'blocks'. Here cognitive and latent learning occur and revision exercises and tests are used to reinforce and correct their knowledge.

The effect of environment

Modern man is distinguished from other creatures by having a larger cerebral cortex, the centre for our thinking and language. This larger cortex must have evolved by the adaptive processes inherent in Darwin's theory of natural selection.

Clues to just how this occurred were given by the work of social psychologist David Krech and his group at UC Berkeley (Packard, 1978).

In this they provided a group of rats with an "enriched environment" of large cages with various things rats enjoy such as slides, wheels and the like. Then a maze with a sugar reward at the end was added. This had a dark and a lighted alley and the rats soon learnt which led to the sugar.

Then the maze lighting was reversed regularly so that the rats had to relearn the 'sugar route'.

A second control group of rats lived normally and a third group was kept in a deprived dark and noiseless area.

After 90 days it was found that the 'enriched' rats had developed thicker cerebral cortexes.

This was perhaps the first evidence that the brain is modified by experience. The enrichment conditions caused the following changes (Atrens & Curthoys, 1982):

[1] The size of the cerebral cortex was increased.

[2] The size of the cortical neurons increased.

[3] The size and number of synaptic contacts increased.

[4] The quantity of acetylcholinesterase, the compound responsible for breakdown of the neurotransmitter acetylcholine, increased.

Therefore, the rats which had experienced environmental enrichment were apparently anatomically and biochemically superior to those which had endured a deprived environment.

This result provided laboratory evidence that environmental enrichment could physically and chemically alter the brain. This ability of neural tissue to change because of its activation is called *plasticity.*

It seems likely, therefore, that as early man discovered fire, began to make tools and advanced in many other ways his brain gradually evolved into that of *Homo sapiens sapiens* or

Conditioning

Much early learning occurs by:

(a) Imprinting, that is selection of a person to imitate.

(b) Imitative learning, that is, imitation of others.

Parents and teachers also use a good deal of *conditioning,* that is, repetitive presentation of information to be learnt, accompanied by occasional doses of positive and negative reinforcement. Conditioning, therefore, is discussed in more detail in the next chapter.

☺☻☹☺☻☹☺☻☹☺☻☹☺☻☹

Chapter 3

CONDITIONING AND MEMORY

You are told a lot about your education, but some beautiful, sacred memory, preserved since childhood, is perhaps the best education of all. If a man carries many such memories into life with him, he is saved for the rest of his days. And even if only one good memory is left in our hearts, it may also be the instrument of our salvation one day.
Feodor Dostoyevsky (1821–81), Alyosha Karamazov,
in The Brothers Karamazov, vol. 2, "Epilogue" (1880).

Introduction

The preceding chapter dealt briefly with modeling which plays a crucial part in the early learning of infants. Mention was also made of how we also instinctively use *conditioning*, for example repetitive presentation of items associated with simple skills to be learnt, often followed by praise when satisfactory progress is made.

Conditioning is a fundamental learning process but it also has applications in psychotherapy, for example behaviour modification using *aversion therapy,* and thence more sinister ones in 'brainwashing' prisoners of war or crime suspects to obtain information from them or to make them 'switch sides'.

In the modern era, however, it is more relevant to everyday life than ever as conditioning is used to some extent in advertising to repetitively expose people to a brand name. They quickly develop recognition of the brand and, before long, some degree of acceptance, if not approval.

Much of the excessively long and drawn out education process is also conditioning for obedience and routine. Military training, of course, is one of the more extreme examples of conditioning.

Some understanding of the mechanics of conditioning is therefore well worthwhile in an age when we are confronted with it almost at every turn.

Classical conditioning

Classical conditioning, or learning by association, was first demonstrated by Ivan Pavlov's celebrated experiments with dogs in the 1890s.

In these he noted that a caged dog's mouth salivated when it saw food on a pan swung within its reach. Here the food is the *uncontrolled stimulus* (US) and salivation is the dog's *uncontrolled reaction* (UR)

Next, a bell was rung shortly before presentation of the food and the dog's saliva collected in a cup to measure the amount. Here the bell is the *controlled stimulus* (CS).

It was found that the after a few repetitions of the paired stimuli of bell and food the dog would begin to salivate with the ringing of the bell alone, this being the *controlled reaction* (CR).

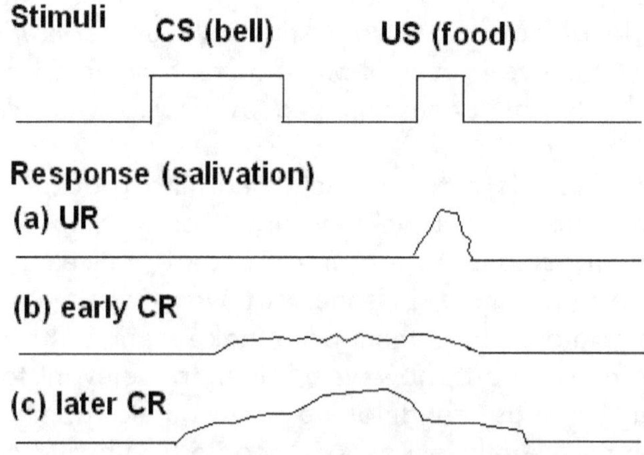

Figure 3.1. Pavlov's classical conditioning experiment:
(a) Bell precedes food presentation.
(b) Bell the only stimulus.
(c) US resumed temporarily - then only CS giving result shown.

Similar results can be obtained with almost any stimulus that consistently evokes a reflex response such as electrical shock.

For example, a dog or a human given a mild shock to a leg will quickly withdraw the leg.

If the electrode giving the shocks is attached to the leg, on the other hand, flexion of the leg will occur in response to shock, the US. Then when a prior conditioned or 'neutral' stimulus is given as warning conditioned response is developed and remains after the US is removed.

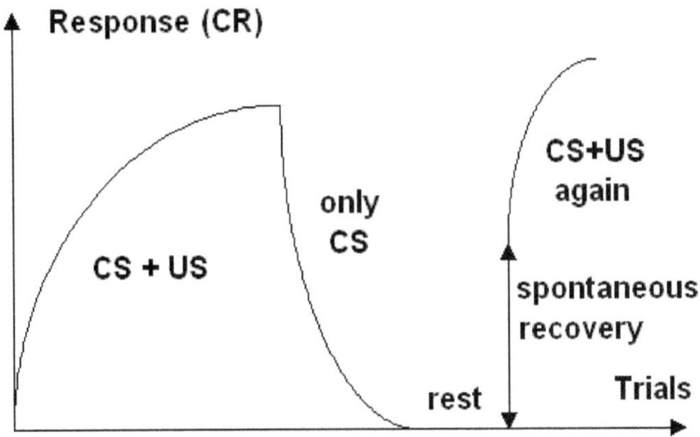

Figure 3.2. Conditioning, extinction and recovery.

After many trials the results can be graphed as a *learning curve.* Typically this takes the form shown in Figure 3.2 where the curve gradually flattens as the number of trials increases.

Here the US and CS remain paired. If the US is removed, however, *extinction* occurs and the response (the CR) decreases. Then, if the US is again added after the CS, the response recovers, the initial amount of response being called the *spontaneous recovery.*

Advertising often uses classical conditioning by repeatedly associating a product with positive ideas and images, thereby encouraging people to have positive feelings towards the product itself.

Operant conditioning

Operant conditioning, or learning by consequences, is characterized by the use of *reinforcement* which encourages a response in which the subject *operates* in some way, rather than just exhibiting a passive reflex response as in classical conditioning.

The classical experiments in operant conditioning were conducted in the 1940s by Skinner, a Harvard psychologist. In these he placed a rat in a box in which there was a lever that delivered food to it when pressed.

Initially the lever was operated from outside and soon the rat learnt the association between seeing the lever move and the appearance of food.

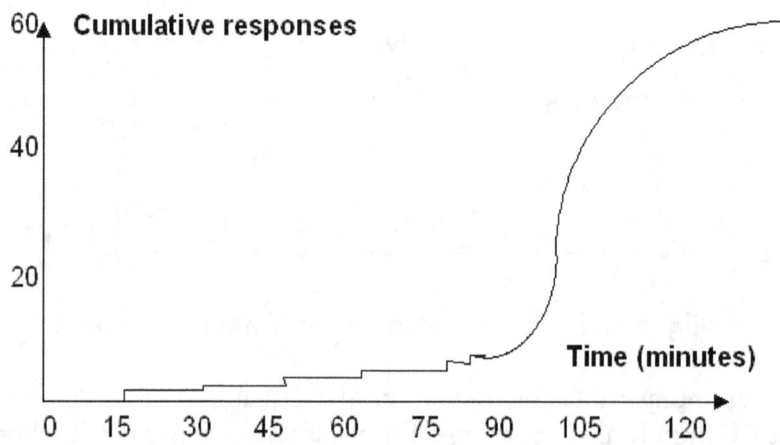

Figure 3.3. Operant conditioning responses by rat in Skinner Box. First response at 15 minutes, second at 30, third at 45, but after 75 minutes the rate of response becomes high.

After a while it operated the lever itself to obtain food and continued to do so with increasing frequency as it became more familiar with the routine, as shown in Figure 3.3.

In the result of Figure 3.3 the rat in the 'Skinner Box', as it came to be called, took 15 minutes to successfully operate the feed lever.

Four more intervals of about 15 minutes occurred before following operations when, the rat having fully learnt the procedure, the rate of operation accelerated markedly.

We instinctively use operant conditioning in bringing up children, the reinforcement to encourage desired actions being smiles and vocal approval.

Note that the timing of reinforcement is important. In a Skinner box, for example, the greater the time delay between the rat pressing the lever and the delivery of the food the longer it will take the rat to associate the two events and thus learn the feeding operation.

As with classical conditioning, *extinction* occurs when reinforcement ceases. This 'unlearning' process may be stronger still when *negative reinforcement*, typically some form of punishment in the educational context, is used.

Conditioned physical responses may be accompanied by emotional feelings or responses and many of our feelings are developed by conditioning.

In the case of classical conditioning *conditioned emotional responses* (CERs) may develop. Indeed, our feelings about many people and other things in our lives develop in this kind of way.

Advertising is also a case in point where an ad reminds us of a familiar product, evoking feelings of recognition and approval whilst the implications for education are all too obvious.

Generalization and discrimination

When alternative conditioned or 'signal' stimuli are used in classical conditioning the subject may learn to *discriminate* between them and respond more strongly to one than the other.

In Pavlov's classical experiments, for example, he found that dogs also responded to a buzzer as a CS instead of a bell, but less strongly.

This is called *generalization* and the more similar the alternative CS the better the response. Sometimes, however, the conditioned responses occur when a new but similar CS is used that has never been paired with the US previously.

In this way a child can develop a fear of dogs after being bitten by a black dog. It may then generalize that fear into a phobia about other harmless black objects.

When two stimuli are used but pairing of the US or 'reward' is not maintained with the second stimulus the subject develops *discrimination* and begins to learn to ignore the second stimulus.

Behaviour shaping

In operant conditioning *shaping* can be used to speed up the process. In Skinner's rat experiment, for example, shaping might begin by remote operation of the 'food lever' only when the rat gets close to it, gradually decreasing the distance of the rat from the lever before the lever is operated.

Then the lever is only operated when the rat touches the lever. Next the lever is only operated when the rat attempts to depress it.

Thus behaviour shaping involves reinforcing *successive approximations* to the desired behaviour pattern.

In this way conditioning can be accelerated and quite complex patterns of behaviour can be taught, a familiar example being circus bears that have been taught to ride bicycles in this way (Lindzey, Hall, & Thompson, 1978).

Packard (1978) reported that up to 20% of teachers in the eastern USA were systematically using behaviour modification techniques that involved systematic use of rewards and punishments in their classrooms.

Two teachers in Montana went too far by extending the 'Skinner box' idea to a four-foot high box for miscreant students. It had no lighting and no ventilation other than two small holes for observation. The relatives of a retarded child that had been locked in this box complained and the teachers were sacked.

A better example of 'behavior-shaping' was tested by University of Kansas researchers. They had the teacher divide the class into two teams, and the team which incurred fewer violations of several rules for good class behaviour was given various rewards. The researchers reported good results.

Objections to such applications of behaviour shaping are that they focused on restricting behaviours such as talking in class whereas advocates of 'open' classrooms encourage a freer learning environment.

The advent of the PC in schools, however, has brought a highly mechanized learning process, some aspects of which progressive educators are pleased with.

With the use of appropriate teaching software, PCs become a 'teaching machine' with which students can learn at their own pace and receive instant reinforcement for correct answers.

Reinforcement schedules

To this point we have assumed reinforcement, when used, was applied on a continuous basis, that is, after each response.

In operant conditioning reinforcement can also be made according to some fixed schedule. Examples include:

[1] The *fixed-ratio schedule* gives reinforcement after a certain number of responses.

[2] The *fixed-interval schedule* where reinforcement is given after a fixed interval of time, regardless of how many responses are made.

[3] In *variable-ratio* schedules reinforcement might come, for example, after three, then six responses, then three again. Similarly *variable-interval schedules* vary the time intervals between reinforcement.

Another obvious alternative is *random interval reinforcement,* that is, choosing an average interval and multiplying it by a random number between 0 and 1 produced by successive applications of a random number generator such as the RND( ) function of BASIC and other computer programming languages.

As might be expected, extinction is slower after cessation of scheduled reinforcements. This is the situation in human life where, for example, parents can only occasionally reward or punish a child's behaviour.

The result is that we may continue doing things we were shaped to do early in life long after reinforcement has ceased.

Primary and secondary reinforcement

A primary reinforcer, or unconditioned reinforcer, is effective for an untrained subject, for example food as a positive reinforcer or electric shock as a negative reinforcer.

A secondary reinforcer, or conditioned reinforcer, must be learnt by being paired with a primary reinforcer.

In a Skinner box, for example, a gong could be sounded every time the primary reinforcement of food was obtained. As in classical conditioning, the subject would associate the gong with the food and soon it would become an effective secondary reinforcer.

A better example occurs in child rearing where parents typically reward children for good behaviour with food treats or presents as primary reinforcers, accompanied by praise as secondary reinforcement. Ultimately the secondary reinforcement of praise may become the most frequently used and important form of reinforcement.

Contiguity of reinforcement, that is the time interval, is also important. The smaller the interval in time between the two reinforcements to be associated, the sooner the secondary reinforcement is learnt.

Understanding the workings of the brain

The role of chemicals

An example of the power of conditioning is cited by Packard (1978). This came about from experiments with flatworms whose brains have only about 400 cells. The worms were conditioned to "scrunch up" when seeing a light go on when this was followed by electrical shocks. It was found that when the worms were cut in half, or even several pieces, the pieces regenerated brains that remembered the conditioning.

Similar results were then obtained with various species of vertebrates.

Even more startling was the 'memory transferability' achieved by making soup of the brains of rats conditioned to shun darkness and feeding it to hamsters. The injected hamsters soon began to shun darkness!

This led before too long to the suggestion that students should eat their professors!

Later Georges Ungar and coworkers detected a peptide compound ¶ in the brain of a conditioned rat that caused it to avoid darkness.

[¶ Peptides link chains of up to thousands of amino acid molecules to form *polypeptides*. Proteins are naturally occurring polypeptides].

They pooled the brains of 4000 rats to obtain a sample of this compound large enough for analysis and synthesis of the compound (Ungar et al., 1972).

Subsequently Ungar's group reported discovering several other brain peptides that seemed to transfer learning from one animal to another (Jonas, 1974).

The role of electricity

That electrical stimuli in the brain play an important part, however, was demonstrated graphically by Jose Delgado by rigging a bull for radio-triggered mild electrical stimulation of a part of its brain (Delgado, 1971). He then stood in front of the animal. When it charged the tiny electrode in its brain was triggered and the bull stopped. After triggering the stimulation several times the bull was so pacified that it allowed witnesses of the experiment into the ring without charging them.

In humans electrodes implanted in the brain have been found to cause recall of long forgotten memories.

It has been found that the speed of conduction of impulses or *action potentials* in nerves is approximately proportional to the square root of the fibre diameter, a result familiar in cable theory (Schmidt-Nielsen, 1979). In myelin coated axons, however, the conduction speed is approximately proportional to the fibre diameter.

The 'strength' of memories

Memory storage is sometimes so effective and indelible that sometimes we can't forget things we would like to such as bad habits.

Sometimes *motivated forgetting* suppresses memories of traumatic experiences but this generally occurs subconsciously and we are not able to control the repression process at will.

One clue is that when we do consciously forget certain things we quickly dismiss them from our thoughts as soon as they enter them. When happier thoughts cross our minds, on the other hand, they may linger a little longer and almost involve a euphoria comparable to that which might be induced by small doses of tranquilizers like alcohol.

In other words we use processes like elaborative rehearsal to 'tag' memories with appropriate emphasis as important, good, bad and so on.

It is also clear that we have different 'layers' of memory so that past memories are in 'background memory' and take from seconds to days to recall.

Presumably items in foreground memory are chemically tagged and, over time, the pathways and neurons that store them become depleted in these markers.

Supporting this view, research in Sweden found changes in RNA in rat's brains compared to those of a control group after they had been given a learning task.

Such work clearly demonstrates that, just as DNA stores genetic coding, macromolecules of RNA play an important role in memory processes.

Effect of experience

The environment enrichment experiments with rats of Krech's group at Berkeley were mentioned in Chapter 2. These were perhaps the first physical evidence that the brain is modified by experience.

Memory structure

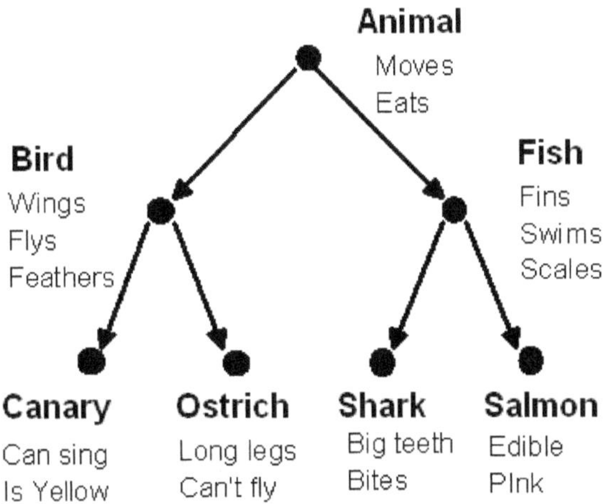

Figure 3.4. Hierarchical organization of the mental lexicon.

Figure 3.4 shows a proposed structure in which the brain stores information about animals as categories and sub-categories with properties attached to each 'node' in the structure (Collins et al., 1969).

Some experimental results do not fit this model, for example Ripps et al. (1973) found that people were quicker to agree to the truth of the statement: *A cat is an animal* than they were to the truth of the statement: *A cat is a mammal.* They argued that MAMMAL should be closer to CAT than ANIMAL in the hierarchy.

More important, however, is that the word ANIMAL is much more frequently used than the word MAMMAL and frequency of reference to a memory certainly does enhance the speed of recall.

The present author would also argue that the brain almost certainly must store memories in a *precedence network* based on the order in which learning occurs.

In such a network a memory search that succeeds in finding a 'connection' or *common* property shared by a 'new' item in short term memory and an item in long-term memory might then store the data on the new item in the same physical area.

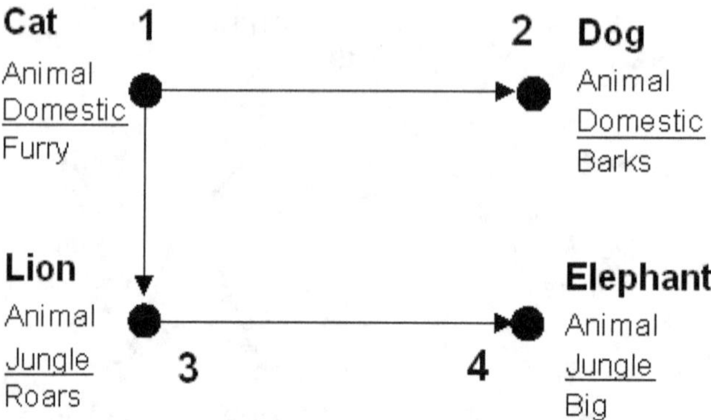

Figure 3.5. Precedence memory network.

For example, the first animals that most children encounter are domesticated cats or dogs so that they will begin forming the memory structure shown in Figure 3.5.

Here four memories have the *common property* 'animal' and cat is the first animal encountered by an infant and thence the first memory stored (at node 1, perhaps one or more brain cells). The second memory is dog, the third lion, and so on. Then cat and dog are associated by the property *domestic* (in the child's language perhaps 'house' or 'home') whilst lion and elephant are associated by the common property *jungle*.

Such memories have a considerable visual 'content' and the ease of recall of a memory will depend its 'strength' which will depend on such factors as the degree of elaboration with which it was committed to long-term memory and the frequency and recency with which the memory has been revisited.

Long-term potentiation

In practice a signal between two neurons is an electrical impulse passed along the axon of the first to the dendrites of the second via a synaptic junction. At this junction neurotransmitter chemicals pass the signal across a 'synaptic gap.' Evidently these chemicals react with RNA or peptide macromolecules in the neurons that play a role in memory *coding*.

In the case of classical conditioning, therefore, with frequent 'dosing' in this way the storage of a memory is made more permanent, an effect called *long-term potentiation* (Vander et al., 1994).

Conclusions

Conditioning, or at least some form and degree of it, is used in many areas of life, for example, in training infants in the basics of life, educating young children, and in 'brainwashing' the public through repetitive advertising to become "consumer zombies", as discussed in Chapter 8.

Behaviour shaping, essentially for form of conditioning, is also much used in training and educating young children, also requiring reinforcement to be effective.

Chapter 4

GROWING UP WITH HOPE

*Children also need something to hope for
- - big or small - - as long as it teaches them
to look forward with positive expectation.*
Shane J. Lopez, *Making Hope Happen* (2013).

The early years

Piaget borrowed from psychoanalysis to define two types of thought (Gillespie, 2017):

> ➤ *Directed or intelligent thought* is based on experience and logic and has realistic and communicable goals.
> ➤ *Undirected or autistic thought* via images, myths and symbols aimed at satisfying unconscious and unrealistic desires.

The directed mind sees objects as having certain properties and obeying certain laws, whereas for the autistic mind objects are simply there to be seen or enjoyed.

Piaget felt that children from 3 to 7 are largely egocentric and indulge in autistic thought, whereas from 7 to 11 they begin to develop the perceptual intelligence of the adult mind.

The formative years

The period from age 12 to 30 has been termed the *critical period* for formation of attitudes and it can be divided into two parts (Morgan et al., 1979):

(a) Adolescence, during which parental, educational, peer group, advertising and sociological influences are largely responsible for development of most of the attitudes a person will form through life.

(b) Young adulthood is a time when commitments such as choosing a vocation and marriage occur, and one in which attitudes tend to *crystallize* or 'freeze' for life.

In part this crystallization may involve attempts at *cognitive consistency* in which we tend to make our attitudes relatively consistent with one another and thus avoid *cognitive dissonance* or conflicting attitudes.

Heider's *balance theory* is of the cognitive consistency type and assumes that we try to maintain consistent and balanced or harmonious relationships with other people and our environment. According to this theory we would not marry a person with whom we disagreed on major issues about which we felt strongly, such as abortion (Morgan et al., 1979).

That attitudes do indeed crystallize or 'firm up' in young adulthood was confirmed by a US survey of women college students in the 1930s which, when followed-up 20 years later, found that for most issues on the 'conservative-liberal' dimension the women's attitudes, except for a slight "conservative drift" typical of older people, remained the same as they had been in their twenties (Newcomb, 1963).

That attitudes tend to firm up in adolescence and young adulthood has, of course, important implication for how we are likely to live the rest of our lives.

Preschool education

Children's brains develop rapidly in the first few years and it is important to take advantage of their resulting capacity for early learning to provide infants with a stimulating environment which should include a 'personal learning centre' that includes educational pictures and toys.

By the second year they should be involved in small learning groups supervised by a specialist teacher so that they can begin real learning (Packard, 1978).

In the third year they should begin kindergarten for at least a couple of days a week and these learning efforts should continue. By now they have a modest vocabulary and are capable of *cognitive learning* which processes and stores *abstract* information.

At this stage deliberate effort should be made at 'IQ building', noting that IQ tests include questions testing verbal, spatial and numerical ability. If a child has a problem with numbers, for example, early detection and correction of this will prevent far greater problems later.

Then, given a head start, they should commence school at age four, rather than the usual five in most countries.

Home schooling

In the USA home schooling has increased markedly in recent decades. The number of home-schooled children grew from just a few thousand in the early 1970s to 1.1 million in 2003, having increased 30% between 1999 and 2003 (Penn, 2007).

In 2000, only 52 percent of colleges had formal admission policies for home-schooled students, but by 2005 85% did, in that year a study showing that home-schooled students scored 81 points higher than the national average on the SAT (Penn, 2007).

Enhancing the learning process

The home learning process can be enhanced by such means as the 'Superlearning' recommended by Ostrander and Schroeder (1979). This involves encouraging physical and psychological relaxation with quite background music, slow breathing exercises, and visualizing nice scenes to achieve a reflective and receptive frame of mind.

Then the child is encouraged to affirm: *"I can do it."*

Here, developing a positive attitude is comparable to the 'teacher expectancy effect' where it is found that students who already get good marks are encouraged to do even better by a combination of the positive results, the confidence they obtain from these, and the 'expectation' and confidence the teacher shows about their ability. Here *hope* plays an important part, and students who become accustomed to getting low marks tend to lose hope, and without hope, of course, life is much less bearable.

With the scene set, the parent/teacher reads the material aloud at a careful pace while the child reads it silently. This is repeated again with quiet background music and the child is then tested on the material.

Motivation

Aristotle was first to assert that our goal was to become more nearly what we were intended to be. Psychologists refer to this is as *self-actualization* and Maslow viewed this as striving to reach our potential (Lindzey at al., 1978). He defined two kinds of needs:

(a) *Basic needs* such as hunger, thirst, sex and security.

(b) *Metaneeds* such as achievement, beauty, goodness, justice, order and unity.

Maslow defined achievement as a basic need but the present authors prefer to classify it as a 'higher' or more human metaneed.

First, we must meet our basic or 'animal' needs. That done, we can turn our attention to the higher 'human' metaneeds, and thence self-actualization as a human being.

These needs provide *primary goals* that may motivate us towards *secondary goals* such as money in order to achieve them.

Most of our basic needs are *intrinsic motivations*. Of these, *competence motivation* is perhaps the most basic and is learnt by infants challenged by goals such as standing up in their cot or walking. Most of our metaneeds are *learned goals*. Achievement motivation, for example, can be inculcated by parents or teachers. *Social motivations* such as justice are also acquired in this way.

What has this got to do with thinking? One's motivations will, of course, greatly influence how one thinks and acts.

Some studies have found, however, little correlation between motivation and efficiency of learning, suggesting that genetics and practice are more important factors.

Giving children more attention and hope

Weiss and Mann (1978) refer to a project in Milwaukee that found that children given more attention by the mother or a specially trained teacher, showed markedly higher IQ. This is no doubt the reason that only children tend to have higher IQ and that, in families with more than one child, the eldest child has a slightly higher IQ on average (Vernon, 1960). The youngest child in larger families, on the other hand, does not do too badly compared to those 'sandwiched' in the middle and perhaps most deprived of attention.

Related to this, of course, is the 'teacher expectancy effect,' in which students who get better marks are not only themselves encouraged by getting good results, but also by teachers often openly predicting that they will continue to do well.

As Lopez (2013) puts it: *Children also need something to hope for. They need to be excited about one thing in the future . . . then another, then another.*

As Marta (2004) puts it:

Each of us has a responsibility to have a positive impact on the children we know. Talk about the future – their dreams and aspirations – throughout their lives, not just at important milestones.

Goal setting

As with the teacher expectancy effect, goal setting and positive thinking play an important role in many other activities in life. In sports, for example, coaches do their utmost to encourage positive thinking and goal setting, and much psychological research has been done in this area, Sykes (1995) citing several examples of doctorates in education being granted for dissertations with such titles as:

"The use of goal setting and positive self-modelling to enhance self-efficiency and performance for the basketball free-throw shot" for a PhD at the University of Maryland.

Preferably, however, goals should not be 'commanded'. Rather, they should be 'suggested' and should be personal goals, not 'institutional' ones.

Conclusions

According to Lopez (2013):

Optimism is partly based on temperament – some babies come into the world inclined to embrace experience, while others shy away. The components of hopeful thinking are learned in early childhood; if all goes well, they're in place by age two.

Thus, both because of the rapid rate at which neural connections are made in the brain in the first years of life, (Mohr 2012a, 2014c), and because the very young brain is more open and receptive, the formative years are crucial, and efficient, personal, and encouraging early learning can increase a child's IQ substantially (Mohr, 2012d, 2018f).

In addition, children who are brought up with positive thinking, goal setting, and encouragement are likely to have better, more successful, and happier lives, and thus be far less likely to suffer from depression.

☺☺☺☺☺☺☺☺☺☺☺☺☺☺☺☺☺

Chapter 5

REAL IQ

> *Genius is one percent inspiration*
> *and ninety-nine percent perspiration.* Thomas A. Edison,
> newspaper interview quoted in *Golden Book*, April 1931.
>
> *I have no great intelligence, I have imagination.*
> John Argryis, said to the first author in 1998.

Intelligence quotient (IQ)

In France, asked by the French government to do so, Alfred Binet (1857-1911) and his colleague Theodore Simon developed the first IQ test using questions that tested a child's attention span, recall capability, and problem solving skills.

In 1916, Stanford University psychologist Lewis Terman "tweaked" the Binet-Simon test to create the Stanford-Binet Intelligence Scale. In this, IQ is defined as a person's mental age score on an 'intelligence test' divided by their chronological age, the resulting fraction being multiplied by 100 to obtain the IQ score (Craughwell, 2012).

In the 1930s American psychologist, David Wechsler, developed three IQ tests: the Weschler Intelligence Scale for Children (WISC), the Weschler Preschool and Primary Scale of Intelligence (WPPSI), and the Weschler Adult Intelligence Scale (WAIS). These test results are compared to the results of other test takers in the same age group, and follow a Normal distribution with a median score of 100, with two-thirds of population scores being between 85 and 115, circa 5 percent above 125, and 5 percent below 75.

Multiple IQ tests

Differential aptitude tests (DAT) for verbal, numerical and 'abstract/figural' IQ are preferable, the final IQ being an average of these. Figural tests might take the form of Raven's matrices which typically show 3 rows of 3 simple diagrams with the last diagram omitted, followed by several diagrams, one of which is the correct one to 'complete' the 3 x 3 matrix (Mackintosh, 2011).

Example IQ test

In each question a missing number is to be deduced according to some logical arithmetic operation or sequence. In these example questions the answers are the numbers following a question mark and underlined (Mohr et al., 2017). The test the time allowed for these 10 questions would be circa 8 - 10 minutes.

Find the missing numbers:

[1]   6   7   9   13   21   ?<u>37</u>

[2]   447   (?386)   254
       262   (?<u>518</u>)   521

[3]   4   7   9   11   14   15   19   ?<u>19</u>

[4]   2   10   6
       3   9   3
       1   3   ?<u>1</u>

[5]

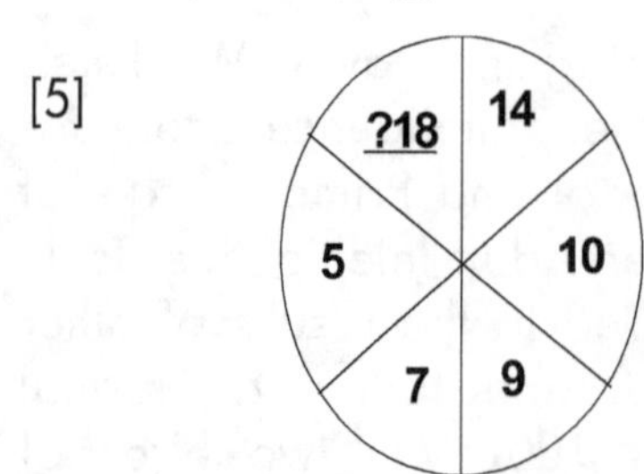

[6]   279   242   205   168   ?<u>131</u>

[7]   13   (?78)   12
      11   (?<u>55</u>)   10
[8]   126   62   30   14   ?<u>6</u>

[9]   7   1   2
       5   4   1
       3   2   ?<u>5</u>

[10]

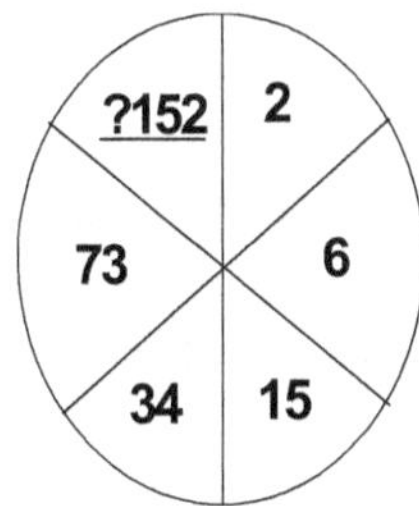

Keys to answers:
[1] The increments double.
[2] Middle number is twice the difference of the others.
[3] Alternate sequences (+3, +2, +1, +0) and (+2, +3, +4).
[4] 3rd # in row = 2nd - 2 x 1st.
[5] Diagonally opposite number is double.
[6] Decrements of -37.
[7] Middle number is half the product of the others.
[8] Next # = half x last # -1
[9] Sum of rows = 10
[10] Going around next # = 2 x last + 2 (then + 3, + 4 etc.).

If the scoring system for Craughwell's 10 item tests is used then 16.5 points are given for each correct answer, ratings for various scores then being (Craughwell, 2012):
165 Genius
148-132 Gifted/superior intelligence
115 Higher than usual intelligence
99 Average intelligence
83 Low average intelligence
70 or below, very low intelligence

For more on IQ tests, for example the SAT test, and 'types' of intelligence (e.g. "Gardner's Eight Intelligences") see *In Search of the Human Mind* (Sternberg, 1998).

How important to success is IQ?

Gladwell cites research that shows that IQ beyond an average of 120 "doesn't seem to translate into any measurable real-world advantage" (Gladwell, 2008).

According to Butler-Bowdon, "You just have to smart *enough*", and beyond this point it is "traits of personality and character" that make all the difference (Butler-Bowdon, 2017b).

British psychologist Liam Hudson said: "A mature scientist with an adult IQ of 130 is as likely to win a Nobel Prize as one whose IQ is 180" if he or she develops more systematic research skills, broader knowledge, and better networking to get ahead in the workplace.

Lewis Termann tracked children with high IQ into adulthood, finding that family background was a more important factor in real-life success than IQ, the most successful coming from homes "filled with books", half of them having a university degree at a time when these were much less common (Butler-Bowdon, 2017b).

Often the most important factor in achieving high levels of success is 'practice', the "ten-thousand hour rule" saying that to be very good at something requires at least 10,000 hours of deliberate practice (Gladwell, 2008).

An example, perhaps, were the Beatles who by the time they toured America in 1964, had performed on stage 1,200 times.

A little luck was also required, however, namely a chance meeting between their manager and a German impresario that led to their period of residency in Hamburg when they sometimes performed two or three times a day.

Thus Butler-Bowdon concludes: *Success is never down to a single thing, but it is rather a combination of talent, work, luck, and environment* (Butler-Bowdon, 2017b).

Real IQ

Intelligence is part inherited and part developed thereafter by learning and experience, often referred to as 'nature and nurture.' It is claimed that IQ tests are "a standardized examination devised to measure human intelligence as distinct from attainments" (Carter, 2007), but many argue that they largely measure learning, not innate intelligence.

It is generally assumed that IQ peaks at age 18, about when 'developmental' school education is finished in advanced countries. I contend that further education and study, however, should be able to increase IQ further so I propose a *real IQ* calculated for those over 18 as (Mohr et al., 2017):

Real IQ = IQ(18) – a(disease/injuries)

+ b(years of learning since 18)

+ c(creativity) - d[(age -18) if over 18]

Here IQ(18) is that one develops, all going OK, by age 18 as a result of hereditary factors and education and 'a', 'b', 'c' and 'd' are constants.

These constants have the following roles:

(a) 'a' is a constant to calculate reduction in IQ resulting from any disease or injuries acquired later which affect the brain, including Alzheimer's disease and psychiatric conditions such as depression.[1]

(b) 'b' is a constant, perhaps circa 0.25, for the effect of learning after the age of 18.

(c) 'c' is a constant for creativity, perhaps circa 1 – 2 if creativity is measured on a scale of 1 to 10.

(d) 'd' is a constant for normal decline in intelligence with aging, perhaps about half the value of the constant 'b'.

---

[1] In contrast to depression, note that positive attitudes may improve real intelligence, an example being the 'teacher expectancy effect.'

In the terms involving the factors 'b' and 'd' the notion of 'use it or lose it' is considered, that is, learning doing intelligent things should help further increase one's intelligence, just as doing more exercise should help strengthen one's muscles.

Creativity is obviously an important factor because if one has considerable ability, but no inclination to put it to tangible use, then one cannot be seen as having much real intelligence.

Whether creativity is, to any extent, in one's genes is debatable, but probably it is mostly a learnt trait, but one that relates to intelligence. In other words, without much ability to create, or intelligence, one is not likely to be very creative.

The foregoing simple equation should, indeed, encourage people to indulge in vicarious learning, surely the best kind for usually people are able to tackle subjects that genuinely interest them with more enthusiasm. In addition, being free to choose when and how one studies may improve results, of course, as this is far less painful than the all too many years spent listening to teachers regurgitate material from text books they have relatively little understanding of.

In my view, it also helps explain how people like Leonardo da Vinci and Isaac Newton, despite having only had very basic schooling, could achieve so much, namely because they did all the work themselves, whereas now most academics have research student slaves [effectively an apprenticeship historically (Mohr, 2013b; Mohr et al., 2018e)] to work on often silly topics they dream up.

Finally, an example of the great 'plasticity' of the brain was a US woman, Michelle Mack, who was found when well into her twenties to have been born with nearly all the left side of her brain missing. Nevertheless, her brain having 'rewired' itself, she had "fairly normal language abilities" and only relatively minor difficulty in coping with abstract concepts and visual-spatial processing.

Social and emotional intelligence

'Social intelligence' and 'emotional intelligence' are closely related, and tests of social intelligence include questions about how people would feel in certain social situations, and questions about the emotions shown in pictures of people smiling or frowning.

Some EI tests use self-report questionnaires, and according to Mackintosh (2011): - *a distinction needs to be drawn between self-report questionnaires, which seem to be a largely measures of well-established aspects of personality, and more objective measures which may more reasonably be called measures of intelligence.*

Performance on the Mayer-Salovey-Caruso Emotional Intelligence Test (MSCEIT), for example, improves with age, and females usually do better than males. Assessments of social behaviour by teachers, friends and managers, however, sometimes show negative correlations with EI test scores (Mackintosh, 2011).

Genetic factors

Genetic defects can, of course affect coefficient *a* of the foregoing formula for Real IQ, for example Fragile X and Down's syndromes, and degrees of mental retardation can fall into four classes:

> Mild.
> Moderate.
> Severe.
> Profound.

Then there are external influences such as malnutrition, lead poisoning and foetal alcohol syndrome, to name just a few. Depressive illnesses, even being slave to a lousy, bullying boss could also be a factor.

What is needed for best results, whether in the home, school or workplace, is an 'enriched environment' and positive attitudes and encouragement to obtain better results, and rewards at least occasionally when better results are obtained.

Finally, as noted in the recent book *Human Intelligence, Learning and Behaviour* (Mohr et al, 2017), such substances as lecithin, magnesium fish oils, zinc, and vitamins A, B-group, C, D and E are helpful in improving brain function, especially in the very young and the very old (Holford & Colson, 2008).

Conclusions

It is generally assumed that IQ peaks at around the age of 18, that is, at about the time when we finish school.

It is important to realize, therefore, that 'real IQ' in fact should increase in later life, rather than decrease as generally assumed, if we continue learning and thus continuing to build both our knowledge and the neural networks in our brains.

It is also important to realize the 'real' or 'effective' intelligence requires creativity, so a factor for this is also included here in the calculation of Real IQ.

Similarly, as argued by Carol Dweck, encouraging a *growth mindset*, rather than a fixed mindset, is important in helping increase children's level of achievement, and this is far more important in life than a single, perhaps once in a lifetime, IQ test result (Dweck, 2006).

☺☹☺☹☺☹☺☹☺☹☺☹☺☹☺☹

PART 2
DEVELOPING ATTITUDES AND HABITS

Chapter 6

ATTITUDE FORMATION
AND MEASUREMENT

> *The body of science described in this book could only have been developed in democratic societies, where attitudinal influence is the form of control that is most often relied upon.*
> Alice Eagly & Shelly Chaiken, *The Psychology of Attitudes,* 1993.

Introduction

The preceding chapter discussed conditioning which has important application in education where forcing pupils to sit out each day conditions them for productive life. Some aspects of conditioning are also involved, of course, in advertising and other forms of persuasion.

In the present chapter a brief introduction to the mechanics of attitude and belief formation is given. Of particular importance in advertising, *mere exposure research* and attitude measurement are also discussed.

Forbes' *contact hypothesis* regarding interactions between ethnic communities is briefly considered, this being of considerable importance in relation to religious persuasion, and, therefore, also having some relevance to advertising.

The formative years

The period from age 12 to 30 has been termed the *critical period* for formation of attitudes and it can be divided into two parts (Morgan et al., 1979):

(a) <u>Adolescence</u>, during which parental, educational, peer group, advertising and sociological influences are largely responsible for development of most of the attitudes a person will develop through life.

(b) <u>Young adulthood</u>, a time when commitments such as choosing a vocation and marriage occur, and one in which attitudes tend to *crystallize* or 'freeze' for life.

In part this crystallization may involve attempts at *cognitive consistency* in which we tend to make our attitudes relatively consistent with one another and thus avoid *cognitive dissonance* or conflicting attitudes.

An example of this might be that a person who goes to considerable effort to maintain good health, for example by exercising regularly and maintaining a healthy diet, is less likely to smoke or condone doing so.

Heider's *balance theory* is of the cognitive consistency type and assumes that we try to maintain consistent and balanced or harmonious relationships with other people and our environment. According to this theory we would not marry a person with whom we disagreed on major issues about which we felt strongly, such as abortion (Morgan et al., 1979).

That attitudes do indeed crystallize or 'firm up' in young adulthood was confirmed by a US survey of women college students in the 1930s which, when followed-up 20 years later, found that for most issues on the 'conservative-liberal' dimension the women's attitudes, except for a slight "conservative drift" typical of older people, remained the same as they had been in their twenties (Newcomb, 1963).

That attitudes tend to firm up in adolescence and young adulthood has, of course, important implication for marketing along the lines of 'get-em young and get-em for life,' an aim exemplified very well by the quotation that opens Chapter 8.

Expectancy-value models of attitude and belief formation

The most popular models of attitude formation towards an object, action, or event, are the expectancy-value models of attitude formation which are expressed as a summation of evaluations of each of several attributes of the object of the form:

$$\text{Attitude}, A = {}_{i=1}\Sigma^n e_i v_i \tag{6.1}$$

where e_i is the *expectancy* about the object for attribute i, that is its score on a simple scale as to the subjective probability or extent to which the object has this attribute, v_i is the *value* or 'evaluation' of the attribute on a similar scale, and n is the number of attributes considered (Eagly & Chaiken, 1993).

For example, a person is reasonably sure that a new soft drink Choke a Dope has nice taste and is trendy but considers that it is too expensive. Using scales of 0 to 10 for e_i and -10 to 10 for v_i he might thus rate the soft drink as follows:

Attribute 1 (taste): $e_1 = 5/10$, $v_1 = 7/10$

Attribute 2 (trendy): $e_2 = 6/10$, $v_2 = 5/10$

Attribute 3 (price): $e_3 = 10/10$, $v_3 = -5/10$

giving an attitude score

$$A = (5 \times 7 + 6 \times 5 + 10 \times -5)/100 = 15/100 = 0.15$$

whereas a 'moderately good' score in which 5/10 is given for each expectancy and value would yield $A = 0.75$, whilst a 'middling' score of zero for each rating v_i would, of course, yield $A = 0$.

In practice there might, of course, be many more attributes and, perhaps, we might average the score as $A = {}_{i=1}\Sigma^n e_i v_i /n$, giving 0.05 in the foregoing example, and such scores have been found to correlate well with attitudes assessed by evaluative semantic differential items (Eagly & Chaiken, 1993).

Information integration models of attitude formation

The information integration theory of attitude formation calculates the response to a series of stimuli *i* as

$$R = w_0\, s_0 + {}_{i=1}\Sigma^n\, w_i\, s_i \qquad\qquad (6.2)$$

where w_i and s_i are respectively the weight and scale of a person's attitude to a set of *n* items of information, and w_0 and s_0 are the weight and scale value of the person's initial attitude (Eagly & Chaiken, 1993).

Here the scale value of information is its location on the evaluative dimension and the weight is its *importance* or psychological impact in relation to the individual's judgment.

Simple summation models such as that of Eqn 6.2 emphasize the importance of using multiple 'selling points' in advertising.

If the sum of the weights is required to be one then the model becomes an averaging model, but averaging models are more generally expressed as:

$$R = (w_0\, s_0 + {}_{i=1}\Sigma^n\, w_i\, s_i)/(w_0 + {}_{i=1}\Sigma^n\, w_i) \qquad\qquad (6.3)$$

The initial attitude parameters w_0 and s_0 may in some instances, that of religion being perhaps the best example, represent 'intergenerational' attitudes acquired from a very early age from family and society at large.

Such initial attitudes, of course, may involve *prejudice*, for example ethnocentricity or racism, and, as history shows, such prejudices are often firmly rooted and perhaps could only be modeled by assigning them an exceptionally large weight.

More important in the modern consumer society, however, is social or imitative learning and in this context w_0 and s_0 represent initial attitude acquired by social learning from a peer or social group.

For example, a person believes that Christianity provides good moral codes (attribute 1) and that Christ did exist and provide a good exemplar of how we should live (attribute 2), but doubts that God really exists (attribute 3).

Even if God did exist, however, in view of man's disastrous history he has a low evaluation of this last attribute, so that, using scales 0 to 10 for both w_i and s_i, he might thus rate Christianity as follows:

Attribute 0 (initial attitude): $w_0 = 5$, $s_0 = 5/10$ (i.e. 'halfway' values)

Attribute 1 (morality): $w_1 = 8/10$, $s_1 = 8/10$

Attribute 2 (good life model): $w_2 = 8/10$, $s_2 = 8/10$

Attribute 3 (God): $w_3 = 2/10$, $s_3 = 1/10$

giving a response score

$$R = [(5 \times 5 + 8 \times 8 + 8 \times 8 + 2 \times 1)/100]/[(5 + 8 + 8 + 2)/10]$$

$$= [155/100]/[25/10] = 1.55/2.3 = 0.674$$

whereas a 'middling evaluation score' with 5/10 for both the weights and scale values for attributes 0-3 would give $1/2 = 0.5$.

In contrast to simple summation models such as Equation 6.2, averaging models emphasize the need to have a limited number of effective selling points in advertising.

Set size effect can be demonstrated by assuming all weights $= 1$ and an initial attitude score of 50 on a scale of 0 to 100. Then if all further pieces of information have a score of 100 the resulting weighted average score for k additional attributes is

$$R = (50 + 100k)/(1 + k) \tag{6.4}$$

giving the values 50, 75, 83.3, 87.5, . . . for 0, 1, 2, 3, . . . pieces of information, resulting in the hyperbola converging towards the asymptote $R = 100$ shown in Figure 6.1.

As might be expected, this hyperbolic result takes the same general shape as a learning curve, emphasizing that there is a diminishing return for each additional piece of information about a given subject, albeit with the unrealistic assumption that every piece of information has the same weight (w_i).

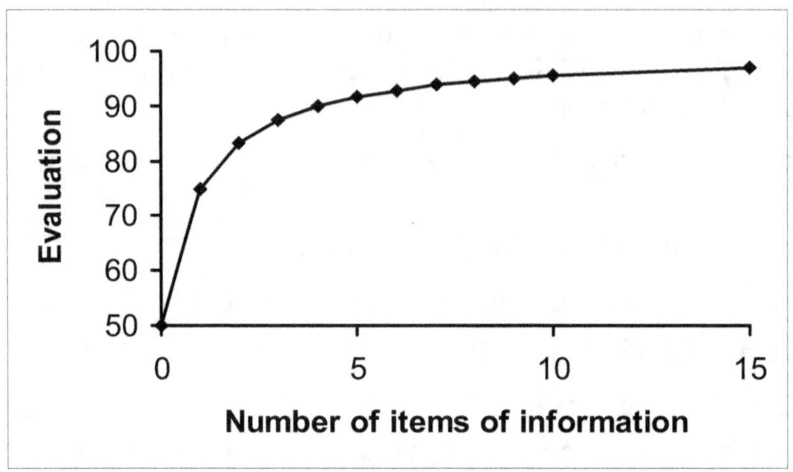

Figure 6.1. Theoretical set-size effect.

The *three hit theory* of advertising that three ads are needed to make people aware of a product, its relevance, and its benefits) would give (with $k = 3$) $R = 87.5$ (on a scale 0 to 100) in Equation 4.4, or $R = 75$ if there is no initial attitude, i.e. $s_0 = 0$ so that the number 50 in the numerator is omitted.

This is a reasonably good result and, indeed, of some relevance, the present author often finds that it takes three goes to remember items of information, presumably because they were not retained in the short term memory register (see Figure 1.2) long enough in the first instance.

Three-value model

A more general 'three-value' model is obtained by combining the expectancy-value and information integration models to obtain:

$$R = b_0 \, w_0 \, s_0 + {}_{i=1}\Sigma^n \, b_i \, w_i \, s_i \tag{6.5}$$

so that three ratings are associated with each attribute (Mohr, 2009):

(1) A *belief* b_i or subjective probability or extent to which the object has the attribute (=e_i in Equation 6.1).

(2) A *weight* or importance rating w_i (=w_i in Equation 6.2).

(3) An evaluation or *scale value* s_i (=v_i in Equation 6.1 and s_i in Equation 6.2).

For example, a woman considers a dress that she has tried on in a ladies fashion shop is 'trendy' and her scores for this attribute might be:

(1) b_i = 7/10 (she is fairly sure that it possesses this attribute).
(2) w_i = 8/10 (trendiness is quite important for a new dress).
(3) s_i = 9/10 (she rates it as very trendy).

Whilst a good deal more difficult to use in practice, this model does emphasize that it is sometimes desirable to consider both *belief* and *importance* considerations in assessing attitudes.

Logical formation of attitudes

McGuire (1960) proposed that people maintain beliefs that are connected by the rules of formal logic. Whilst most of our early attitude formation is via parents, education, peer groups, advertising, etc., it is at least sometimes true that we take 'time out' to think about things and may reassess an attitude, trying to do so in a logical way.

As a simple example consider a confectionery product with the three attributes T = tastes OK, N = looks nice, and P = price is OK, and a positive attitude to the product is denoted as A.

Using a little symbolic logic in which $\rightarrow$ mean 'implies', $\wedge$ means 'and', $\sim$ means 'not', and denoting A = attitude to the product is OK, we can write $\sim P \rightarrow \sim A$
i.e. if the price is not OK then nor is attitude to it.

If $\vee$ means 'or' we might also write:

$(T \wedge P) \vee (N \wedge P) \rightarrow A$

i.e. if taste and price are OK, or if the product looks nice and the price is OK, then attitude is OK.

The example is a little trivial, however, but no doubt we do indeed sometimes reevaluate an attitude and use a little logic in doing so, but, generally, our attitudes are formed by the educational, imitative and information integration processes.

There is, however, scope for educators, religions, and advertisers to try and win us over with a little simple logic along the lines, for example, of: "You like to be comfortable so why not try - - -", an approach compatible with the cognitive consistency theory of attitude formation.

Mere exposure research

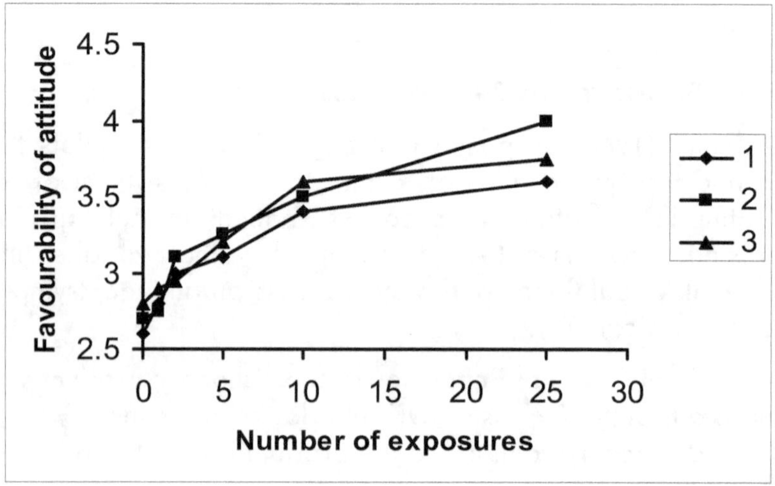

Figure 6.2. Increase in attitude favourability with increasing number of exposures to: 1. Turkish nonsense words. 2. Chinese-like characters. 3. Photographs.

Persuasion studies on message repetition usually focus on the effects of repeated exposure to *information* about attitude objects. In a classic monograph Zajonc (Zajonc, 1968) dealt merely with the objects themselves. Figure 6.2 illustrates the increase in attitude favourability with repeated exposure to three types of stimuli, showing a somewhat asymptotic behaviour similar to that of learning curves.

This result is comparable to the size effect seen in Figure 6.1 insofar as increasing response is seen with increasing amounts of information, albeit repetition of the same information in the case of mere exposure.

It should be remembered, however, that oft repeated attempts at persuasion can be irritating and result in negative attitudes, and some especially loud, haranguing radio and TV advertisements are good examples of this.

Implications of mere exposure in education are obvious, principally that students grow accustomed to new and perhaps difficult at first subjects, if not blasé about them, given time and repeated classroom exposure to them.

The latter observations might remind us that with repeated exposure we become accustomed to, if not hardened to, 'bad things' in life. For example, this is how children endure an excessive number of hours and years in classes and how adults endure jobs which may be, in reality, exceedingly tedious, arduous and boring.

It is also how, unfortunately, individuals become accustomed to essentially bad things such as cigarettes, alcohol, and drugs, perhaps in that order. This is, of course, good news for purveyors of such products.

Measurement of attitudes

One of the earliest methods of psychophysical scaling was Thurston's *method of equal-appearing intervals*. In this a panel of judges rates each of a set of attributes of an object (for example a new product) according to an ascending scale such as 0 - 10. Then the mean value of the ratings of all judges is the scale value of the attribute on the attitude dimension. For example, Table 6.1 shows the scale values that might be established for a new soft drink 'Choke a Dope'.

Then for surveys, the mean of the scale values of the attributes selected by respondents is their assessment of an object. To obtain more reliable results attributes that are rated inconsistently by the judging panel are not used for surveys.

Table 6.1.
Example scale values for new soft drink Choke a Dope.

Attribute	Value on scale 0 - 10
I don't like it.	0
It makes me feel ill.	1
It is very sweet and must have lots of sugar.	2
It has a nice colour.	3
The bottle looks nice	4
My friends like it.	5
it is trendy.	6
The price is good.	7
It tastes nice.	8

Likert's *method of summated ratings* was designed to be much easier to use than the method of equal-appearing intervals but to be at least as reliable. In this approach a large pool of items which are chosen intuitively for their relevance to the attitude object is used (Likert, 1961).

These items usually consist of statements of belief but statements about behaviours or affective reactions can also be used.

Typically each item is presented to respondents in a multiple-choice format such as:
1. Strongly disagree.
2. Disagree.
3. Undecided.
4. Agree.
5. Strongly agree.

Then, for example, a survey on attitudes towards women might contain questions like:

(a) Swearing is more objectionable from a woman.

(b) Intoxication in women is worse than in men.

With scores from 1 - 5 given to each of perhaps a dozen or so such questions the total score is then obtained for each respondent.

Desirably an initial pool of items should be pilot tested on a group of people to eliminate ambiguous and nondiscriminating items which tend to result in neutral responses.

This can be done by examining the *item-total score correlations*, each of which correlates the respondents' scores on an item with their scores summed over all the items. Then a good item will have a positive correlation and better items have higher correlations.

Likert Scaling is widely used, for example to assess the response to political advertising campaigns (Likert, 1961).

Guttman scaling

This approach gives stimulus-person scaling simultaneously and results in a matrix of data called the *Guttman scalogram*. For example, suppose we have five rods of from 5 to 7 feet in length (the exact lengths are not known) and ask each respondent to place a one in the Guttman scalogram matrix shown in Table 6.2 when they are taller than a particular rod. This raw data is then reorganized to give the result in Table 6.3.

Table 6.2. Guttman scalogram.

Persons	Stimuli (rods)				
	C	E	B	D	A
2	1	1	1	1	0
4	0	1	0	1	0
3	1	1	0	1	0
6	0	0	0	0	0
5	0	1	0	0	0
1	1	1	1	1	1
* e.g. person 2 is taller than C, E, B, D but not A					

Table 6.3 is obtained by placing the column with least ones at the left, the column with the most ones at the right, and so on. Then the row with the maximum number of ones is placed at the top (here this is for person '1' in and hence this is the tallest person) and that with the least ones is placed at the bottom.

Table 6.3. Reordered Guttman scalogram.

Persons	Stimuli (rods)					Score
	A	B	C	D	E	
1	1	1	1	1	1	5
2	0	1	1	1	1	4
3	0	0	1	1	1	3
4	0	0	0	1	1	2
5	0	0	0	0	1	1
6	0	0	0	0	0	0

The result is an upper diagonal matrix, as shown in Table 6.3, resulting in a score for each person shown on the right side in Table 6.3, this giving the ordinal ranking for each person.

The preceding example of Guttman scaling was for physical stimuli, when a perfect upper triangular matrix resulted. Generally, however, this is not the case when attitudinal stimuli are considered.

An example is Bogardus' social stimulus scale, illustrated in Table 6.4, in which respondents are asked to judge how closely they would relate to people of various nationalities or races.

Table 6.4. Bogardus' social stimulus scale.

	Acceptance level					
	Would marry	As a friend	Would give a job	Allow as citizen	OK as visitor	No contact
Armenians						
Bulgarians						
Canadians						
etc.						

Such attitudinal stimuli do not yield a perfect upper triangular matrix but it has been suggested that when about 90% of the non-zero entries do appear on or above the diagonal that this *coefficient of reproducibility* value is acceptable.

The Guttman scalogram has the advantage that the degree to which the reordered response matrix is 'triangularized' gives an immediate indication of the reliability of a survey. More complex to use, it is generally only usable for relatively small surveys, such as in-house surveys of consumer groups in advertising offices where it is an ideal tool.

Conclusion

Effective persuasion is all about changing attitude (where this, indeed, is necessary) so that some understanding of theories of attitude formation as cumulative or integrative processes is most important.

The following chapter on the mass media and advertising (Chapter 7) discusses the important trio of cognitive, attitudinal, and behavioural responses and also McGuire's Reception-Yielding model of attitude formation, one that is particularly applicable in such contexts as advertising and religion.

The results of mere exposure research compellingly indicate how attitudes to new stimuli tend to improve given repeated exposure to them, the bottom line being that it is by such means that we are reduced to consumer zombies from cradle to grave.

Measurement of attitudes is, of course, especially important in many areas such as consumer and political campaign surveys. Though perhaps only applicable to relatively small surveys, the Guttman scalogram is useful because the degree of triangularization of the reordered response matrix gives an immediate indication of the accuracy of a survey.

Having a positive attitude and optimistic approach to life will, of course, reduce the likelihood of one suffering from depression, and also reduce the severity of episodes of depression if, and when, they do occur.

☺ ☻ ☹ ☺ ☻ ☹ ☺ ☻ ☹ ☺ ☻ ☹ ☺ ☻ ☹

Chapter 7

THE MASS MEDIA & ADVERTISING

*The idea that the media is there to educate us, or to inform us,
is ridiculous because that's about tenth or eleventh on their list.
The first purpose of the media is to sell us shit.*
Abbie Hoffman, speech at U South Carolina, Sept. 16, 1987.

The print media

The *Acta Diurna* of the Romans contained daily official reports, and the Chinese claim to have had a similar journal of much greater antiquity (Egerton Eastwick, 1896).

The earliest regular newspaper is thought to have been the *Notizie Scritte* published in Venice around the middle of the 16th century. The paper could be seen at various places in the city for the price of a small coin, the *gazeta,* from which came the term Gazette.

Around the end of the 16th century casual publications of various professions, parties and other special interest groups had limited circulation in England. In 1622 the one-page *Certaine News of the Present Week* was first printed and followed by many other one-page weeklies.

Later, two-page newspapers circulated twice a week appeared, eventually being printed daily. In 1785 a newspaper renamed *The Times* three years later was established and by 1829 it was eight pages. During the Crimean war the first war-correspondent letters appeared and the circulation rose to over 50,000. The era of the modern newspaper had begun.

Today's major newspapers are larger than ever and many have large weekend supplements devoted to such things as additional news commentary and the arts.

Articles in major newspapers tend to become a routine mix of such topics as major local and international events, local and international politics and crime, traffic other accidents, business news and sporting news

In most of these areas outcomes or results will be reported, along with editorial comment and discussion of coming events.

The many local and regional newspapers naturally focus more on events in their area so that, for example, plans for alterations to a local park might be a main article.

There are also many magazines which focus on news in special interest areas such as business, cars and computers.

For all newspapers and magazines advertisements are a major source of revenue. There are also a few newspapers and magazines devoted to advertising second hand goods for sale or to advertising products such as cars and computers.

As ever, editorial comment in the major newspapers is usually very guarded so that a rare hint of dissent with government policy is barely noticeable.

Ways in which editorial policy can influence politics, however, include:

➢ By simply giving less coverage to one party than another.

➢ By giving heavy coverage to a mistake or embarrassing incident involving a member of one party.

Over time, therefore, newspapers can have a considerable political effect and always have, so much so that they have often been subjected to government censorship.

Newspapers also play a cultural role, most obviously in discussing local arts and sporting events. The quotation that commences the next chapter is an excellent example of this role and the way in which advertisers can use newspapers to brainwash the young into becoming lifelong consumers of their products.

Radio

Radio has been one of the great advances in human life. It allows international communication of news, embraces the people of most cities and towns, and plays an important role in ambulance, police and other essential services.

Radio has evolved from a novelty in its early days to a habit of modern life. The first author recalls the first 24 hour broadcasting by a radio station in Melbourne taking place in the early 1960s. Since then radio has evolved in major cities to provide a wide variety of 24 hour AM and FM stations such as:

➢ 24 hour news.
➢ Classical music.
➢ Popular music.
➢ 'Old time' music.
➢ Talk-back.
➢ Sports.
➢ 'Traditional' radio: a mix of news, sport, music etc.

Most of these are supported by a good deal of advertising and it is often claimed that many people spend more time listening to radio than they do watching TV and that, therefore, radio ads are more effective.

Radio stations have much smaller audiences than prime time TV, however, though in Australia the government owned ABC radio sometimes has a good sized audience. No doubt, therefore, it will eventually be privatized!

Some of the talk-back stations cater for the sick, deranged, drunk and lonely in the later evening and throughout the early hours of the morning.

Whether radio has much effect politically is doubtful, TV playing a much greater role in this area.

Culturally, however, radio has great influence. The latest styles of pop music are played to the young and this has always had an effect on their behaviour.

Before the 1950s popular recording artists sang in a semi-classical style or were 'crooners' like Bing Crosby who only older people could identify with.

In the mid 1950s the young Elvis Presley was viewed as a potentially bad influence on the young. He was endorsed by such well-known TV personalities as Ed Sullivan, however, and that seemed to overcome early prejudice from the older generation, or at least guarantee the approval of the younger generation.

There is no doubt, however, that rock and roll music has had a bad effect on the young as its performers were often doubtful characters afflicted with all the vices. Inevitably a whole generation was influenced by such behaviour and began themselves to behave less politely and become a little more immoral. If the lyrics of a popular song talked about 'having it off' in the back seat of a car, then young people of that generation would do just that.

Currently we still have stylized singers who 'croon' a song and dress according to some current fashion. We also have bee-bop and other pop music styles that have become more and more 'in your face'. These sorts of songs are accompanied by music clips with scenes of dark alleys in the poor parts of major cities that project an image of loutish behaviour and crime that seems to rub off on young males in particular.

Popular music has occasionally had positive effects, for example through songs protesting war, and there are those that claim that the 'hippie' and 'flower power' movement in the USA of the late 1960s and early 1970s had through a few large pop concerts played an important role in galvanizing public opinion against the Vietnam war and bringing it to an end.

Evidence of the power of pop music is seen in the emergence of radio stations run by religious organizations that play 'nice' pop music for the young with only occasional interviews or ads concerning religious opinions and events.

Finally, some evidence of the power of radio is exemplified by Radio Vatican in Rome which can be heard globally on the Internet. This, no doubt, plays an integral part in the Vatican's ongoing task of propagating Catholic propaganda.

The 'brainwashing' role of radio, however, became relatively limited with the advent of TV because this became a far more potent medium for political and other propaganda.

Television

TV has an enormous impact on modern life and people typically watch TV for at least 3 or 4 hours on most days.

The wide variety of shows on TV includes news, current affairs, interviews, panel discussions, documentaries, movies, sitcoms, children's programs, live sport, sporting panels, quizzes, cooking, home renovation and reality shows.

Most of these types of shows play a cultural role and in Australia they are a mixture of US, British and local products, exactly in line with our traditional alliances.

Many documentary shows, particularly those about past wars and other events in history, tend to reinforce those alliances. A notable example are the almost weekly documentary shows concerning Adolph Hitler which seem designed to keep us 'conditioned' for the concept of justified war and the next 'villain' around the corner that our allies the US or UK want to denigrate as a lead-up to yet another war.

As with newspapers, TV news has editorial controls rarely allowing much criticism of the status quo. The many interviews on current affairs shows allow politicians and others to express a view, but only in short 'grabs' which have little impact.

Occasional panel discussion shows allow groups to express their views but again only in short grabs, a sequence of views contradicting each other having little influence on an audience.

As with any media, however, by judicious choice of material shown the public can be brainwashed most effectively.

In Australia, for example, recent Prime Ministers seem to have had a media team that even Hitler might have envied, one that has them seen on TV almost every day saying a few mindless words on some topic or engaged in some public event to identify themselves with the public. As a result, a typically unlikely politician becomes highly successful.

Children's shows on TV play a positive role. Early morning and afternoon shows help keep very young children occupied and entertained and also have some educational content. In the later afternoon shows which sometimes include quizzes help entertain older children and sometimes have significant educational content.

The purpose of advertising

Nowadays, of course, there are massive media and advertising industries devoted to turning us into *consumer zombies*.

The main objectives of ads, in approximate order of priority, are to:

1. Make the brand name familiar.
2. To give the brand a distinct image.
3. Attribute at least one key attribute to that brand name.
4. Associate the product with certain usages.
5. To convince us that this brand is the best (for us).
6. To persuade us that we should buy the product.

To meet these objectives ads will involve:
slogans, demonstrations, comparisons, testimonials, and repetition.

Comparisons, of course, are usually of price, but sometimes also some sort of semi-official rating, for example safety ratings for cars.

By way of style ad types include basic facts, 'mood', feel-good, social setting, slice-of-life, humour, fantasy, hard-sell, and anxiety/danger/risk or 'fear' ads.

An example of fear type ads are those for household insect sprays, and the TV program *More Hidden Killers Of The Victorian Home* reminds us that fear ads have been around for a long time, ads in the Victorian era selling such products as poisonous Borax (sodium borate) as a household cleanser, the "new science of germs and microbes" helping promote a fear of myriad household 'bugs'.

To make ads more appealing attractive female models, smooth talkers, or sports and movie stars are often used to promote products.

To give ads more authority statements by 'experts' may be used to convince us of the merits of a product.

To make purchase more imperative ads will scream of huge price reductions for a limited time, huge bargains for as little as two days only, and buy on the never-never deals with no interest for a year or two.

Thus ads range from boring to extremely irritating, from dull and routine to the heights of excess and absurdity, from mere suggestion to downright pleading, and from slight desperation to screaming at us to buy the product.

More subtle are 'advertorials' of bought space in newspapers, conspicuous 'product placement' in movies, or internet sites. For maximum tedium there are half-hour infomercials on afternoon or late night TV which sometimes repeat night after night, week after week, and year after year. In these and most other types of ads there are often trial offers, bonus products for quick purchase etc.

The psychology of attitudes

Attitude can be defined as 'psychological *tendency* expressed by *evaluating* a particular entity with some degree of favour or disfavour.'

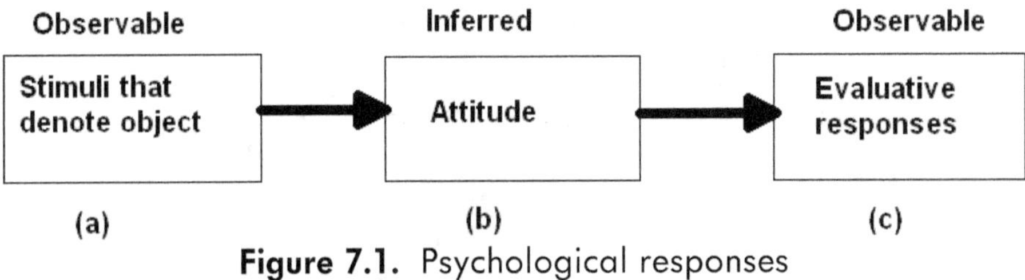

Figure 7.1. Psychological responses

Figure 7.1 illustrates the three types of response involved in attitudinal psychology. These are:

1. *Cognitive response*. This response is that of recognition of, for example, a name, a picture or other stimulus.

2. *Affective response*. This is a hypothetical construct and a latent variable. Here the sympathetic nervous system responds to (1) with feelings or emotions.

3. *Behavioural response*. This is the outward expression of (2) and may be a positive, neutral or negative response of some degree or intensity involving some observable action.

In this context conservatism, environmentalism or racism are objects. Then when we label a person a conservative, environmentalist or racist we infer an attitudinal position. Such attitudes are evidenced and also developed by the 'CAB' mechanism illustrated in Figure 7.1. Schemas are cognitive structures that represent a person's past experience in a stimulus domain by a higher order or abstract cognitive structure. Then attitude is a subset of such a schema.

Schemas have a selective effect on the remembering of information so that people have a better remembrance of stimuli that 'fit' their schemas and also for those that 'oppose.' This same selectivity applies to the 'output' of information as well as its input.

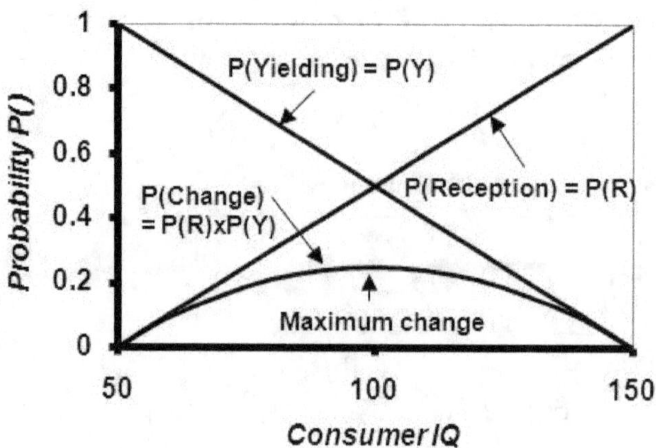

Figure 7.2.
Probability of reception, yielding and attitude change.

Figure 7.2 illustrates the reception-yielding model of attitude formation (Eagly & Chaiken, 1993). Here 'reception' refers to comprehending a 'message', for example an advertisement. This model postulates that the probability of attitude change is given by:

$$P(C) = P(R) \times P(Y)$$

so that a maximum change is obtained where the reception and yielding curves intersect, as shown in Figure 7.2.

One application of this idea is to 'get them young' so that advertising companies target the young and naive before they have the maturity or 'consumer intelligence' to develop resistance. Indeed, this is why the present author believe that the horizontal axis in Figure 7.2 should be labeled 'Consumer Intelligence' or 'Consumer IQ'.

The following quotation is an excellent example:

The chief customers of the public house today are the elderly and middle-aged men. Unless you can attract the younger generation to take the place of the older men, there is no doubt that we shall have to face a steadily falling consumption. If we begin advertising in the press we shall see that the continuance of our advertising is contingent upon the fact that we get educational support as well in the same papers. In that way it is wonderful how you can educate public opinion, generally, without making it too obvious that there is a public campaign behind it all.
Sir Edgar Saunders, Director of the Brewers' Society, Birmingham, 1930 (Sargent, 1979).

Once an idea like 'beer is for men' is buried in a boy's brain he may become a beer drinker for life, the habit occasionally reinforced by ads that make the habit look completely appropriate.

The basic mechanism of persuasion, therefore, is to 'get them young' (and naive or 'less intelligent consumers') as Figure 7.2 suggests. To do this ads need only persuade/brainwash some of the target audience and then imitative or 'social' learning ensures that many of the rest follow them.

Advertisements having achieved this, regular advertising reminds the audience of a product. Then in Figure 7.1 the 'C' response will be one of recognition of your brand, the 'A' response will be one of approval of it, and the 'B' response will be to make a mental note to buy it.

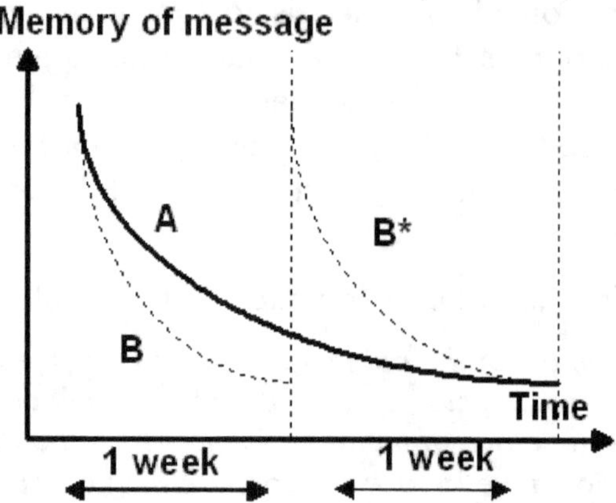

Figure 7.3. Forgetting curves.

Learning curves were discussed in Chapter 3 and in advertising it is important to have sufficient repetitions of an ad to ensure adequate average learning by the audience. The forgetting curves of Figure 7.3 also have important application in developing long-term marketing plans. Here curves A and B are for two messages and curve B* is the result after the second message is repeated.

Then, when time has elapsed after an advertisement its 'residual' effect depends upon both the *primacy* (strength) of the ad compared to others and its *recency.*

In Figure 7.3, after two weeks ad B* has greater recency than ad A, but less primacy so that they have nearly equal effect.

Such repetition of ads will ensure long-term potentiation of the remembered message, an important objective (Vander et al., 1994). Correlation between retention and persuasion, however, is by no means guaranteed and ads can be tailored to these two ends.

Targeting advertising

Maslow defined two kinds of needs (Lindzey at al., 1978):

(a) *Basic needs* such as hunger, thirst, sex and security.

(b) *Metaneeds* such as achievement, beauty, goodness, justice, order and unity.

Maslow defines achievement as a basic need but the present author prefers to classify it as a 'higher' or more human metaneed.

First, we must meet our basic or 'animal' needs. That done we can turn our attention to the higher 'human' metaneeds and thence Maslow's 'meaning of life' goal of 'self-actualization' as a human being.

These needs provide *primary goals* that may motivate us towards *secondary goals* such as money in order to achieve them.

Most of our basic needs are *intrinsic motivations* whereas most of our metaneeds are *learned goals*.

Advertising usually targets the metaneeds of your *ego*.

A Coke ad, for example, is not designed to remind you that you may be thirsty. If so, you might rush to the fridge and grab whatever drink you can find to satisfy that thirst. No, a Coke ad makes it look 'cool' to drink Coke with your friends and being 'cool' is a metaneed! So next day a young boy will want to be 'cool' when hanging out with his friends so they will all drink Coke and act foolishly, just like the actors in the Coke ads

Here again we see the down side of advertising, namely that increasingly ambitious executives will stop at nothing to sell their product, even if it has to brainwash the young into acquiring both bad behaviour and bad teeth.

In marketing to children, of course, familiar cuddly looking cartoon figures are often displayed on packaging and used to speak the lines of TV ads. Here, however, ads usually target the *Id*, the basic 'animal' personality that has basic needs like hunger. Young children tend to eat in smaller doses and often so that almost any time they are awake is a good one to put a picture of confectionery in front of them.

One of the best examples of brainwashing, however, is the use of *consumer panels* of children in marketing research. The children are often asked what they will say and do to persuade parents to buy them the product.

Finally, the extent to which children are exposed to advertising is incredible:

- - "*it is estimated that children between two and 11 years old may see over 20,000 advertisements in a year,*" (O'Guinn et al., 2006).

Advertising, therefore, will brainwash someone in your family, even if it doesn't brainwash you!

In marketing to adults well known sporting identities are often used to market such things as golf clubs, household appliances and cars and houses. Indeed, this was the basis of Mark McCormack's very successful IMG (McCormack, 1986), and one of his earliest clients was Greg Norman who, marketed as 'The Shark', was made out to be a much better golfer than he was and he made an awful lot of money from TV ads.

Addiction

There is no doubt that advertising has the effect of conditioning people. Just as Pavlov's dogs were conditioned to associate a bell with the appearance of food so that they then salivated when only given the stimulus of the bell, so too will a psychological 'trigger' be thrown in our minds when the 'CAB' responses to an ad are invoked.

In the same way advertising seeks to develop *habits*. Habits can be quickly formed and very hard to break. It only takes as little as one or two first exposures to learn something. Then only a few repetitions are needed for the memory to become *long-term potentiated* (Vander et al, 1994) and more easily recalled than most other memories in your brain.

In young children the result of confectionery advertising is often a virtual addiction to sugar. In teenagers this continues but junk food and Coke are added to their habits, soon followed by bourbon and Coke and then beer for the boys and perhaps some of the new vodka based mixed drinks for the girls.

Booze ads often *associate* booze with celebration so that at 'rave' parties for young people primeval music seems to go hand in hand with drugs and booze.

The psychology of this sort of behaviour is doubtless based on imitative learning from adults. In other words, as long as adults are stupid enough to drink booze children will too.

Since cigarettes are now discouraged in the media teenagers will smoke marijuana, arguing that it is not as harmful. This is not only an intoxicating drug but a hallucinogenic one as well. So, why not harder drugs like a little cocaine after that?

Then addiction quickly becomes likely. From booze to most other drugs, poisons have two problems:

(a) They don't really taste nice unless diluted enough by other things such as water and sugar in the case of booze.

(b) They alter the metabolic rate, resulting in changes in pulse rate and blood pressure, and contraction or dilation of blood vessels in the brain and elsewhere. Thus every fair sized dose of most drugs gives you withdrawal symptoms, whether you realize it or not.

If you have a booze overdose, for example, you might want some 'hair of the dog' (that bit you) as alcoholics call a dose of booze early in the day to help overcome a hangover.

Celebration is not the only excuse for booze. Wine goes well with food, it is said, so that is another.

The reality is that, because alcohol is a poison, wine will tend to eat at your stomach so it is best to line your stomach with a little food to ease the discomfort that you should be able to feel after a few glasses of wine.

This somewhat corrosive property of alcohol is the reason why it causes stomach ulcers and cancer of the oesophagus and stomach. It is also the reason why it was used to dissolve the connective tissue in the frontal lobes of the brain in the first lobotomy operations.

One way or the other, booze is inculcated as a daily habit, whether that be granny's tot of fortified wine, a bottle or two of wine with dinner or while watching TV afterwards, or a six pack of beer at a party or a sporting event.

In other words *advertising* does reduce us to brainwashed zombies who will enjoy drinking poison if told to. We will leap about to primitive music like savages if told to. Many of us still smoke because ads used to tell us to.

All too many of us take drugs like marijuana, heroin and cocaine. All these addictions are practices that supposedly more civilized European explorers learnt from primitive societies and took back to Europe with them.

Push and pull marketing

Some marketing campaigns use *push strategies* which concentrate on the availability of products. In this case the ads are 'basic' and concentrate on telling you the product name and where to get it.

Examples of such ads on TV are:

➢ A presenter reads a script while holding the product in question up in front of the camera.

➢ Ads with only text messages and a voice-over.

➢ Semi-humorous ads which sometimes use cartoon characters to present their message.

➢ Ads targeting children which involve cuddly characters and fantasy scenes and the like.

➢ Ads for junk food which play on having a high 'reward/effort' ratio (Govoni et al., 1988). That 50 million people a day eat McDonald's stuff is testament enough to the success of their advertising.

➢ Ads where the reader just about screams at you not to miss some bargain sale or to go to some cheap store.

Advertisements for 'basic' food, junk food, confectionery, clothing and home appliances are usually of the 'push' type.

Marketing campaigns often use *pull strategies* which promote the product in order to attract buyers.

In this case the ads concentrate on 'image' to attract the audience to the product and the product name is secondary and *associated* with the imagery. Examples of this sort of ad on TV are:

➢ Sophisticated ads that show the product in 'classy' surroundings with actors dressed stylishly.

➢ "Laid back' ads were the presenter extols the virtue of the product with, for example, an island resort as a backdrop.

➢ Ads that use glamorous people such as movie stars as actors.

This type of advertising is usually used for higher priced or more 'up market' products, including fashion clothing, cosmetics, expensive furniture, luxury cars and overseas holidays.

One of the most important 'levers' in advertising, undoubtedly, is *keeping up with the Jones's*. This is exploited heavily in marketing cars and new gadgets of which the mobile phone is the supreme example at present.

Another powerful inducement is selling on the 'never-never', for example with no repayments for a year.

Ubiquitous advertising

Today advertising is literally everywhere.

On TV in Australia there used to be regulations limiting the amount of advertisements per hour to something bearable. Now there seem like 20 minutes or more of ads per hour at times. Worse still, owing to the increasing cost of TV advertising time a truly bewildering string of ads appears in each ad break, sometimes up to about a dozen.

It is almost as bad on radio where there are sometimes as many as half a dozen ads at once on the higher rating commercial stations.

Junk mail from supermarkets and other retail chains has reached epidemic proportions. Other 'direct marketing' is done by phone and is increasingly irritating, often involving requests to complete lengthy market research surveys over the phone.

In addition, free local papers almost totally full of advertisements are also stuffed into millions of letterboxes in major cities.

Trams, trains and buses carry plenty of ads, as do train stations and tram and bus stops.

Taxis and trucks all carry signage, as do many vehicles belonging to small businesses.

Shopping strips are becoming more and more cluttered with advertising signs above the shops, and sandwich boards and often products on the footpath.

More and more restaurants, coffee shops and juice bars have also spilled out onto footpaths, sometimes making little room for the pedestrians for which they were originally intended.

Shopping malls are filled with advertising and more and more stalls with spruikers have appeared in them.

Sporting grounds carry more and more advertising and sporting teams now carry prominent advertising on their clothing.

Casual clothing often comes complete with the brand name writ large upon it.

The Internet is full of advertising, of course, some of it of a lurid nature.

Then there is the despicable practice of placing confectionery and soft drinks near the checkouts at supermarkets, resulting in many a tantrum as young children taken shopping throw a tantrum to get another dose of perhaps the first 'drug' of addiction, sugar.

Perhaps the most predatory advertiser of all, Coca Cola, has its vending machines just about everywhere, including pubs and clubs, office buildings, stations and heaven knows where else (they are probably there too!).

Using religion

In the West Christianity has been heavily exploited in marketing for example by:

➢ The use of religious symbols such as stylized crosses in the jewelry business.
➢ The confectionery industry makes heavy use of Easter to sell chocolate. Bakeries join in by selling Easter buns and industries such as the entertainment and travel industries rely heavily on the Easter holiday period.
➢ Christmas, of course, is a bonanza for business and has become almost completely devoid of its original meaning. For example, the image of Santa is actually from a 19th century cartoon of a rich robber baron with some of *his* toys which he certainly isn't going to give away (Solomon, 1992).
➢ Not too distantly related to this are Mother's Day and Father's Day which are also exploited by, and were probably created by, big business.

Religion also makes increasing use of TV and radio programs for promotion and in the US some religious sects have also spent large sums of money to employ advertising companies to run PR campaigns to promote themselves.

New trends in marketing

Some of the many new trends of late include:
1. Healthy foods, for example low fat products.
2. Recycling.
3. Pollution free and environmentally friendly products.
4. Diets and weight watching.
5. Alternative therapies. Of these the list grows daily:
   a. Aromatherapy.
   b. Herbal remedies.
   c. Acupuncture and Chinese medicine.
   d. Group therapy.
   e. Exercise therapy, for example Yoga and Pilates.
   f. Transcendental meditation.
   g. Reflexology - and so on.

In many large cities where house prices have tended to become unaffordable to new entrants to the market there is a growing 'live for today' approach to consumer spending and this is seen in:
1. The growing fast food industry, including take-away food and packaged 'heat only' meals sold in grocery stores.
2. Increasing diversity in consumption of alcohol.
3. Increasing use of drugs which may perhaps be encouraged by the legalization of marijuana.
4. Increasing use of leisure industries such as gambling.
5. Increasing use of restaurants by young childless workers (who may remain childless).
6. Greater spending by young and independent working women on cosmetics, clothes, jewelry and other beauty and fashion products including hair dressing and magazines.
7. Greater spending on magazines, videos, books, computer games, music and other home entertainment products.
8. Greater spending on cars, holidays and other major items by young childless couples or unattached persons.

In these and many other areas there seems to be a growing market which advertisers are busy exploiting. In some communities, however, one or two of the foregoing examples may be on the wane.

The disastrous sociological results

The extent to which advertising has reduced us to consumer zombies strolling around in jeans and carrying a mobile phone in one hand and a bottle of drink in the other is mind boggling.

An article in *The Australian* newspaper on 23 May 2005 reported that psychologists had found that regular use of text messaging on mobile phones could reduce IQ by as much as 10 points, a staggering outcome.

More important, advertising corrupts young minds by showing young people behaving irresponsibly, for example a recent Pepsi Cola ad showing a few youths riding a large wheeled garbage container down a steep street and into a harbour.

In the early 1960s a US Department of Justice official expressed alarm at the "startling" pace at which youthful lawlessness was increasing and concluded that by 1962 a million American teenagers would be arrested each year.

The same official remarked (Packard, 1963):

We seem to have misplaced the sense of values which made this a great nation. Self-indulgence and the principle of pleasure before duty on a vast and growing scale have become a phenomenon of the adult world. These are warning symptoms of the decadence disease which has contributed to the decay of so many civilizations throughout history.

The role that advertising has played in promoting decadent movies, music and behaviour has resulted in a more violent, lawless, indebted, miserable and brainwashed society.

Propaganda has always painted socialism as communism which permits little freedom. How free are we when we are all brainwashed to dress and behave in the same, often stupid way?

Advertising contributes heavily to the increasing debt levels carried by families in the West. Many people have half a dozen credit cards and get way above their heads in debt, often leading to family disunity and breakups.

The disastrous environmental results

Closely related to advertising is the slick packaging of many products, an example being the easy to use 'heat in the tray' packaging of frozen pizza and lasagna. The economic cost of such packaging is enormous and the environmental consequences drastic.

Another example of this are the thin plastic supermarket bags used in Australian supermarkets. Unbelievable numbers of these are used each year and many of them end up littering streets and parks and clogging creeks and storm water drainage systems, and only now (mid-2018) is some action being taken on this issue.

Atmospheric pollution has reached serious levels in many large industrialized cities and global warming has already been significant not long after the term was first coined.

Parkinson's well known law: *work expands so as to fill the time available for its completion* is generalized to obtain Mohr's Universal Law:

Junk fills the time and space available.

This covers a wide range of the problems of mankind including:

➢ Bureaucratic inefficiency, as in Parkinson's Law that work expands to fill the time available, when people are the junk.

➢ The Peter Principle problem of the most incompetent people being those that rise in hierarchies. Here those rising are the junk.

➢ The problems of pollution.

➢ The problems of resource depletion as a result of excessive consumption of 'junk products' which are unnecessary, extravagant and wasteful, and have planned obsolescence built into them.

Four wheel drives and other cars with massive engines are a good example of the latter issue.

The Club or Rome Report (Meadows et al., 1974) pointed out that we were then running out of chromium, once so heavily used by ostentatious American cars. That we are now running out of oil promises to be a major catastrophe because we have built our major cities around the car.

All this has occurred because we have long been brainwashed into becoming mindless zombies consuming not for our own benefit, but for the benefit of insanely greedy and highly overpaid executives whose motivation is an even bigger multimillion dollar bonus.

Though the world was already becoming overpopulated by then, "adman-columnist" E.B. Weiss commented in the 1950s (Packard, 1963):

Ever since I've been regaled with the current multitude of wonderful forecasts of a population future sparked by a remarkable growth of our population I have wondered about the magical powers of a large population automatically to assure eternal prosperity at successively higher peaks. The most populous regions of this mortal coil tend to be the most poverty-stricken.

In other words, capitalist industry has been happy to brainwash us into mindless consumption and has even been happy to count on excessive population growth to help boost profits even further, all the while ignoring the finite nature of the world's resources and its finite capacity to absorb the waste products and pollution arising from extravagant consumption.

Depression

An understanding of the cognitive-attitudinal-behavioural response model of Figure 7.1 can help people suffering from depression realize that whether they respond positively or negatively to certain stimuli is in large part up to them, and they can try and make a habit of forming a more positive attitude to situations and memories that tend to cause depression.

The important reception-yielding model of Figure 7.2 suggests that, in trying to treat depression and other mental health problems, one should, of course, pitch any suggestions of how sufferers might reduce their problems in a simple, encouraging, and easy to follow way.

Finally, the forgetting curves of Figure 7.3 remind one that bad/depressing experiences etc. can be quickly forgotten, and that, if repeated, there effect can be reduced by developing a more positive attitude to them.

☺ ☺ ☺ ☺ ☺ ☺ ☺ ☺ ☺ ☺ ☺ ☺ ☺ ☺ ☺

Chapter 8

THE PSYCHOLOGY OF HABITS

*Television has spread the habit of instant reaction
and has stimulated the hope of instant results.*
Arthur Schlesinger Jr, In *Newsweek,* 6 July 1970.

*A habit cannot be tossed out the window,
it must be coaxed down the stairs one step at a time.*
Mark Twain, attributed.

Accommodation

Piaget used the term 'accommodation' to describe how infants come to terms with their environment of a cot, etcetera, and also become familiar with the small group of faces that they regularly see often smiling at them so that, of course, ere long the infant copies this behaviour and smiles back. Thus WordWeb 6 dictionary defines accommodation as:

In the theories of Jean Piaget: the modification of internal representations in order to accommodate a changing knowledge of reality.

This early adaptation to a small group of 'familiar faces', and the copying behaviour associated with it, is an early form of social and imitative learning, a process by which we develop many of the habits we adopt throughout our lives.

Then, of course, the many years most of us spend in the all too long and drawn out education system inculcate many other habits, whilst throughout our lives we are literally bombarded with advertising and religious and political propaganda, from which many lifelong habits are acquired.

Early learning

A great deal of what a child learns, of course, is taught by parents, other relatives, and teachers in a relatively formal didactic manner. Indeed, modern societies rely almost totally upon teaching at schools, colleges and Universities to train children and young adults for a vocation that in many cases will occupy them for most of their life.

Indeed, for many people learning becomes a habit, and they continue to learn throughout life by reading and studying subjects related to their jobs, or subjects that simply interest them, such interests often having been 'adopted' from parents and other life role models.

Imitative learning

Young children learn many behaviours by imitating or 'modeling' those of their parents, siblings, teachers and friends etcetera. Such imitation ranges from manner of speech to eating and recreational habits. Thus many children take up the same sports as their parents, whilst others may learn swear words and such bad habits as smoking from friends at school.

Social learning

Social learning is simply imitative learning that takes place in the larger context of society, rather than the confines of home or the classroom. It includes social groups such as friends, religious groups, and sporting and other clubs that a person might belong to.

It is by a combination of imitation of parents and social learning from a small group of friends that children may acquire an interest in beer and/or wine, for example, or worse still and far more dangerous to their health in the long run, illegal drug habits usually begin with social learning, for example at teen dances and parties etcetera.

Studies have also found that children with only one parent are more likely to smoke or drink by the age of 11.

Religion

Throughout history religion has played a major role in instructing adherents in how to behave according to guidelines established by each religion. An example of this, a Pope in the 1960s said something along the lines of: *Give me a child before the age of five and I will make him a Catholic for life.*

The current plague of Islamic conflict and terrorism that afflicts much of the world at present is, of course, in part a result of Islamic teachings based on the Koran's frequent advocacy of jihad against "unbelievers" in order to establish caliphates for a particular Muslim leader.

An example of the satanic Muslim religion, in one "barbaric" episode in Mosul 'Islamic State' captured a group of fleeing women and children and burned them alive.

Political propaganda

In like fashion to that of religion, political propaganda has played a major role in human history, usually with disastrous results as often clearly insane and greedy leaders seek power over more and more people and territory, often using religion as a pretext for their aims at greater self-glorification.

Hitler was perhaps one of the best examples, the Nazis doing an excellent job of 'brainwashing' the German people with a constant hail of propaganda to support them. The Nazis also provided their troops with massive amounts of amphetamines to 'energize' their military efforts, whilst Hitler became addicted to a cocktail of drugs including cocaine during WW2, perhaps contributing to increasing depression as the war turned bad for his forces, and ultimately contributing to his suicide.

Two factors in his hate of the Jews were:

(a) The centuries old European prejudice against them because, when they had trouble being employed by Christians, they would go into such businesses as running pawn shops and banking, thereby getting rich.

(b) Rumour had it, and we tend to believe it, that he had contracted syphilis from a Jewish prostitute during WW1. Syphilis not being curable then, because antibiotics had not been discovered, the later stages of it no doubt added to his madness gradually as the years rolled by.

A globally widespread example of propaganda of sorts is the use of the terms 'right' and 'left' to compare capitalist sympathetic political parties and parties with more socialist policies, the term 'right', of course, being intended to sound 'right' in the sense of 'correct' or the 'right thing to do'. Here then is a major example of how the mass media in the West promulgates its bias towards the capitalist system that runs it.

The mass media and advertising

As discussed at modest length in Chapters 7 and 8, the mass media and advertising are the main means by which modern society is fed information, whether to 'sell' a particular religion or political party, or a household or other product.

The persuasiveness and effectiveness of advertising is, of course, sometimes remarkable, the Reception-Yielding Model of Figure 8.2 illustrating quite well why advertising is so successful in appealing to more 'gullible' or less intelligent consumers.

Recognition and *approval* are important factors in how 'consumer zombies' are brainwashed into lifelong habits of consumption, as emphasized by the 'CAB' model of Figure 8.1 in which cognitive, attitudinal and behavioural responses follow exposure to a stimulus such as that of an advertisement. Then, positive attitude or 'approval' is likely to lead to consumption of a product, and perhaps habitual consumption of it.

Indeed we are creatures of habit, much of our lives being spent in the company of just a few friends or family, consuming certain products we have come to like, and spending our spare time in certain adopted pursuits, for example going to the same pub or restaurant, and following a particular sporting team regularly.

Psychopathic behaviours

This is the largest category of abnormal psychological types, the pathology of which may involve such traits as:

[1] Assertiveness, aggression and bullying.
[2] Dishonesty and lying.
[3] Alcohol and drug addiction.
[4] Excessive sexual behaviours.

Psychopaths usually have two or more of the above traits, but are not normally classified as mentally ill, in part perhaps because such behaviours are so common.

Bullying may be learnt by an eldest brother or sister, and the first author knew examples of both cases both within his own 'nuclear family', his extended (by his own marriage) family, and people with whom he was friendly for a while.

Evidently the eldest is able to boss younger siblings around from an early age, and often stays bossy with both these siblings, and perhaps other people throughout most of the rest of their life until too old and feeble to be bossy anymore.

Bullying usually involves a 'superior' or boss, or somebody with psychopathic aggressive tendencies based on feelings of superiority, 'bad mouthing' the victim to their face with brief but hurtful and disturbing insults. These insults are repeated regularly to both the victim, often a 'loner' in an isolated situation, and to the bully's small group of friends and supporters who then repeat the same insults to the victim, increasing his or her feelings of isolation and helplessness.

In the schoolyard, for example, the bully is often bigger and stronger than the victim, who may be of the 'nerd' type. Indeed, the bully is often better at sport, but jealous of the victim getting better marks in class and perhaps occasional praise from teachers and others.

In the workplace the reasons for bullying by bosses or 'superiors' in the workplace hierarchy are often less clear, but often, for example, involve male bosses abusing women with 'sexual insults' that they are ugly, or that women in general are in some way inferior.

Addiction

Addiction to legal substances such as nicotine, a brain stimulant, or alcohol, a vasodilator and thus subtle tranquilizer, is, of course, very common.

Alcohol abuse can lead to problems in the workplace, home or social venues. Heavy drinkers suffer unusual brain shrinkage of both white and grey matter, reduction of the latter giving rise to the widespread belief that alcohol kills neurons (Sweeney, 2009).

Western governments have taken several measures to limit smoking, particularly limitation if not prohibition of advertising of cigarettes, in part to reduce the huge impact that the long-term health effects of smoking have upon public health system budgets.

Similarly, measures such as tougher drink-driving laws, earlier closing of some late night clubs and bars, and tougher penalties for family violence, have been put on place to limit some of the harmful consequences of drinking to excess.

Drugs, including alcohol and nicotine, have two problems:

(a) They don't really taste nice unless diluted enough by other things such as water and sugar in the case of booze.

(b) They alter the metabolic rate, resulting in changes in pulse rate and blood pressure, and contraction or dilation of blood vessels in the brain and elsewhere. Thus every sizable dose of most drugs gives you withdrawal symptoms, whether you realize it or not. If you have an overdose you will realize it and you might want some 'hair of the dog' (that bit you) as alcoholics call a dose of booze early in the day to help overcome a hangover.

As for quitting smoking and moderating booze consumption, the first author devoted a chapter to this subject in several books (Mohr, 2012c; 2013a; 2015; 2018a; 2018b).

Increasingly, addiction to pharmaceutical drugs such as Valium prescribed for anxiety, or the raft of drugs prescribed for relatively newly 'invented' conditions such as ADHD and OCD, is commonplace and, indeed, something of a modern medical scandal comparable to that of the practice of lobotomy and leucotomy 50+ years ago.

The global illegal drug industry is now, unfortunately, along with the global arms industry, one of the world's largest. Some of the most widely used illegal drugs include:

[1] Cocaine and its derivates, including morphine, are highly addictive and have been widely used for more than a century. High quality cocaine, however, is very expensive, so that users often turn to crime to 'feed' their habit.

[2] Heroin, a narcotic that is considered a 'hard drug', is a highly addictive morphine derivative, intravenous injection providing the fastest and most intense 'rush'.

[3] LSD became quite popular in the 1960s but is rarely used now. It binds to serotonin receptors, only very small amounts having profound effects, including altered states of consciousness and hallucinations. In some cases LSD has been associated with psychosis, particularly when taken by a person with an existing mental disorder (Sweeney, 2009).

[5] Marijuana grew greatly in popularity from the 1970s, and is still widely in use, being easily able to be grown on country farms, and in suburban backyard and sheds.

Marijuana's active ingredient delta-9-tetrahydrocanniabinal (THC) inhibits release of the glutamate and GABA neurotransmitters, reducing cognitive function. Caffeine has the opposite effect of increasing neuronal release of glutamate and GABA, thereby slightly increasing cognition.

As noted in Chapter 16, marijuana use has been found to correlate with the incidence of schizophrenia.

[5] Methamphetamines, particularly crystal meth or 'ice', have become widely used in the last two decade, and are easily able to be manufactured with quite small and simple chemistry apparatuses in suburban houses and garages.

Gambling

Gambling is now a massive global industry, ranging from gambling on various sports to the growing casino industry. Gambling on horse racing has ruined the lives of many people, but it is gambling on poker machines that has ruined many more.

Many millions of people around the Western world are addicted to poker machines which might be likened to Skinner boxes in which rats quickly learn to press a lever to obtain a food reward, soon increasing their rate of lever pressing to hundreds of times per minute.

The video screens are part of the addiction no doubt, just as they prove to be in laboratory experiments with pigs and, of course, TV and PC screens have proved to be highly addictive with many humans.

Habits and hope

Many of the most common habits involve some degree of addiction, smoking, alcohol and gambling being some of the best examples. Most habits, however, such as the foods we like, the sports we play or follow, and the types of movies we like, are generally seen as relatively harmless.

A substantial proportion of the most common habits can be seen to involve hope, particularly gambling, when we hope to win, and in supporting a favourite sporting team, when we hope that it wins.

Regrettably, however, most habits are unproductive pastimes at best, often expensive, and all too often downright harmful.

For a better quality of life, therefore, we should seek to develop habits that are likely to have positive outcomes, for example a good work ethic which we could hope would ultimately be rewarded with better job satisfaction, better pay, and perhaps a better job and life.

Conclusions

Behaviours and habits are learnt from the outset by accommodation, modeling and imitative and social learning, as well, of course, by formal learning whether this be in the home or at school.

Such often lifelong habits as interests in and perhaps participation in music, reading, movies, and certain sports are acquired by both imitative and social learning, as well as teaching in many cases.

The mass media and advertising, of course, play a key role in modern society, informing us of current events, and also persuading us to adopt a particular religion, support a particular political party, or buy an advertised product.

Indeed, the extent to which we in today's consumer society are 'brainwashed' has all too many negative consequences and led the first author to coin the term *consumer zombie* (Mohr, 2013b; Mohr & Fear, 2016; Mohr et al., 2018e).

For a better quality of life, therefore, we should make a habit of focusing on productive and positive goals that, if achieved, will improve our lives.

Such goals might include, for example, a better job, making more money, and a better, happier, and healthier lifestyle as free as possible from bad habits.

☺☹☹☺☹☹☺☹☹☺☹☹☺☹☹

8. The Psychology of Habits

CHAPTER 9

HOPE IMPROVES LIFE

Hope against hope, and ask till ye receive.
James Montgomery, "The World Before the Flood",
The Poetical Works of James Montgomery (1840-41).

Scientific proof

A home-based study of almost 800 people included the simple question:

Are you hopeful about the future?

Regardless of their sex or ethnicity, 91% of the respondents replied "yes", the other 9% replying "no" (Lopez, 2013).

The two groups, the "hopeful" and the "hopeless", were almost the same age (averaging respectively 69 and 70), had the same levels of education and health, with "no significant differences in blood pressure, body mass index, and drinking behaviour".

The hopeful, however, had higher levels of physical activity, fewer were smokers, tested for much lower levels of depression and higher measures of social well-being, had more social contacts, and were slightly better off financially.

About a decade later only 11% of the hopefuls had died, compared to 29% of the hopeless, the principal researcher concluding that: "If you are hopeless you are less likely to keep doctor's appointments" (Lopez, 2013).

103

Hope vs. optimism

The 2nd edition of the Macquarie Dictionary defines hope as:

1. expectation of something desired; desire accompanied by expectation.

2. a particular instance of such expectation or desire: *a hope of success.*

It defines optimism as:

1. disposition to hope for the best; tendency to look on the bright side of things.

while defining optimistic as:
1. disposed to take a favourable view of things.

Here optimism is a mood, a state of mind, usually without a specific goal, whereas hope is usually associated with a particular wish or ambition.

According to Lopez, however, hope is more important:
But when life throws us a curve, when the going gets tough, optimists get stuck and frustrated. Hopeful people shine in negative situations. They are energized to act and they find meaning and dignity in moving ahead, whatever the challenge.

Leading with hope

Lopez (2013) cites a telephone Gallup poll of more than 10,000 people which asked them what three words best described how bosses or community leaders contributed positively to their life. It turned out that words such as *wisdom* were rarely mentioned, but that respondents said *"they want the people they serve to meet four psychological needs: compassion, stability, trust, and hope."*

Lopez concludes that most leaders *"do not spend enough time making hope happen"* but spend more time reacting to problems rather than planning for a better future.

The Gallup poll found that 69% of people who said their workplace leader make them enthusiastic about the future rated highly on measures of their involvement with and enthusiasm for their work. They were also more innovative, productive, and likely to stay longer with the company.

On the other hand, only 1% of those who did not find their boss made them enthusiastic about the future were committed to and enthusiastic about their work. They were also likely to be physically and mentally unhealthy, and to undermine the work of others.

Teacher expectancy effect

The teacher expectancy effect is based on the observation that students aware of the fact that the teacher considers them 'bright' tend to do better than they otherwise would, even if they are not actually exceptional. In addition, teachers tend to mark students they consider bright more favourably (perhaps we could call this 'teacher's pet syndrome'). Thus we have a double barreled effect.

For the present discussion, however, we shall merely consider an *expectancy effect* for which we write

$$\text{Motivation} = (\text{Valence}) \times (\text{Expectancy})$$

where *valence* is the desire for marks (or in other spheres for $) and *expectancy* is the person's notion of the probability of obtaining a certain mark (perhaps enhanced by the teacher or, just as likely, by knowledge of their own record).

This expectancy is of a first level outcome (obtaining certain marks) with a second level outcome expected to follow from the first outcome (such as approval by parents).

This theory emphasizes the different levels of motivation that will exist in different people and managers should, if possible, have some idea of the motivation of their staff and, in addition, make some effort to enhance this by increasing their expectancy.

Things we hope for

There are many things people hope for in life, some of the key ones being:

> ➢ Good marks at school.
> ➢ To do well at sports.
> ➢ To get a good job.
> ➢ To make money.
> ➢ To own a house.
> ➢ To find love and marriage.
> ➢ To have children.
> ➢ To be healthy.
> ➢ To be content, if not happy, with life.
> ➢ To have a long life.

There are many less important things we hope for, of course, including that our favourable sporting team wins, that the weather will be nice, to have a nice outing at the weekend, to have a holiday before long, etcetera.

A major issue, of course, is how we deal with disappointment when are hopes are not realized.

When this happens we should consider whether the hope in question was realistic. If on further consideration we believe it was realistic/achievable, then we should:

> ➢ Extend the timeframe for achieving the goal.

> ➢ Consider alternative means of achieving it.

> ➢ Consider getting help to achieve it.

and examples of the sorts of decision making processes that might be employed are given in Chapters 23 and 24.

Conclusions

In his 1994 book *The Psychology of Hope,* Charles Snyder postulates that hope has three key elements:

1. The ability to envision goals.
2. The understanding that there are alternative pathways to a goal.
3. Self-efficacy, that is, the capacity to muster up power and energy in pursuit of that goal.

Hope, of course, is very important in life, and perhaps there is no better example than the teacher expectancy effect because it gives a good example of how greater hopes and expectations can lead to better results and greater happiness.

Indeed, extensive research has repeatedly shown that more optimistic, more hopeful people are much less likely to suffer from depression and tend to live longer, happier and more fruitful lives.

The first author recalls a pertinent remark made to him when talking to a lady in an employment bureau about being bullied into 'walking the plank' by a nasty new HOD several years earlier. She said: *You can't change the past.*

Unsympathetic as it sounded at the time, it is useful advice and, when one is pondering the misfortunes of one's past, as most people often do, it is usually best to limit the time spent grieving over past problems and move on to thinking more positively about the future, hoping to avoid or deal with any problems along the way more effectively.

Despite our best hopes things sometimes go wrong, of course, but even when a particular goal becomes seemingly unachievable, it is usually possible to find another way, perhaps also finding help along that way, to achieve that goal.

Chapter 10

BUILDING SELF-CONFIDENCE AND HOPE

> *Faith is a charisma not granted to all; instead man has the gift of thought, which can strive after the highest things.*
> Carl Jung, *A Psychological Approach to the Dogma of the Trinity*, (1958), *Collected Works*, vol. 2 (1969).
>
> *Hope against hope, and ask till ye receive.*
> James Montgomery, "The World Before the Flood",
> *The Poetical Works of James Montgomery* (1840-41).

Self-esteem and self-confidence

Some psychologists argue that self-esteem has two components: *self-efficacy* and *self-respect* (Krapp, 2005), and in order to increase self-belief often counsel patients to:

(a) Repeat to themselves such statements of affirmation as: "*I believe in myself*" to increase self-belief.

(b) Associate with positive people to obtain encouragement and support.

(c) List their past successes and review this list periodically to increase their levels of optimism.

Dr Robert Anthony in his 2010 book *The Ultimate Secrets of Total Self-Confidence* describes a "simple but very effective learning technique" in which over a period of only 21 days patients "break an old destructive habit and form a new positive one."

Various chapters encourage readers to:
➢ "Dehypnotise" themselves.
➢ Develop self-reliance.
➢ Think positively.
➢ Use "creative imagination".
➢ Develop a "direct action worksheet".
➢ "Get the smile habit".

The final chapter concludes that a positive mental attitude gives a person self-confidence.

It could also be added, of course, that a positive attitude givens one hope, and with hope comes some degree of confidence.

Self-regulation

Bandura's social-cognitive theory holds that people are capable of self-regulation and thus controlling their own behaviour, and that the self-regulation process has three parts (Krapp, 2005):

[1] Self-observation: tracking one's own thoughts, feelings and behaviours.

[2] Judgment: comparing oneself to standards set by oneself or, preferably, others.

[3] Self-response: rewarding oneself for doing well and punishing oneself for doing badly.

For example, a student doing poorly at mathematics can self-regulate their performance by (Krapp, 2005):

[1] Write down their negative thoughts associated with maths classes, homework, and tests.

[2] Set a realistic goal for improvement, for example if the student is getting C grades, they should be somewhat optimistic and aim for B grades, not C+ as this is not a sufficiently rewarding goal, and not A+ as this is not a realistic goal.

[3] Note but not dwell too much on any lack of improvement, but celebrate improvement when it comes.

Self-assessment

Sensible and accurate self-assessment is, of course, very important throughout life, and this should include several of the key facets of one's life, and Table 10.1 is an example 'life-assessment' for a married person in their mid-30s with a job and two children.

Table 10.1. Self-assessment for married person.

Factor	Present situation	Score/10
Job	OK	6
Marriage	OK	7
Family finances	?	5
Home life	Good	8
Child 1	Problems	4
Child 2	Good	8
House	OK	7
Car	Old	6
Social life	Very little	3
Total score/100		**54**

The total score is mediocre, to say the least, and perhaps a better job could be hoped for to improve it, and thence the family finances and situation in general.

If weights were added to each factor, as in the Expectancy-Value and Information Integration models of attitude formation discussed in Chapter 6, then a better assessment is obtained. A relatively high weight would be given to the 'job' factor, of course, as this affects most, if not all, of the other 9 factors.

In the case of a school-age child, of course, the factors would by very different, including marks at school, friends, extra-curricular activities such as sports, 'pocket money', and perhaps food as children, of course, have to do as they are told on most things, including what they eat, and their earliest signs of discontent are often diet-related.

Social support

When things go wrong it is, of course, helpful to have supportive people, whether they be relatives, friends, or counsellors, to turn to for advice and moral support.

Such people can provide help and encouragement that may provide hope in the most difficult of circumstances, and hope alone in most cases will help one cope in the short term.

Then, in the longer term, one can begin to fix the problem(s) in question, or 'move on' from them to work towards new goals.

Successful businesswoman Lillian Vernon recalls: *My father told me I had talent and a good idea for starting a business and I should never let anything get in the way of fulfilling my dream, or I would regret it for the rest of my life,* concluding: *So don't let challenges, setbacks, or detractors defeat or discourage you. If you believe in yourself and think positively, you will succeed* (Trump, 2004).

Creating goals

Happy and successful lives are far more likely if we plan them by creating goals. These should be realistic in terms of time and resource requirements, and goals which we are enthusiastic about are, of course, more likely to receive attention and thus be achieved.

When a goal involves solving a problem it is best to think positively about it. If one is having problems with a co-worker Jim, for example, rather than think:

I want to have less trouble with Jim

it is better to think: *I want to make friends with Jim*

and act positively by, for example, paying him polite compliments occasionally.

It is also best, of course, to choose goals that your abilities are best suited to, and Chapters 23 and 24 detail some systematic methods of planning for a successful life.

When things go wrong

There are many bad things that can happen in life, some of which can be most upsetting, for example:

> ➢ Getting bad marks at school.
> ➢ Failing and having to repeat a year at school.
> ➢ Losing a job.
> ➢ Marriage and family breakdown.
> ➢ Psychological problems.
> ➢ Physical health problems.
> ➢ Financial problems.
> ➢ Excessive use of, and addiction to alcohol or drugs.

When one has such problems one should always seek advice and help from family, friends, and professional to think difficult situations through and find solutions to them.

In the case of physical health problems, of course, one's GP should be the first port of call, whereas for problems at school teachers should be consulted. Family and friends may be able to help deal with minor psychological problems, but for major ones professional help should be sought.

For married couples with children, the 'breadwinner' losing his or her job can be a major catastrophe, of course, one that often leads to marriage and family break-up.

Whilst marriage counsellors often help with marital difficulties, finding a 'good' job can be very difficult, especially when one has been unemployed for a substantial period of time, in part because answering questions at interview such as: "What are you doing now?" honestly will greatly reduce one's prospects, especially if reference statements from previous employers are not highly supportive.

Indeed, in such situations, one really needs a credible advocate or supporter to accompany one to the interview for support and to help plead one's case.

Conclusions

Optimistic and hopeful attitudes make success more likely and depression less likely.

Self-assessment and regulation, and creating achievable goals will also help reduce the likelihood of depression.

Building one's self-esteem and self-confidence, and having a supportive social network will also greatly improve one's mental health.

Chapter 11

THE WORKPLACE

> *People ask the difference between a leader and a boss.*
> *The leader works in the open, and the boss in covert.*
> *The leader leads, and the boss drives.*
> Theodore Roosevelt, speech 24 Oct. 1910, Binghamton N.Y.

Introduction

In the workplace leadership or management style, and communication are important issues. The following chapter briefly discusses some of the key requirements for good leadership, and how good communication and group loyalty improve workplace performance.

Leadership

According to Bennis (1989), becoming a leader involves:

➢ Ongoing curiosity and learning.

➢ A motivational vision.

➢ Communicating that vision to inspire others to follow it.

➢ Being prepared to take risks.

➢ Maturity, honesty, and willingness to accept criticism.

➢ Searching for solutions to problems.

➢ Seeking success in small, incremental steps rather than waiting years for "Big Success".

In *The One Minute Manager* three keys to good management are proposed:

1. Agree on up to 6 goals with staff and put them in writing.

2. Staff should provide detailed records of progress to management.

3. When there is a lack of progress, management feedback should focus on any poor results, not the persons responsible, and should encourage staff to keep trying (Blanchard & Johnson, 1981).

Leadership and group performance

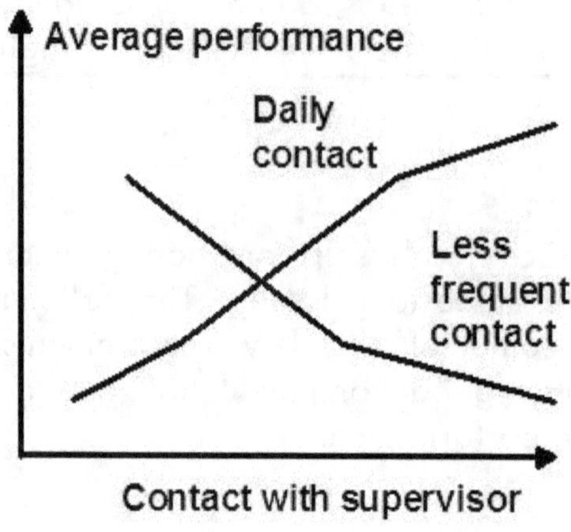

Figure 11.1. Communication with management.

Formal communication within a company will tend to follow the corporate structure. Effective communication can considerably improve productivity and morale.

Figure 11.1 shows the results of a study of the relationship between mean or average performance (or productivity) and amount of contact with the group supervisor. Clearly relatively frequent and regular management contact improves productivity as one would expect (Mohr, 2017, 2014b, 2018d, 2018f).

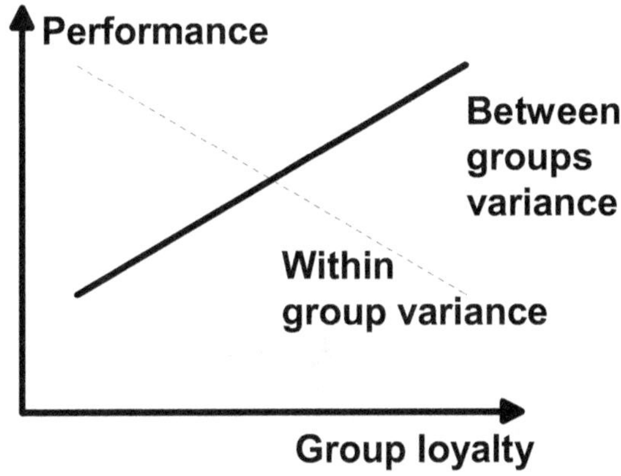

Figure 11.2. Performance and communication
with boss vs. group loyalty.

Figure 11.2 shows the type of result obtained in a correlation of worker performance and group loyalty, indicating that productivity improves if group loyalty is high. In part this improvement results from the (necessary) emergence of 'team leadership'.

The study of Figure 11.2 also found that correlation between the proportion of workers who took their complaints to the boss and group loyalty took the same form (that shown).

In addition, the correlation between how easy the group found communication with the boss and group loyalty also took the same (ascending) form shown in Figure 11.2.

Effective communication (and hence loyalty) within the group and with the supervisor, therefore, both lead to improved productivity. In addition group loyalty improves communication with the supervisor, that is, the factors of group loyalty, amount of supervisor communication, quality of supervisor communication, and productivity are all interwoven in such a way as to suggest that if communication is optimized considerable improvements in productivity might result.

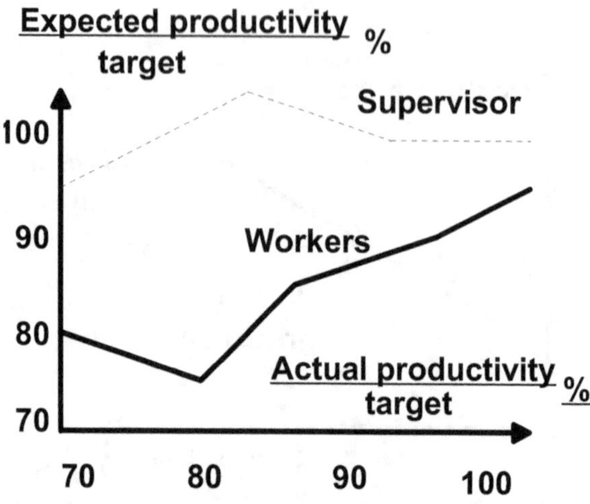

Figure 11.3. Expected vs. actual productivity

Figure 11.3 shows expected productivity compared to actual productivity for both the supervisor and the workers. Clearly the expectations of the supervisor are greater than those of the workers and are always fairly close to the target productivity.

The expectations of the workers, on the other hand, are for improvement when productivity is low and for slowing down when productivity is high, and are perhaps more realistic.

Unfortunately, however, there is no data from this study on the correlation between supervisor and worker expectations though this, of course, would depend on communications and, in any case, productivity variation is our main concern.

Figure 11.4 shows the results of a study of the effect of attitude of supervisor on productivity. There was a considerable spread in the results but there was sufficient correlation to support the finding that the more favourable the attitude of the supervisor (to both the workers and the job) the greater the productivity, as one might expect.

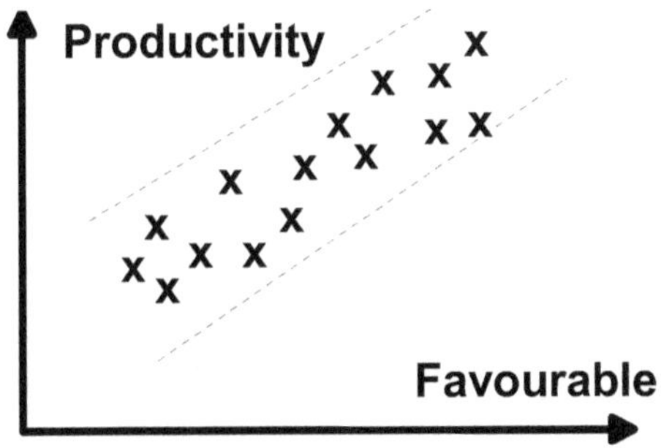

Figure 11.4. Dependence of productivity on supervisor attitude.

We might also expect that favourable supervisor attitude resulted in more favourable worker attitude and that the latter also results in greater productivity.

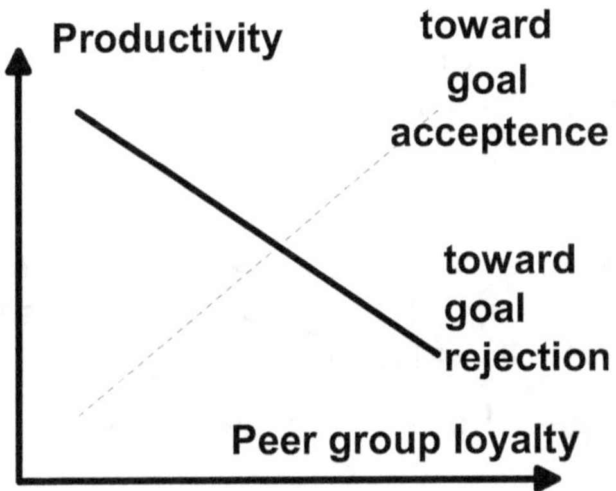

Figure 11.5. Loyalty towards company goals vs. productivity

Figure 11.5 shows the relationship of peer group loyalty to productivity when motivation is towards accepting versus rejecting company goals. Clearly peer group loyalty towards company goals results in greater productivity as one would expect.

The results of Figure 11.5 are related to those of Figure 11.2, showing that group loyalty is a very important factor in productivity.

Surviving in the workplace

In Table 12.1 I score two bad bosses who did much to ruin my life.

One key moment was, having had an important promotion unfairly and dishonestly delayed, and then been bullied into resigning.

Had I talked to another colleague about the issue, however, I would have been advised not to resign, but get help in dealing with the new HOD who had caused me problems.

Indeed, when doing my PhD in Cambridge in 1975 – 76, I talked of returning to Australia to finish it in May of 1976. He advised me against this, so I stayed, submitting my thesis in December 1976, adding a couple of pages of addenda after the 'viva' about a month later.

There is, of course, an important lesson to be learnt from these two contrasting experiences.

Conclusion

Besides those conclusions already made in the foregoing discussion, the following recommendations are suggested as worthwhile by the results of Figures 11.1 – 11.5:

[1] There should be effective communication of productivity goals.

[2] There should be thorough assessment of productivity results.

[3] Groups and tasks with low productivity should be identified.

[4] Group loyalty should be encouraged and groups should be motivated to accept new staff and 'loners' in a group.

[5] Leadership audits should be used.

[6] Supervisors should exhibit favourable attitude and communicate frequently and regularly with their staff.

[7] Group loyalty toward company goals should be sought.

[8] Supervisors should make themselves freely available to staff with complaints and other feedback and make themselves easy to communicate with.

Generally, therefore, good leadership involving sufficient efficient communication of goals and team attitudes is likely to result in very considerable improvements in productivity.

It is also important, however, that measurements are made of productivity, group loyalty and management efficiency. The results will then be useful in identifying problems requiring correction and productivity results when favourable, for example, can be used as motivational information for supervisors and their groups (Mohr, 2014b, 2018d, 2018f).

As shown in Figs 11.1 to 11.5 effective communication that improves productivity will:

[1] Be regular.

[2] Promote communication and thence loyalty between workers.

[3] Communicate realistic production targets.

[4] Project a positive management attitude to both the work and the workers.

[5] Promote worker loyalty to the company and thence acceptance of company goals.

Developing detailed business policy, therefore, requires a lot of thought and the ongoing operation of a company requires a good deal of communication and, in turn, much thought about feedback etc.

Effective management and communication leads, of course, to better results, and also to a happier and more productive workplace with people taking less time off work for mental health issues such as anxiety and depression.

☺ ☻ ☹ ☺ ☻ ☹ ☺ ☻ ☹ ☺ ☻ ☹ ☺ ☻ ☹

11. THE WORKPLACE

Chapter 12

HIERARCHICAL ORGANIZATIONS

I'm the boss. I'm allowed to yell.
Ivan Boesky, q. in *Den of* Thieves, James B Stewart, 1991.

In every one of those little stucco boxes there's some poor bastard
who's never free except when he's fast asleep
and dreaming that he's got the boss down the bottom
of a well and is bunging lumps of coal at him.
George Orwell, *Coming Up For Air,* pt 1., ch. 2 (1939).

Corporate structure

Corporate structure is the hierarchical structure and communication channels giving rise to the chain of command and response in a company or organization.

Most companies have a functional structure, larger companies having a divisional structure, with a functional structure for each division, as in the example of Figure 12.1.

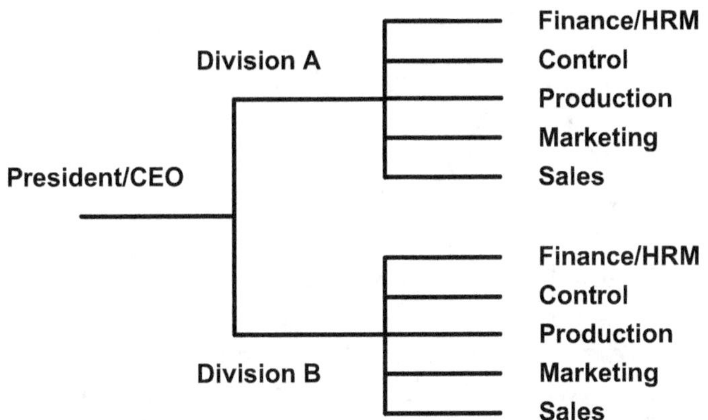

Figure 12.1. Divisional corporate structure.

The Peter Principle

Dr Laurence Peter drew on his experiences in the education sector to try and explain why we always seem to have lousy leaders (Peter & Hull, 1969). The result was his celebrated *Peter Principle:*

> ### *In a hierarchy every employee tends to rise to his own level of incompetence.*

In other words, *the sour cream rises.*

A corollary is: *In time every post tends to be occupied by an employee who is incompetent to carry out his duties.*

In his often tongue-in-cheek book Peter gives a few excellent historical examples of his celebrated principle, including:

(a) Socrates was a brilliant philosopher but a lousy defence attorney.

(b) Hitler was a brilliant politician but a lousy general.

Mohr's Law of Hierarchies

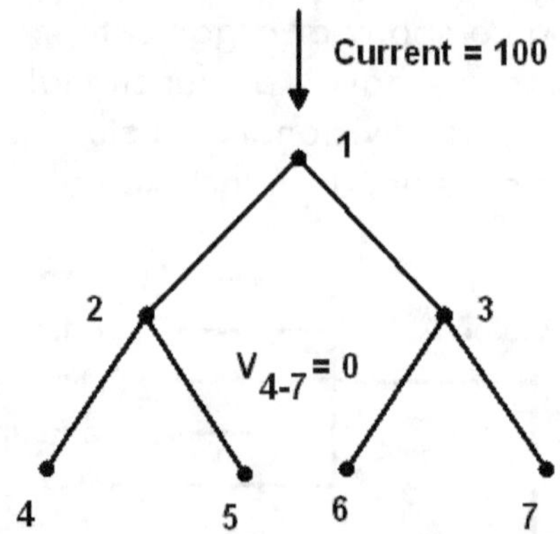

Figure 12.1. Hierarchical network.

This can illustrated by the small (hierarchical) DC network shown in Figure 12.1 which can be modeled as a DC network using a simple Finite Element Method program (Mohr, 1992, 2012a, 2018e).

At node 1 we have the pyramid building and lunatic 'boss' and a current 'load' of 100 is input. This is done by specifying the voltage at node 1 as 100, this being equivalent to adding a 'load' to the network.

Then zero datum voltage is specified at nodes 4-7 and unit resistance is given to all 6 elements so that the results from the program are:

Voltage 75 at node 1.
Voltage 25 at nodes 2 and 3.
Zero voltage at nodes 4 to 7.
Currents 50 in the top two elements and 25 in the rest.

This illustrates what the 'econobabble' of economists and politicians calls 'the trickledown effect', that is, the boss of this very small hierarchy has 3 times the voltage (or power, money and status) of his subordinates (the front line managers) one rung below. The workers at the bottom have no status at all.

If we add a further bottom row of 8 nodes in Figure 12.1 then now the 'voltage hierarchy' is 87.5, 37.5, 12.5, 0 so that the boss now does 7 times as well as the 'front line managers' on the row above the bottom row.

Then if we add a further fifth row of 16 nodes the voltage hierarchy is 93.75, 43.75, 18.75, 6.25, 0 and the boss does 15 times as well as the front line managers and infinitely better than the workers at the bottom!

The latter 'voltage hierarchy' is the fundamental principle of modern management, leading to Mohr's Law of Hierarchies:

> *In hierarchical organizations the amount of real material-producing work people do is inversely proportional to their rank or level in the organization.*
> *The amount of compensation they receive, however, is proportional to their level, sometimes to an exponential degree.*

For such people their earnings might be expressed as an exponential function: $\$ = C \exp(kR)$

where $\$$ = salary, R = rank, and C and k are constants.

This, of course, is not fair at all.

In ancient times philosophers felt that nobody should be paid more than about 10 or 20 times as much as anybody else, and even that is a great difference, of course, but it might be justified in the case of an elected national leader who must be able to present a strong, powerful image and might have only a relatively short term in office.

In the case of big business, however, things have got out of hand and remuneration of CEOs is often tens of millions, on top of which they get huge share issues as annual bonuses, huge 'golden handshakes' when they retire, and gigantic 'golden parachutes' then the company collapses.

To add insult to the injury of poverty, the worker-slaves endure 'top-down one-way' (TDOW) communication as they did all through their long years at school, in other words, they are treated like shit.

This is grossly unjust as the poor peasants who work on farms, in factories or on building sites produce what is essential to human life, that is: food, clothing, housing etc.

So those posters often seen in the USSR decades ago which pictured the workers as heroic perhaps made some sense. Then, of course, the hammer and sickle on their flag was also symbolic of the importance of the workers.

So the bottom line is that we have to create fairer societies which have real or *direct democracy* and leaders who 'check their ego at the door'. In these greed, hunger, famine, war and other evils will not be tolerated by the people.

Power corrupts

As figure 12.1 illustrates, the higher up you are in a hierarchy the more 'power' you have, which might be stated symbolically as:

$$P = C R^n$$

where P = power, R = rank, and C and n are constants.

Assuming the value of n is 2 then when one is twice as high in the hierarchy one has four times as much power.

Then, as we all know, power corrupts, one of the major factors in mankind's endless history of conflict.

As noted in the previous section, salaries may increase exponentially in hierarchical organizations and this result can be related to Mohr's Law of Capitalism which is the exponential growth law of money ($) with time (T):

$d(\$)/d(T) = c_1(activity)$ where $activity = c_2\ \$$

Here the rate at which money is made is proportional to the rate of business activity, this in turn proportional to the amount of money available to fund this activity.

Combining the two constants above as $k = c_1 c_2$ we have

$d(\$)/d(T) = k\$$ where k is the *growth factor.*

where $\$$ = money made.

This last equation is *separable* which means that it can be integrated in the form

Integral $[\ d(\$)/\$\ ]$ = Integral $[\ k\ d(T)\ ]$

giving, with the inclusion of the initial values, the exponential growth law $\$/\$_0 = \exp[k(T - T_0]$

If, for example, the growth factor is 10% per year, that is k = 0.1, then over 10 years we obtain the growth ratio $\$/\$_0 = 2.7$, so that we have nearly *tripled* our money.

The only real beneficiaries, however, are those higher in the hierarchy. The workers at the bottom who do all the *real work* (sitting and raving at sometimes boozy board meetings is not hard work) can't usually save any money and thus are slaves to all intents and purposes.

This is an intolerable situation and the CEOs who earn 'megabucks' are, of course, corrupt, and such corruption has always sown the seeds of discontent that have always, sooner or later, ended up as revolutions.

Thus socialism tends to be ruled by a single dictator, but capitalism by a multiplicity of petty dictators:

> *Capitalism tends to produce a multiplicity of petty dictators each in command of his own little business kingdom. State Socialism tends to produce a single, centralized totalitarian dictatorship, wielding absolute authority . . . through a hierarchy of bureaucratic agents.*
> Aldous Huxley, *Ends and Means* (1937).

Politicians too are often corrupt, of course, often being found to take bribes from big business.

Monarchs and dictators, of course, have nearly always been the greediest of all. Not only do they help themselves to plenty of money and live in grand palaces, but throughout history their hunger for power and thence territorial gain has led to one war after another.

How hierarchies operate

Hierarchies operate through a chain of command, leaders meeting with a chosen few top-level executives responsible for overseeing the various operations of the organization. In the case of government, for example, there are ministers for defence, treasury, education, health, and so forth.

In each of these areas there is a permanent and hierarchical bureaucratic department with several levels of seniority ranging from head of the organization and department heads to front-line managers who manage teams of workers.

Through the whole chain of command there is an implicit level of intimidation and fear that usually makes sure that everybody does as they are told. At the front line, however, things often get ridiculous, for example the traditional screaming of army sergeants at their miserable subordinates.

It is through such bullying and intimidation, of course, that soldiers are brainwashed into following orders without question or delay, essentially becoming expendable slaves to satisfy the whims of their leaders. Don't worry about 'executive stress,' therefore, worry about 'slave-stress.'

Indeed, our many sports with a relationship to conflict, for example absurd rugby with its 'charge at the enemy' no matter what the risk of injury, or archery and rifle shooting, all relate to our historical predilection for conflict.

Throughout hierarchies there is, of course, ambition to rise, often leading to a good deal of competitive behaviour, much of it often downright dishonest and unfair. In politics, for example, plenty of 'backstabbing' goes on day in and day out.

This corresponds quite closely, perhaps, with the alpha-male behaviour seen in several animal species, notably our close relatives, gorillas. The result is, of course, that those who end up as leaders may well be the most rotten people in the organization and, indeed, historically in both government and business this has always proved to be the case to some extent at least. That is, leaders are always greedy and bossy to some extent at least, but often they are exceptionally so.

Within hierarchical organizations there is also conflict, particularly over the 'rat race' involved in rising in the hierarchy.

Indeed, often ambitious, driven people are psychopathic, the pathology of their condition involving lying, cheating, aggressiveness, and bullying to get to the top.

Given power, it seems, they become psychotic with dreams of greater wealth and power and thus superiority. Alexander the Great, for example, began to think that he must be divine.

The problem is that, being people who have proved themselves good at the 'rat race', they tend to be the worst leaders, exactly in accordance with the Peter Principle.

Not only that, power not only corrupts, it makes people vain, self-centred, neurotic, obsessive, and, basically, mad. Here I must hasten to note Mohr's 10th Law, that is, that things such as madness must be judged on a scale of 1 to 10, not merely as a true-or-false judgment.

Furthermore, I like to make the important distinction between *bad mad* (depression etc.) and *sad mad* (Mohr, 2012b, 2018c; Mohr et al., 2018), and all too often political leaders have been bad mad, for example Nero and Hitler.

Diagnosing psychopaths

Table 12.1. The Hare checklist for psychopaths.

	TRAIT	SCORE
	Facet 1: Interpersonal	
1	Glibness or superficial charm	1
2	Grandiose sense of self-worth	1
3	Pathological lying	2
4	Cunning or manipulative	1
	Facet 2: Affective	
5	Lack of remorse or guilt	1
6	Emotionally shallow	1
7	Callous or lack of empathy	1
8	Failure to accept responsibility for their own actions	1
	Facet 3: Lifestyle	
9	Need for stimulation (easily bored)	1
10	Parasitic lifestyle	1
11	Lack of realistic, long-term goals	0
12	Impulsivity	1
13	Irresponsibility	0
	Facet 4: Antisocial	
14	Poor behavioural controls	0
15	Early behavioural problems	0
16	Juvenile delinquency	0
17	History of conditional prison release being revoked	0
18	Criminal versatility	0
	Other traits:	
19	Many short-term marital relationships	0
20	Promiscuous sexual behaviour	0
TOTAL SCORE		**12**

In 1980, Canadian clinical psychologist Dr Robert Hare, who worked in prisons, released the first version of the Hare checklist for identifying psychopaths, and several further versions followed.

As shown in Table 12.1, it divides 20 personality traits into four groups: interpersonal, affective, lifestyle, and antisocial, these measuring traits including charm, propensity to lie, lack of remorse, and need for stimulation.

After an interview each trait is scored as 0 (not present), 1 (present but not dominant), or 2 (dominant), so that the maximum possible score is 40.

Average people score from 3 to 6, non-psychopathic criminals score from 16 to 22, whilst in the UK and US respectively, scores of >25 and >30 are taken as a positive diagnosis of psychopathy (Gillespie, 2017).

In Table 12.2 the first author has scored a couple of bad bosses he once had, both of whom were too young and inexperienced for being HOD, and played a major role in destroying his promising University career when he was less than 40.

Their total score of 12 seemed too low, as both seemed at least somewhat psychopathic, suggesting that Table 12.1 might apply more to hardened criminals for which item 17 relates to a form of 'treatment', namely continued imprisonment, presumably because of little or no sign of rehabilitation or remorse. Similarly, items 16 and 19 relate to past history.

Thus criteria for judging a bad boss should include:

➢ Bossiness.

➢ Assertiveness.

➢ Dishonesty and lying.

➢ Selfishness and greed.

➢ Vanity.

➢ Bullying.

The recent book *The Psychology of Life* discusses the alternative Mohr Checklist for Psychopaths (MCLP), this working better for the two bad boss example cases scored in Table 12.1 and referred to above (Mohr, 2018f).

Dealing with psychopaths

Gillespie (2017) suggests that organizations which are run using 'Management by Objectives' (MBO) are conducive to psychopathic bosses:

"The only way for a psychopath to succeed in a structure based on MBO would be to fall in with the objectives of his team and his superiors. Anything else would mark him out for removal from the organization."

Alternatively, Gillespie suggests that persons deemed to be psychopaths can be got rid of by getting them 'fired', but this, of course, is very difficult to bring about when the only person in the part of the organization in question able to do firing is a psychopathic boss, as is often the case.

When you do go above his or her head seeking to get them fired they counterattack, usually resulting in the person or persons complaining being disciplined or fired.

Most workers, therefore, simply have to endure bad and mad bosses and a 2016 study of Australian workplaces with "toxic leaders" concluded that the following strategies were unwise (Gillespie, 2017):

➢ Confronting the leader.

➢ Avoiding, ignoring or bypassing the boss.

➢ Whistleblowing.

➢ Worrying to excess about the boss.

➢ Continued anger and frustration.

➢ Focusing on work to try and forget about the boss.

➢ Taking sick leave (giving only short-term relief).

Instead, Gillespie says one should behave as a polite and compliant employee and do whatever one is told, no matter how much one dislikes it.

Then to survive in this way one should also:

- ➢ Think about a future, better job.

- ➢ Make sure your fellow workers don't 'tell' on each other.

- ➢ Check the accuracy of what the boss says.

- ➢ Don't show any anger and frustration.

- ➢ Build a support network.

- ➢ Document every bad thing the boss does, noting the time, date and names of any witnesses.

In this way one can survive for the medium term, at least, and perhaps build a case against the bad boss that might result in him being disciplined, demoted or shifted sideways, or even fired.

The bottom line, of course, is that there is a lesson to be learnt by any reader from this, that is, if having problems with a bad boss, give plenty of thought and get as much help as needed to deal with the problem and, hopefully, resolve it somehow, whether that help is simply support from one or two other staff members, or help from people above the bad boss in the hierarchy, and, if need be, lawyers.

Conclusion

Hierarchies are difficult to deal with over the long term.

When one is young, and not long out of the education system, they are simply a learning experience at first. Over time, however, grudges over being treated badly, and impatience over lack of promotion, grow and grow to the point at which getting another job may seem the only hope of improving one's life and career prospects.

If one has a psychopathic 'bastard boss', however, it may be impossible to get a halfway supportive reference from them, without which getting a decent job, or any job at all in line with your abilities, qualifications and experience, may prove difficult.

Some of the concepts and suggestions made in the foregoing chapter may be of some help, however, to workers with bad bass problems.

Primarily, of course, one needs at least one or two helpers within the organization in question. A problem here is that the workers at the same level in the hierarchy are also competing for the same promotion that you are. Thus, if you are in a group of, say, 10 seeking promotion to 'Senior xyz', then one might establish a mutually supportive relationship with just one of them, hoping that you will both be the next two workers promoted.

With the recent rise of the ME TO movement, bullying in the workplace has, like sexual abuse in the Catholic Church, become a prominent issue.

In dealing with a bad boss it helps to:

> Identify any psychopathic behaviours of the boss.
> Try to speak carefully to the boss about the problems, perhaps with a friend or colleague to back you up.
> Get as much as possible from the bad boss in writing.
> Consider recording bad behavior somehow.
> Ask advice from friends and family about any problems.
> Go above the bad boss in the hierarchy about problems.
> Speak to counselors and perhaps lawyers about problems.
> Consider using a simple 'person scaling' survey of fellow workers to get a 'rating' of the bad boss which might then be given to people higher in the hierarchy.

The bottom line, however, is that when one suffers bullying, threats etc. from bad bosses, one should make careful records of such behavior and seek help in dealing with the issue, being careful to behave at a professional and courteous manner at all times, hoping not to exacerbate the situation, but to resolve it as well as possible, and to the benefit of all parties.

☺☻☹☺☻☹☺☻☹☺☻☹☺☻☹

Chapter 13

HOME LIFE

Introduction

People who live alone are, of course, more prone to depression and anxiety because quite simply, living alone means that one has more to worry about, ranging from shopping, cooking, cleaning etc.

Today, of course, younger people often share flats and houses and, of course, that is a way of meeting other people.

It is also a way of meeting the opposite sex. Indeed, it is my experience more than once that advertising a room in a house is a quite likely way of finding a friend and women know this full well. They are fully aware of the possible consequences of living in the same abode as another man and, indeed, often seek to meet a man in this way.

Share houses can be chaotic, to say the least, and most people would prefer to have just one 'partner' in life to live with. This raises the question of 'love' etc.

Love at first sight?

When a single person looking for a partner meets a person of the opposite sex they should try to form a sound opinion of the person by considering such factors as:

- Looks.
- Body language. This is especially important, including how does it feel to have the person close to you?
- Personality.
- Do they seem relaxed or nervous meeting you?
- Do they seem genuinely pleased to meet you?
- Their age, occupation and educational background.
- Have they been single for long? If so, why?
- Where did their parents come from?
- What do her parents do?

This is quite a lot of data to gather and it may take more than one meeting to acquire it. At the first meeting a kiss or hug or two is OK but nothing more than that should be considered. If either person is too drunk to care about this limitation then that should end the first meeting. If polite refusal causes offence that is good reason to end the first meeting and never have another one.

If a second meeting is had that allows time to complete the foregoing data list and assess the person and also assess your own feelings for the person. The second meeting, however, is still too soon to sensibly consider having sex with the person.

Evaluating your response to a new acquaintance is important, as is estimating what you think their response to you is. In both cases the cognitive response should be instant recognition, followed by facial expressions and body language that indicate attitude, and finally behaviour such as, for example, turning away from you which, of course, is probably a sure sign of negative feelings.

If things go so far as meeting two or three times you should be in a position to make a decision table to evaluate the new friend and thus decide whether to continue the relationship for a significant period.

Table 13.1. Decision table.

	Scores/10	
Attribute	**Person A**	**Person B**
Looks		
Body language		
Personality		
Talkative		
Apparent IQ		
Family background		
Education		
Occupation		
Honesty (perceived)		
Good worker?		
Generous		
Friends or a loner?		
Sex OK		
TOTAL		

Table 13.1 is a decision table comparing the attributes of two people using Likert Scaling (Likert 1961; Eagly & Chaiken 1993). Obviously if one has a much better score than the other then that might suggest them as a better partner for a long-term relationship.

Believe it or not, a woman I once met when divorced put me under a tiny bit of pressure on the commitment issue and I responded by suggesting such a table. She duly compiled one and in the column for me the score for sex was blanked out, perhaps mercifully!

On a more serious note, communication depends in part sometimes in what two people have in common to talk about, for example, what to have for dinner, or their children. At the beginning of a relationship, however, it is far more important to assess whether there is much in your respective personal and family backgrounds to talk about.

Do you for example, have similar tastes in music, literature and sport? Are you both the 'arty' or the scientific types? And so on, but very important.

Communication will also depend, in part at least, on intelligence. When you talk about a certain subject does the other person sometimes quickly respond with new information or a useful suggestion? If so, that is a sign of intelligence.

Jencks et al. (1975) report that men with IQs of 120 have wives with an average IQ of 111 and that wives with an IQ of 120 have husbands with an average IQ of 111.

Thus they have not married randomly for, had they done so, their partners would have an average IQ of 100.

Living together

The decision whether or not to live together should be based on data such as that required for Table 13.1 and, of course, should not be made in haste.

Only a few decades ago unmarried men and women living together were deemed to be living in sin and whether or not to get married usually took years to decide.

This has changed greatly but still the decision on whether to live in a de facto marriage situation should not be taken lightly and only after the relationship has lasted at least a few months without problems.

When a couple do decide to live together that is only a beginning of sorts. Presumably sex has been tried out a good deal before cohabiting, hopefully with effective contraceptive measures in place. Such measures should continue, of course, until the relationship has lasted for, preferably, a few years.

At that point the relationship can be carefully reassessed and a decision made as to whether it should be continued.

If so, the question of children might be considered, but only after careful thought and planning, including careful consideration of whether the job and financial prospects of one, if not both, partners are secure for the long term.

On the important question of children advice is essential from friends, relatives and preferably a professional counselor, the bottom line being that marriage and relationship guidance counselors are needed before marriage, and most certainly before having children, not when the marriage strikes problems.

Indeed, independent advisors can consider the physical, emotional, and financial conditions of the relationship and thus take a 'potential child's' point of view in deciding whether it should be had.

Similarly, I would urge couples with children considering breaking up to be more democratic and consider their children's view of the matter also.

Communication

Lack of effective and constructive communication is the great problem of the human race. What makes us unique amongst animals is our enlarged cerebral cortex that stores the semantic memory required for our advanced languages.

Yet throughout history we have continued to behave just like the chimps that Jane Goodall (van Lawick-Goodall, 1971) was so disillusioned by, we have periodic conflicts with other groups of people, be it tribes, nations or followers of another religion.

This is largely because of a lack of *effective* communication and thence *understanding* of other people.

Such understanding is, of course, made more difficult when people speak a different language, but men and women also, in effect, speak different languages to some extent at least, in part because of their different upbringing, and thence different issues and related vocabulary.

As a result of their different, somewhat socially stereotyped, upbringing, men and women have different values. Women, of course, care more about children, in part owing to the powerful 'maternal instinct'. Men, on the other hand, care more about the football team they follow winning, and such comparatively trivial pursuits tend to alienate them from many women.

There are many more minor differences. Women care much more about their appearance, having been brought up supposed to look beautiful. Men's business suits, on the other hand, relate to army uniforms and are designed to make them look stupid, not hard to do.

These differences, of course, make communication difficult. As a somewhat tongue-in-cheek test of this, try sending a member of an all-male board to a meeting dressed as a woman!

In a marital-type relationship, however, I would recommend that the partners have some sort of discussion every day or two. At this they can air their respective gripes about each other, if any, and it is far better to bring them out in the open in this way than risk the other partner complaining to other people about you as this may result in rumours which may be damaging to your reputation.

Perhaps more important, the partners should discuss any problems they may be having at work as these may pose a risk to a partner's career. Problems with their children should, of course, also be discussed.

Finally, financial matters should be discussed occasionally to make sure that the family financial situation is sound.

Partnership

A marital-type relationship should, of course, be a partnership and the work should be shared. In the traditional male breadwinner scenario housewives would always complain that they were still busy cooking and dealing with children after the man had finished work, giving rise to the old saying:

"A woman's work is never done."

Today, a high proportion of wives are also employed at least part-time, often requiring expensive day care for children, and this places a considerable financial stress on many families that are also struggling to pay substantial rents or mortgages.

Even when both partners work full-time, however, most women find themselves doing most of the housework, men are now encouraged to spend more time helping with both housework and caring for and teaching children.

If the working woman cum housewife then has a little more spare time that can be spent relaxing and talking with their partner, thus helping keep the relationship working congenially and effectively.

Healthy life

Healthy lifestyle should be a primary objective in every family, this including sound diet, watching one's weight, getting enough exercise, getting plenty of quality sleep, and getting enough relaxation time.

A healthy diet should, of course, include plenty of vegetables and a little fruit, limit fat (particularly saturated and trans fat) and thence meat (especially red meat), limit fatty fast food, limit fatty and salty snack foods, and limit sugary confectionary and drinks.

Children should limit sugar, of course, to protect their teeth, also brushing them soon after eating. Indeed, I find it lamentable that there is no provision for this at school.

Watching one's weight and exercise, of course, go together, and it is important to keep one's weight fairly close to that recommended for one's height and sex (Mohr, 2012c, 2013a, 2015, 2018a, 2018b).

To help build strong bodies children should have about an hour of exercise daily, including walking, and when old enough they should be encouraged to do an average of half an hour of more strenuous exercise daily.

For good health the same exercise requirements apply to adults, regular medium intensity exercise being required for a healthy heart and circulation system, for example.

A few hours of relaxation time is also necessary and this, of course, can include such entertainments as TV, music and reading.

For adults circa 8 hours of good quality sleep is necessary for good mental and physical health. Here the shared double bed can be a problem. If, for example, one partner snores, as is often the case, that can pose serious problems. Lonely young children invading the room in the middle of the night is another problem lessened (roughly halved, in fact) if the parents have separate rooms.

Sexual intercourse is merely an act of breeding which humans, being in most respects the most stupid creatures on the planet, as our always troubled history suggests, attach much too much importance to.

On the issue of satisfactory sex, according to the landmark Kinsey report, 10 percent of married women had never had orgasm during sexual intercourse, and 25 percent had not had orgasm during the first year of marriage (Lindzey et al, 1978).

Some people think that a couple's sex life might be better if they slept in separate beds, if not separate rooms, especially if one partner snores. Then, refreshed by sleeping well each night, a little 'mucking around' could be done on a more occasional basis if both partners had a double bed, even if in separate rooms, but perhaps with a shared bathroom between them.

The bottom line is that sharing a bed for life with the same ultimately 'rotting' thing is arguably somewhat insane, and certainly physically unhealthy, if not distasteful, if one had half one's wits left that is.

Conclusion

One problem in marriage is that young men are not brought up thinking about children and romance. Often they are really just finding their way in the world a little when they have their first sexual relationship or two with women. When they all too often end up with unplanned for children they are completely unprepared for the situation.

Young women, on the other hand, have been brought up playing with dolls, and for them children are a raison d'etre.

In addition, they see getting married to some nice man and having children as being romantic. Indeed, much of the huge publishing and movie industries are based on this.

Thus, when the somewhat humdrum reality of marriage with wailing children emerges women are often quite disillusioned.

No doubt that is why we call that holiday taken after marriage the honeymoon, because reality will hit when the honeymoon ends, of course.

For marriage to work the relationship must have been a carefully chosen one in the beginning. Then the marriage should only have been made after careful thought and advice, and after the relationship has endured for a substantial amount of time.

More important still, children should only be had if the relationship is likely to last, and after plenty of thought, discussion, advice and counseling, along with proper career and financial planning.

Then one should also note that, with the world already overpopulated with humans, it is best to have only one or two children, also noting that only children and children from smaller families tend to have higher IQ (Vernon, 1960).

Then, to keep the partnership working well, frequent and effective communication and planning is required, along with optimism or 'hope' (GA, RS & PE Mohr., 2018), to ensure a healthy and happy life for the whole family.

☺ ☺ ☹ ☺ ☺ ☹ ☺ ☺ ☹ ☺ ☺ ☹ ☺ ☺ ☹

13. Home Life

Chapter 14

SOCIAL LIFE

> *Compare society to a boat. Her progress through the water*
> *will not depend upon the exertion of her crew,*
> *but upon the exertion devoted to propelling her.*
> *This will be lessened by any expenditure of force in fighting*
> *among themselves, or in pulling in different directions.*
> Henry George, *Progress and Poverty*, bk. 10, ch. 3 (1879).

Social norms

Social norms are standards or expectations that govern people's actions in various social situations. Generally, we learn about social norms by observing what other people in our culture say and do. In almost every culture there is a norm holding that to be selfish is wrong, and to be helpful is right.

Two norms that encourage us to be helpful are (Grivas & Carter, 2005):

1. The *reciprocity norm*, which is based on the notion that we should be prepared to give to others what we receive, or expect to receive. We should, therefore, help others that help us, but many people, such as children and the elderly may not have the resources or capability to give as much help as they receive.

2. The *social responsibility norm* prescribes that we should help those that need help. Whether we do, in fact, help people in need depends on many factors, including the urgency of their need, and how much 'implicit' social pressure we feel to help them.

Social support

Social life is generally considered important, solitude being associated with loneliness, depression etc.

More important, perhaps, is that when things go wrong it is helpful to have supportive people, whether they be relatives, friends, or counselors, to turn to for advice and moral support.

Such people can provide help and encouragement that may provide hope in the most difficult of circumstances, and hope alone in most cases will help one cope in the short term.

Then, in the longer term, one can begin to fix the problem(s) in question, or 'move on' from them to work towards new goals.

Successful businesswoman Lillian Vernon recalls: *My father told me I had talent and a good idea for starting a business and I should never let anything get in the way of fulfilling my dream, or I would regret it for the rest of my life*, concluding: *So don't let challenges, setbacks, or detractors defeat or discourage you. If you believe in yourself and think positively, you will succeed* (Trump, 2004).

There are many activities, hobbies etc. via which one can meet and socialize with people, some of these being briefly discussed in following sections.

Sporting clubs and associations

An Australia, Australian Rules Football (AFL) is very popular, membership of some Australian Football League clubs totaling circa 100,000 members (for Collingwood it is 180,00 members), attendances at many games often being circa 90,000.

In Eastern states Rugby is also very popular, having two 'codes', the Australian Rugby Union, and the Australian Rugby League. Attendances for ARU and ARL games are typically 20,000 to 30,000.

In several countries cricket is a major sport, the "Ashes" tests series between Australia and England, and the Indian Premier League being of particular note, and having large attendances of up to 100,000.

Tennis remains a very popular sport globally, as evidenced by large attendances at the four "Grand Slam" tournaments in England, France, the USA, and Australia, and there are tennis venues and clubs in almost every suburb and town of substantial size in Australia.

Lawn bowls is also popular in many countries, Australia having lawn bowls clubs in most major suburbs of large cities with substantial memberships, mostly retired and elderly people.

Golf remains popular in many Western countries, the many suburban golf courses in Australia having substantial memberships and large clubhouses for social activities.

Horse racing is also a major sport in several countries, also providing an opportunity for plenty of socializing between races, as well as afterwards.

Several other sports also provide opportunities for socializing, including trotting (horses), greyhound racing, surfing, shooting, gyms, basketball, and netball.

Social clubs

There are many clubs formed for purely social purposes, examples in Melbourne, Australia, including the somewhat exclusive Melbourne Club, and the Atheneum Club.

Clubs and pubs

Pubs have a long history of providing social contacts between 'regulars', and an opportunity to meet people and make new friends.

In Australia there are now there are many "clubs" with dozens of poker machines which provide most of their revenue, with old-fashioned pubs with only a bar now regularly closing down.

These clubs also have bars and restaurants, and often have organized social groups which meet regularly.

Nightclubs and dances

In the central suburbs of major cities nightclubs provide late night booze and an opportunity socialize, and in particular meet and dance with members of the opposite sex.

There are also regular weekend dances organized at council-owned premises, most of these attended by young people with, or looking for, a girl or boy friend.

Writers groups

In many major cities many major cities there are several writers groups where people who have writing as a hobby meet once a month, some groups publishing a book of collected works by members every year.

Some members of such groups do write a book or two, sometimes using the growing 'self-publishing' industry to publish their books, and occasionally succeeding in find 'traditional' publisher to print and market their books.

These writers groups, however, are largely a social exercise providing an opportunity to meet like-minded people.

Art clubs

Few in number, there are a few arts clubs in which both amateur and professional artists meets and socialize and share ideas.

Religious activities

Religious services, of course, provide a regular opportunity to meet people afterwards, some churches, for example having a community lunch after their weekly Sunday service.

Many churches, synagogues etc. also hold occasional social evenings for members of the congregation.

The use of 'confessionals' by the Catholic Church is worth note, but the author believes it would be more helpful if churches provided a 'complaints service' instead in which people could air their problems. Not far from where the first author lives, however, the Anglican Church runs a community consultation service where people can discuss life problems.

Political meetings

Politics, of course, is very much about meetings, ranging from local branch meetings to the farcical 'raving clown show' of the antiquated and Westminster Parliamentary system of two major opposing parties yelling at each other from opposite sides of the "chamber".

Membership of the local branch of a political party, however, does provide a good deal of social contact with plenty of opportunity for discussion and sharing of views and opinions.

Helping in election campaigns, for example by 'door knocking', or handing out flyers at shopping centres and on election day, also provides opportunities to meet people and perhaps make a few new friends.

Regular local government council meetings can also be attended, perhaps providing an opportunity to meet people and make new and useful contacts.

The workplace

Workplaces, of course, often provide a good deal of opportunity for social contact. Typically, one has at least one or two friends in the workplace, and regular, if not daily, opportunities to chat with them over lunch, over drinks after work etcetera.

In a typically 'obsessed with sex' type of statement of the kind that made him infamous, Sigmund Freud said:

Laying stress upon the importance of work has a greater effect than any other technique of living in the direction of binding the individual more closely to reality; in his work he is at least securely attached to a part of reality, the human community. Work is no less valuable for the opportunity it and the human relations connected with it provide for a very considerable discharge of libidinal component impulses, narcissistic, aggressive and even erotic, than because it is indispensible for subsistence and justifies existence in a society.

Civilization and Its Discontents, 1930 (tr. Joan Riviere),
q. in *The Oxford Book of Work,* ed. K. Thomas (1999).

Conclusion

There are many activities, clubs, and other organizations that provide an opportunity for social contact.

Many of these organizations have regular meetings, sometimes purely for social purposes.

Branch meetings of political parties are, however, are usually relatively formal but usually have an informal chat session over drinks and snacks afterwards, as do meetings of many other social, sporting etc. organizations.

Chapter 15

RETIREMENT AND OLD AGE

> **Neural Darwinism.** A term coined by Nobel laureate Gerald Edelman, this describes the process in which neurons that receive constant stimulation grow and those that do not atrophy. MS Sweeney, *The Complete Mind* (2009).

Introduction

Globally, the human population is growing rapidly, and between 2015 and 2050, the proportion of the world's population over 60 years of age will nearly double from 12% to 22%, or in absolute terms from 900 million to 2 billion.

Over 20% of adults older than 60 year suffer from a mental or neurological disorder, causing about 7% of all disability, and accounting for almost 20% of years lived with disability.

34% of adults over 70 have at least one mental disorder.

The most common mental and neurological disorders in older people are dementia and depression, affecting 14% and 9% of people over 70 respectively. Anxiety disorders affect about 12% people over 70. Substance abuse problems affect almost 1% of people over 60, and about a quarter of deaths from self-harm are among people aged 60 or more.

Mental health problems in the elderly result from such factors as: illness, frailty, loss of independence, death of loved ones, financial stress, changing living arrangements, and social isolation.

Social isolation can be lessened by the activities discussed in the previous chapter, and ways in which physical and mental health can be improved are discussed in following sections.

Reducing aging

Unhealthy arteries not only means development of atherosclerosis, and with it the risk of heart disease, but also increased aging of the brain, the cerebral cortex losing up to 30% of its neuronal activity with aging, though dendrites lengthen to compensate in part for this.

To reduce physical and mental aging one should establish a sound diet, dietary supplements, exercise and relaxation routine to normalize cholesterol and homocysteine levels, including plenty of antioxidants to reduce DNA mutations and thence cancer risk (Mohr, 2012c, 2013a, 2015, 2018a, 2018b).

A truly healthy lifestyle will also reduce the effects of any harmful food substances and any genetic disadvantages you may have concerning, for example, predisposition to heart disease or breast cancer.

Research in recent decades has shown that *neurogenesis,* the growth of new neurons by cell division, occurs in birds, tree shrews, primates, and humans, whilst the nervous systems of some fish and amphibians continue to grow in size throughout life. Neurogenesis may have been lessened in primates to retain past learning more efficiently, but humans can create neurons in brain areas such as the hippocampus, amygdala, and cerebral cortex for new learning (Cozolino, 2002).

Memory loss with age

Jane Durga at Wageningen University in the Netherlands gave 818 people aged 50-75 800 mg of folic acid (about 3 times the RDA) a day, or a dummy pill. Three years later the supplement users did as well as people 5.5 years younger on memory tests, and as well as people 1.9 years younger on cognitive speed tests (Holford, 2009).

As this improvement no doubt related to reduction of homocysteine levels, homocysteine being one of the main villains in both atherosclerosis and neural pathway deterioration, other homocysteine-lowering nutrients such as B6 and B12 should be likely to reduce brain aging as well and, indeed, studies are in progress on this issue (Holford, 2009).

Research has shown that antioxidants improve IQ in children. They also reduce memory loss with aging, much of which is owing to reduced liver function, and antioxidants reduce the 'detox burden' on the liver (which may include excess alcohol).

Well-known now, DHA and EPA oils improve brain function. The herb ginkgo biloba is also helpful and a double-blind placebo-controlled French trial found that giving 320 mg a day to 60 to 80 year-olds improved cognitive processing speed to that of healthy young adults (Holford, 2009).

Acetyl-L-carnitine (ACL) boosts energy production in the brain, improves the brain's glutamate receptors responsible for learning, and may stop formation of lipofucian, an "age spot" in neurons that interferes with memory (Gottlieb et al., 1990).

ACL is expensive and glutamine, the most abundant amino acid in the cerebrospinal fluid surrounding the brain, is an alternative. One US study of healthy volunteers found glutamine enhanced problem-solving ability.

Phospholipids are also helpful in reducing age-related problems. Acetylycholine is derived from phosphatidyl choline (pure lecithin) and deficiency of this is probably, after high homocysteine levels, the main cause of declining memory with age, and Holford (2009), who calls acetylcholine "the memory molecule," recommends 5 to 10 gm of (commercial) lecithin to maximize mental function.

Gottlieb notes that 300 mg/day of another phospholipid, phosphatidyl serine (PS), has been found to reverse the chronological age of the outside layers of neurons by up to 12 years (Gottlieb et al., 1990).

Thus, to combat memory loss with age take[2]:

➢ Folic acid and B12, and also B6 and B1, B2, B3.
➢ Lecithin [5 - 10 gm], phosphatidyl choline (pure lecithin) or phosphatidyl serine. Linseeds will help absorption of lecithin (Mohr, 2012c, 2013, 2015).
➢ 1000 mg DHA and EPA, i.e. two fish oil capsules.

---

[2] Daily dosages recommended by Holford (2009) shown in [ ] brackets.

- Antioxidants A, C [3 gm], E [100 IU/decade of age], selenium and zinc.
- Glutamine [5 - 10 gm].
- Ginkgo biloba, 160 – 320 mg.
- ACL, 250 – 2,000 mg.

Finally, sustained stress is harmful to the brain[3] so relaxation and exercise (including mental exercise) will help reduce memory loss with age.

Alzheimer's Disease

Alzheimer's disease results in 'senile dementia of the Alzheimer type' (SDAT) which affects an ever-increasing number of people as the world's human population grows older.

Supplements required for this are, of course, similar to those of the preceding section:
- Folic acid [10 mcg], B12 [250 mcg] and B6 [20 mg] to reduce homocysteine levels.
- Lecithin (+ linseeds for absorption) to provide phospholipids. Firshein (1998) recommends phosphatidyl serine dosage of 150-300 mg/day.
- Omega-3 from fish oils.
- Turmeric.
- Antioxidants as in the preceding section.
- DHEA [15 mg], a precursor to testosterone and oestrogen.
- N-acetyl cysteine which is converted into the brain's primary antioxidant glutathione.
- Hyperzia serrata [200 mg], a moss which is an ancient Chinese remedy. This helps keep the neurotransmitter acetylcholine in circulation.
- ACL, 500 – 2,000 mg/day.

Turmeric's active ingredient is anti-inflammatory curcumin which breaks up plaques in Alzheimer's patients' brains (Holford, 2009).

---

[3] Because the stress hormone cortisol shrinks dendrites (Holford, 2009).

Parkinson's Disease

The conventional treatment for Parkinson's disease is the drug L-dopa which is a direct precursor of the neurotransmitter dopamine which is linked to mood and behaviour.

As with Alzheimer's, also a neural issue, homocysteine levels are linked to Parkinson's and B6 plays an additional role independent of its homocysteine-lowering one in preventing Parkinson's.

Indeed, Geoffrey and Lucille Leader tested patients with Parkinson's and found that "literally 100 percent of them had nutritional deficiencies based on tests that measure what is going on in the cells" (Holford, 2009).

Antioxidants help prevent free-radical damage to brain cells, slowing progression of Parkinson's disease, a 7-year pilot study finding that 3 gm C and 3,200 IU of E delayed the need for drug therapy by up to 2 or 3 years (Holford, 2009). This study published in 1992 used alpha-tocopherol; much better results would be expected with the much more potent tocotrienol forms of vitamin E.

Coenzyme Q10 is also helpful, being one of the most important antioxidants for protecting mitochondria, and a US study of 80 patients found that 1200 mg of CoQ10 slowed loss of motor function by 44%, 300-600 mg slowing it by 20% (Holford, 2009).

Thus useful supplements for Parkinson's disease include:
➢ B6, folic acid and B12.
➢ CoQ10 [1200 mg].
➢ Magnesium.
➢ C [3 gm], E [3,200 IU], selenium and zinc.

In addition plenty of protein should be had, perhaps some of it as supplements, because protein is converted with the aid of B6 to L-phenylalanine.

This, with the aid of folate, magnesium, manganese, iron, copper, zinc and C, is converted to L-tyrosine which the same substances convert to L-dopa which is used in drug form for conventional treatment (Holford, 2009).

B6 and zinc then convert L-dopa to dopamine, C converts this to noradrenalin, which B12, folate and niacin then convert to adrenalin.

It also helps to reduce stress levels, avoid environmental and other toxins, and reduce auto-intoxication from constipation by taking magnesium, perhaps as cheap Epsom Salts, magnesium also being helpful for muscle, arterial and brain function.

Finally, according to Gottlieb et al. (1990), Parkinson's patients have low levels of the hormone DHEA (dehydro-epaindrosterone) and medically supervised supplementation (10 mg/day for women and 25 mg/day for men) may reduce symptoms.

Other diseases involving the nervous system

Homocysteine not only attacks arteries, perhaps being the initial instigator of atherosclerosis, but also nerves and neural pathways in the brain. Many of the supplements cited in this chapter should be helpful in treating MS, in particular B12, injections of which totally eliminated symptoms in one patient (Firshein, 1998), and perhaps vitamin D now being trialed for MS treatment.

The author also believes it likely that trigeminal neuralgia and Carpal tunnel syndrome may be caused by the cyst-like fibrolipid plaques of atherosclerosis. Initially these extend inside arteries, but with further growth they bulge outside the artery, perhaps interfering with adjacent nerves in the face, in the case of trigeminal neuralgia, or adjacent nerves in the hand in the case of Carpal tunnel syndrome which "results from median nerve entrapment as it passes through a tunnel in the wrist" (Walther, 1988).

Vitamin B6 deficiency has been found to cause the symptoms of carpel tunnel syndrome and it has been found that B6 dosage of 2 mg/day reduced symptoms, whilst 100 mg/day of pyridoxine for 12 weeks has been found to "correct" the condition. Applied kinesiology treatments involving appropriate manipulations of the hand and wrist have also been found helpful (Walther, 1988).

Carpal tunnel syndrome may also result from trauma to the hand such as stopping a fall with the hand extended, from regular 'wear and tear' in occupations such as carpentry or typing, the latter being a classical cause with heavy old-fashioned typewriters which required significantly more pressure to operate them than modern PC keyboards.

Shingles is an acute and painful inflammation of the spinal nerve ganglia, often associated with a prominent, itchy and painful rash around the middle of the body, and sometimes on the face, neck, arms and legs as well. The rash usually goes after 2-3 weeks, sometimes leaving scars, but the pains which are known as post-herpetic neuralgia can persist for much longer. Therapies for shingles include acupuncture, aromatherapy, reflexology, 'visualization' (of the rash vanishing), and hydrotherapy. Such treatments, and also 'colour therapy', acupressure, yoga and massage are helpful for trigeminal neuralgia and carpal tunnel syndrome (Shealy, 1999)

Strokes

A stroke occurs when a blood clot or ruptured blood vessel cuts off blood flow to the brain, which requires about 20% of the body's oxygen supply. Without oxygenated blood, brain cells die, resulting in loss of cognitive and/or motor functions.

There are four types of stroke:

[1] Thrombotic strokes - when an artery supplying the brain is blocked by fatty deposits.

[2] Embolic strokes - when a fatty clot forms elsewhere in the body, moves and gets stuck in a brain blood vessel. Types [1] and [2] account for 80% of strokes.

[3] Haemorrhagic strokes occur when an artery ruptures in the brain, usually as a result of high blood pressure.

[4] Transient ischemic attacks or TIA's are a temporary obstruction with mild and temporary symptoms.

Table 16.1. Stroke symptoms.

Damaged brain region	Symptoms
Right hemisphere	Weakness or paralysis on left side; confusion; disorientation; denial of paralysis; impaired judgment/reasoning; emotional instability
Left hemisphere	Weakness or paralysis on right side; reduced vision for objects to right; impaired thinking; difficulty speaking or understanding others; depression
Cerebellum	Impaired balance; nausea, vomiting; dizziness; extreme weakness of arm and leg on same side as cerebellum injury
Brain stem	Unstable BP & pulse, leading to coma; difficulty swallowing, pronouncing words; vertigo & impaired walking; weakness or paralysis on both sides

Table 16.1 shows the effects of stroke-induced damage to different regions of the brain (Sweeney, 2009). When a stroke cuts off blood to part of the brain, neurologists can estimate the location of the damage by the patient's symptoms.

Aging of the sensory system

The senses become less acute with age as a result of changes in the sense organs as well as in the brain. Minimum levels of stimulation, called thresholds, are required before the brain perceives a sensation. Thresholds increase with age, requiring greater stimulation before sensations register so that the aging brain is slower in both IQ tests and in life in general.

The working memory of the brain also decreases, so that an abundance of lights and sounds can overwhelm the elderly brain so that, for example, driving in heavy traffic becomes difficult for the elderly (Sweeney, 2009).

The eyes and ears, the primary means of information gathering, suffer most from aging:

[a] Common eye diseases in the elderly include glaucoma, cataracts, and macular degeneration. The eyes also tend to become dry, eye muscles become less efficient, and the lenses lose clarity.

[b] A high proportion of the elderly suffer some degree of hearing loss, and many older people require hearing aids.

Mental illnesses

Many of the supplements noted in earlier sections are helpful with mental illnesses, including B-vitamins, vitamin C, phospholipids, fish oils, magnesium, and zinc.

Several other supplements are also helpful, including niacin, manganese, and chromium (Holford, 2009).

Thoughts of suicide, especially if relatively frequent, may be indicative of a need for supportive counselling etc., but under certain circumstances euthanasia may be a realistic and justified option.

The importance of sleep

One study showed that sleep-deprived adults had significantly reduced cognitive function.

Getting plenty of quality sleep, which is said to have a "dishwasher effect" on the brain, is also important because in old age we tend to sleep only about circa 6 hours per night (with 20% of this REM sleep) whereas mature adults get about 8 hours/night (again with 20% REM), whilst infants get about 14 hours/night, with 40% of this being REM sleep to help the young brain develop (Sweeney, 2009).

Many children and adults suffer from sleep disorders including (obstructive) sleep apnoea, insomnia, sleep hypoventilation, restless legs syndrome, sleep talking, and sleepwalking. The prevalence of sleep apnoea, which interferes with breathing, has increased because many more people are obese, but there are new remedies for sleep apnoea such as facial attachments to aid breathing.

Conclusion

In addition to diseases of the nervous system, there are many physical ailments common in old age such as arthritis and osteoporosis which can also contribute to depression etc..

Sound programs for diet and diet supplements including plenty of antioxidants, exercise, and relaxation will all help combat some of the key causes of aging such as reduced immune function, atherosclerosis, deterioration of collagen and thence skin, DNA mutations, and memory loss which can begin to occur as early as the mid-40s.

For relaxation, sitting in a comfy chair listening to quiet relaxation music, perhaps involving nature sounds, is far preferable to noisy music, movies or sporting crowds. Indeed, scientific research has shown that listening to pleasurable and relaxing music causes a short-term increase in the ability to solve spatial problems, and may also increase cognition at many levels, from simple perceptions to deeper thoughts (Sweeney, 2009).

B vitamins, phospholipids, fish oils, antioxidants, amino acids, glutamine, magnesium, hormones, turmeric, ginkgo and hyperzia serrata help deal with neurological problems, along with getting plenty of sleep and sound diet, exercise and stress reduction regimes.

Chemicals have also been developed that 'turn on' brain growth factor genes which don't change brain size, but may slow the neuronal wear and tear of aging, perhaps enabling humans to retain a greater percentage of their original memory capacity well past middle age (Lynch & Granger, 2008).

More important, thinking young won't hurt, along with plenty of continuing learning to keep the brain in some sort of shape, noting the equation for real IQ given in Chapter 5.

☺☺☹☺☺☺☹☺☺☹☺☺☹☺☺☹

PART IV
PSYCHOLOGY AND PSYCHIATRY

Chapter 16

PSYCHOLOGY AND PSYCHIATRY

*Starting in the late 1950s and early '60s, the psychoanalysts set out
to convince the public that we were 'all' walking wounded,
normal neurotics, functioning psychotics ...
and that Freud's teachings contained the secrets
to eradicating inner strife and reaching our full potential.*
Jeffrey A. Lieberman, *Shrinks, The Untold Story of Psychiatry,*
Little, Brown & Co., NY (2015).

Introduction

Psychology is defined as the 'science' of the mind, and psychological as 'mental' or 'emotional' as distinct from physical in nature. Psychiatry is defined as the branch of medicine dealing with the 'diagnosis' and 'treatment' of 'mental disorders'. In the last couple of decades psychologists have far outnumbered psychiatrists and they consult with patients about 'mental health' issues, whilst psychiatrists mainly deal with more serious 'mental illnesses', though the line between the two practices is now somewhat blurred.

The present chapter discusses some of the early history of psychiatry, then discussing a range of common mental illnesses.

Chapter 21 then briefly discusses some of the main methods by which psychological problems are diagnosed.

Psychiatry

Sigmund Freud (1865 - 1939) believed human beings to be wholly driven by their unconscious minds, and developed what he called "the talking cure" or psychoanalysis which some regard as the first method of examining the human mind. He also proposed the division of the psyche into ego (our outer self), super-ego (our conscience) and id (our inner self).

Alfred Alder, on the other hand, saw us as social beings who create a style of life in response to the environment and what we feel we lack (Alder, 1927).

Modern psychiatry now assesses a wide range of mental disorders, several of which are discussed in following sections.

The field of psychiatry, however, has a disgraceful history. As late as 1815 the Bethlehem madhouse in England exhibited lunatics every Sunday and made a considerable amount of money in the process (Youngson & Schott, 1996).[4]

At the Bicêtre hospital in France attendants used whips to make the mad perform dances to provide traditional entertainment. At the Charenton asylum the infamous Marquis de Sade presided over theatrical performances by the inmates.

In the USSR dissidents were often confided to asylums for the insane, a policy no doubt practiced elsewhere.

The practice of lobotomy was particularly scandalous.

It can be traced back to Dr Gottlieb Burckhardt, the superintendent of a psychiatric hospital in Switzerland, who in 1890 drilled holes in the head of six severely agitated patients, thereby altering their behaviour.

Then in 1935 John Fulton at Yale University removed the frontal lobes from two chimpanzees, changing their behaviour greatly. Dr Walter Freeman, an American neurologist, was recovering from a nervous breakdown when in July 1935 he attended a seminar given by Fulton.

---

[4] The word Bedlam is a corruption of "Bethlehem."

Egas Moniz, a celebrated Portuguese neurosurgeon also attended the seminar and two months later in Portugal he performed the first *leucotomy* by drilling a small hole in the skull and injecting alcohol into it to destroy the fibres in the frontal lobes of the patient.

The operation succeeded in making the patient less agitated and overtly paranoid but made her more apathetic and dull than Moniz had hoped. Nevertheless, further operations were performed and the procedure was refined by drilling six holes in the skull.

When he published he gave no hint of the downside of his procedure and Walter Freeman was bursting with enthusiasm to try it and he enlisted the aid of neurosurgeon James Watts to carry out his first leucotomy on 14 September 1936.

A week later the patient became incoherent and could not even recite the days of the week and when asked to write could only scribble nonsense. Her speech improved in following days and they operated on another five patients.

In November 1936 Freeman and Watts published a report in which they wrote: *In all our patients there was a ... common denominator of worry, apprehension, anxiety, insomnia and nervous tension, and in all of them these symptoms have been relieved to a greater or lesser extent.*

Freeman and Watts renamed the procedure *lobotomy* and made it more drastic by drilling only two holes in the side of the head and using a canula, the tubing from a six inch heavy-gauge hypodermic needle, to pave the way for a cutting tool to destroy targeted brain tissue.

Watts became so proficient that he could thread the canula through the brain from the small hole on one side of the head to that on the other. Though not qualified to do so, Freeman began to perform lobotomies on his own and became a celebrity in the process. He also simplified the procedure by using electroshock to subdue the patient and then plunging an ice pick into their head, usually producing a zombie-like person.

Often the procedure was repeated a second and third time and Freeman, a neurotic with severe depressive symptoms who needed 3 Nembutal to sleep at night, enthusiastically continued his crude procedure years after it had been discredited.

Such surgery had been performed on more than 40,000 people in the USA alone by 1955. Fortunately, lobotomy has fallen out of favour though it is probably still practiced occasionally.

The misinformation that allowed this brutal procedure to be performed for some 30 years, however, is all too typical of a world in which we are fed misinformation and brainwashed into accepting any new procedure or product no matter how dangerous.

Little better, however, is widely used electroconvulsive shock therapy (ECT) in which electrodes are placed on either side of the head and short bursts of high-frequency and high intensity electrical current passed through the brain. ECT can produce a strong amnesic effect, but it is not clear by what means this occurs (Atrens & Curthoys, 1982).

Psychopaths

This is the largest category of abnormal psychological types, involving the following behaviours such as (Davies, 1971):

[1] Assertiveness, aggression and bullying.
[2] Dishonesty and lying.
[3] Alcohol and drug addiction.
[4] Excessive sexual behaviours.

Psychopaths usually have two or more of the above traits, but are not normally classified as mentally ill, in part perhaps because they are so common.

Through their assertiveness, dishonesty etc. psychopaths often rise high in the hierarchies of business. Gillespie (2017), having had "many good managers" in his "various careers", cites a personal example of a psychopathic boss:

He was constantly meddling - - micromanaging the workplace - -. He trusted nobody and his impact on the workplace was devastating.

This boss made a habit of giving select people subtle but excruciating public punishment. - - The longer I knew him the more convinced I became that everything he said was a lie.

He cites a few examples of famous people from the past and present who might be described as psychopaths, including Caligula, Lance Armstrong, and Donald Trump, quoting Tony Schwartz, the co-author of Trump's autobiography, as telling the "*New Yorker* that if he were writing *The Art of the Deal* today, he'd call it 'The Sociopath'.

Mania

Typical manic behaviour involves a period in which an expansive, elevated, or irritable mood, along with enhanced activity and reactivity persists abnormally. During this episode symptoms such as increased talkativeness and grandiosity, distractibility, decreased need for sleep, inflated self-esteem, and excessive involvement in pleasurable yet risky activities may be present.

Such symptoms occur during normal mood changes, but it is their magnitude and frequent recurrence that may indicate a psychiatric problem. The frenetic and driven behaviour of mania results in a non-functional individual who cannot work effectively (Atrens & Curthoys, 1982).

The neurochemical alterations in mania are less clearly understood, but it is well established that drugs effective in the treatment of mania are those that antagonize dopamine and serotonin. The mechanism responsible for the therapeutic efficacy of lithium for the treatment of mania is not yet clear. Although mood disorders tend to have a familial background, the evidence for a genetic component is not convincing.

Manic depression or bipolar disorder, involving both manic 'highs' and depressive 'lows' is discussed in Chapter 19.

Depression

Depression is very common, and it is normal to feel depressed from time to time. Severe depression, however, is characterized by despondency, diminished interest in most or all activities, weight fluctuation not due to dieting, disruption in sleep patterns, psychomotor agitation or retardation, feelings of worthlessness, excessive quiet, and recurrent thoughts of death or suicide.

A professional diagnosis of depression is made, however, when a person suffers frequent and/or prolonged bouts of depression of more than usual severity, perhaps associated with thoughts of self-harm or suicide.

Major depression is associated with decreased brain levels of the neurotransmitters norepinephrine and serotonin, and the most effective therapy consists of drugs that inhibit the breakdown of these compounds.

Much less common, manic depression, or bipolar disorder, involves both manic 'highs' of greater energy and activity, alternating with bouts of depression or 'lows'. Manic depression is often treated with lithium salts.

Writers and artists, many of whom work in relative solitude, have often been associated with depression (Thomas & Hughes, 2006), Vincent van Gogh being a notable example (Sweeney, 2009).

Depression is discussed further in Chapter 18, and manic depression or bipolar disorder is discussed in Chapter 19.

Anxiety

It is normal to feel anxious about things ranging from minor issues such as getting behind with one's work or household chores, to worrying when a child is late coming home from a party. Many people, however, have abnormal levels of anxiety, including phobias and fears, and tranquillizers such as Valium, which enhances the inhibitory actions of the neurotransmitter GABA, are used to relieve anxiety and relax muscles.

Hypochondria

Hypochondria is an anxiety disorder in which people worry excessively about their health, for example just hearing someone mention a certain illness triggering fears that they might have that illness.

Obsessive Compulsive Disorder

Obsessive Compulsive Disorder (OCD) is a form of anxiety which makes people worry about certain things and 'overreact' to their concerns, the two most common behaviours being washing and checking, for example some people wearing away skin on their hands by frequently washing them, others repeatedly checking such things as whether the door is locked when they leave home.

One OCD sufferer, for example, feels compelled to do many things four times, another to count to seven between each mouthful of food (Carter, 2000).

Panic disorder

Panic disorder involves recurring, unexpected attack of anxiety called *panic attacks* in situations that would not concern most people. Attacks may occur without obvious cause and last from a few minutes up to an hour or more, with the person feeling sick, dizzy, breathless, tight in the chest and disoriented.

Panic disorder is often accompanied by *agoraphobia*, a morbid fear of being alone in public places.

In severe cases agoraphobics are not prepared to leave their home for fear of a panic attack, often being unable to keep a job or have a social life.

Anti-anxiety medications such as depressants are sometimes prescribed for panic disorder, but don't treat the cause of the anxiety. Cognitive Behaviour Therapy (CBT), which is discussed in Chapter 22, is often used to help treat agoraphobia.

Teaching patients how to relax with *relaxation training*, and how to use *slow breathing technique* (SBT), may also help in reducing hyperventilation which often accompanies panic attacks.

Phobias

Phobias are irrational and excessive fears of a particular object or event that disrupt normal functioning, and can be reduced by avoiding the object and thoughts about it.

Feared objects may be potentially dangerous, such as snakes, spiders, or being in high places. They may have little or no associated danger, such as flowers (anthophobia), computers (cyberphobia), or daylight (phengophobia).

Social phobia is an irrational fear of social or performance situations in which embarrassment may occur.

People are not normally classified as having a specific phobia unless symptoms of it have lasted for at least six months.

Specific phobias can be treated using CBT or *systematic desensitization,* in which patients are taught to gradually replace their fear response with a relaxed response.

Tourette's syndrome

Tourette's syndrome is also an anxiety disorder, and certainly sufferers do appear anxious and disturbed when they have a bout of Tourette's and stressfully utter a nonsensical word while some part of their body, usually the face, has a 'tic' or twitches.

Asperger's syndrome

This is a psychiatric disorder usually noted during early school years and characterized by impaired social relations and by repetitive patterns of behaviour.

Autism

This an abnormal absorption with the self marked by communication disorders, short attention span, and inability to deal with other people.

In 2016 a Finish study of 258 people found that religious people could be compared with those with autism because they didn't view the world realistically, many believing in such supernatural phenomena as demons, gods and inanimate objects being alive in some way.

ADD and ADHD

Attention Deficit Disorder (ADD) and Attention Deficit Hyperactivity Disorder (ADHD) are normally associated with school children who have difficulty sitting through classes without feeling distracted and wishing to be elsewhere doing something else. They thus have trouble concentrating and their learning is affected adversely.

There is much current controversy about these condition, many feeling that it is diagnosed too freely with children needlessly being put on long-term medication that may do more harm than good (DePaulo, 2002).

Dyslexia

This is an impaired ability to comprehend written words usually associated with a neurological disorder. The cause of dyslexia is believed to involve both genetic environmental factors and it often occurs in people with ADHD and is associated with similar difficulties with numbers. It may begin in adulthood as the result of a traumatic brain injury, stoke or dementia. The underlying mechanisms of dyslexia are problems within the brain's language processing.

Dyslexia is diagnosed through a series of tests of memory, spelling, vision, and reading skills and should not be confused with reading difficulties caused by hearing or vision problems, or insufficient teaching.

Treatment involves adjusting teaching methods to meet the person's needs which, while not curing the underlying problem, may decrease the symptoms. Treatments targeting vision are ineffective.

Dyslexia is the most common learning disability and occurs all around the world. It affects 3–7% of the population but up to 20% may have some degree of symptoms. While dyslexia is more often diagnosed in men, it has been suggested that it affects men and women equally.

Dyslexia should not be confused with 'mirror writing', for which Leonardo da Vinci was famous, some believing that he wrote in this fashion deliberately as a sort of coding.

Schizophrenia

Schizophrenia is a chronic neurological disease of distorted thoughts and perceptions which usually begins during adolescence or early adulthood (Sweeney, 2009) It has a strong genetic component, one which research shows may be largely physiological, and not a result of a "disturbed environment" (Atrens & Curthoys, 1982).

Schizoid people worry obsessively about being watched by others and being talked about, fearing that people know too much about them and have invaded their 'space'. When walking in the street, for example, they will worry that other people are watching them, in this way 'distorting' reality.

Schizophrenia is relatively common, occurring in about 1 percent of the general population worldwide. Because the incidence of schizophrenia among parents, children, and siblings of patients with the disease is increased to 15 percent, it is believed that heredity plays an important role in the genesis of the disease (Atrens & Curthoys, 1982). However, other studies suggest that non-genetic factors such as a "disturbed environment" are also influential.

In the last decade or two, for example, a correlation between excessive and prolonged marijuana use and the development of schizophrenia has been observed.

The biochemical basis of the disease may be an excess of the neurotransmitter substance dopamine, as high levels of dopamine and its metabolites, as well as increased dopamine receptors, are found in the brains of persons with schizophrenia. Further evidence for this hypothesis is that the drugs most effective in treating the disease are those that have a high capacity to block dopamine receptors.

Psychosis

Psychosis is any severe mental disorder in which contact with reality is lost or highly distorted, including severe schizophrenia. The drug chlorpromazine was developed and widely used to treat psychosis, by 1964 ten thousand peer-reviewed articles having been published on it. According to Lieberman (2015),

Like a bolt from the blue, here was a medication that could relieve the madness that disabled tens of millions of men and women - - the widespread adoption of chlorpromazine marked the beginning of the end for the asylums.

The commercial success of this drug encouraged pharmaceutical companies to search for new antipsychotic drugs, leading to the massive pharmaceutical industry of today.

Hysteria

This is a neurotic disorder characterized by violent emotional outbreaks and disturbances of sensory and motor functions. The term hysteria comes from the Greek word *hustericos* meaning 'of the womb' because ancient Greeks associated such highly emotional and neurotic behaviour with childless women. This indicates that man has long had an interest in trying to understand human psychology and behaviour.

Dementia

Dementia is simply mental deterioration usually associated with old age. Senile dementia of the Alzheimer type (SDAT) is a result of advanced Alzheimer's disease, a progressive form of pre-senile dementia that is similar to senile dementia except that it usually starts in the 40s or 50s, the first symptoms being impaired memory which is followed by impaired thought and speech, and finally complete helplessness.

Homosexuality

Homosexuality is on the increase. Once a trait one had to keep secret it is now rampantly displayed at gay Mardi Gras festivals, at gay bars in major cities, and in late night TV ads for homosexual dating services.

Some claim that homosexuality is inherited and a study of 113 people in 33 families in which at least two brothers were homosexual found a genetic marker on the X-chromosome (Xq28) that had a very high correlation with sexual orientation (Galton, 2001).

Genes may play a minor 'predispositionary' role but, largely, homosexuality is a learnt behaviour. Typically, for example, the normal heterosexual male has one or two homosexual experiences in adolescence (Robertson, 1981), and no doubt the same applies to women.

Those who become homosexuals, therefore, presumably do so as a result of imitative learning at an early age. There are, no doubt, also psychological factors involved, for example a lack of confidence in approaching the opposite sex coupled with the fact that there are earlier homosexual experiences to draw upon as an alternative behaviour model.

If alcoholism is to be regarded as a psychiatric illness, as it often is (Davies, 1971), then homosexuality is even more obviously a treatable psychiatric condition as well.

That said, most of our heterosexual behaviours are also learnt ones, many of them hardly natural or healthy, an example being 'tongue kissing', a truly revolting and very unhealthy practice like many other modern sexual practices.

Post-traumatic Stress Disorder (PTSD)

PTSD is caused by events of great stress and trauma in a person's life, perhaps the best-known example being that of Western Vietnam war veterans, whose vulnerability to symptoms of PTSD such as depression and suicidal thoughts was no doubt increased by feelings of isolation as a result of having fought in a war which many thought to be mistake in the first place, and which the West ultimately lost.

Losing one's job, or the death of a spouse or young child are also common causes of PTSD.

According to Cozolino (2002):

Someone suffering from PTSD is, in essence, in a continual loop of unconscious self-traumatization, coping and exhaustion. When these symptoms are experienced on a chronic basis, they can devastate every aspect of the victim's life, from physical well-being to the quality of relationships to the victim's experience of the world.

Symptoms of PTSD may be *intrusive* and include:

➤ Distressing memories or dreams of the event.
➤ Mentally reliving the event.
➤ Distress when reminded of it.
➤ Physiological reactions including sweating and high pulse rate when reminded of it.

Avoidance and *numbing* symptoms to block unpleasant memories and feelings associated with the trauma include:

➤ Avoiding thinking and talking about the event.
➤ Avoiding things and places that remind one of the event.
➤ Feelings of detachment from reality.
➤ Restriction of emotions such as kindness and love.

Hyperarousal symptoms may include:

➤ Difficulty in sleeping.
➤ Difficulty in concentrating.
➤ Irritability and anger outbursts.
➤ Hypervigilance or always looking out for signs of danger.

Typically, people with PTSD have one or more symptoms from each category.

PTSD is often accompanied by other physical and psychological problems, including feelings of panic, depression, and abuse of alcohol and other drugs.

PTSD can be treated using Cognitive Behavioural Therapy (see Chapter 22) and stress management techniques, for example mindfulness meditation slow breathing, and anti-depressant and anti-anxiety medications may also be used.

Conclusion

Freud has often been accused of an obsession with sexual feelings (Gillespie, 2017), whilst both he and Jung seem to have been overly obsessed with the importance of dreams, leading many people to distrust formal "talk therapy". Chapter 22, therefore, discusses a range of treatments for psychological problems.

Chapter 17

PERSONALITY

> *Man's main task in life is to give birth to himself,*
> *to become what he potentially is.*
> *The most important product of his effort is his own personality.*
> Erich Fromm, *Man For Himself*, ch. 4 (1947).

Freud's components of personality

Freud believed that a person's basic personality is fully formed by about five or six years of age, and that it only undergoes slight refinement thereafter.

He proposed that personality had three basic parts:

1. The *id*, or inner self, representing the innate, biological needs we are born with such as hunger, thirst, sleep and sex.

Conceptually the id is the 'force' of the demanding, impulsive, illogical, irrational and selfish part of our personality, and it seeks satisfaction regardless of the feelings of others.

Freud believed that a newborn child's behavior is dominated by the id, the child crying immediately some need is experienced, whilst most young children's behavior is mostly driven by the id, resulting in them often being demanding.

2. The *ego*, or outer self, develops as infants move into childhood and begin to acquire some understanding that needs can't always be met immediately, if at all.

The ego is realistic, logical and orderly, and considers the 'real-life' restrictions that must be considered in dealing with the demands of the id.

3. The **superego** is our 'conscience' or personal understanding of what is right or wrong.

The superego develops by learning from parents and others what are acceptable forms of behaviour.

Freud believed that the id, ego, and superego forces are at a state of constant interaction within us, and that all our behaviour is governed by this interaction.

The most frequent interaction is between the self-satisfying urges of the id and the moral views of the superego, "the ego often playing the role of mediator trying to find a way to satisfy the id without upsetting the moral of the superego, within the limitations of the real world" (Grivas & Carter, 2005).

According to Freud, in a 'balanced' personality the id, ego, and superego play relatively equal roles.

When the id is somewhat dominant, one's personality may be self-centred, demanding, sulky, and childish.

When the ego is stronger than the id or the superego, one may be logical and practical, and perhaps somewhat introverted.

When the superego dominates the id and ego, a person may be moralistic and strict, often feel self-guilt, and be antisocial.

Defence mechanisms

According to Freud, the ego uses 'defence mechanisms' which take a slightly distorted, more optimistic view of reality to reduce anxiety. Some of the most common defence mechanisms are:

- ➢ Denial: denying painful thoughts.
- ➢ Repression: preventing bad thoughts from becoming conscious.
- ➢ Rationalization: finding an explanation for one's thoughts and actions that justifies them.
- ➢ Intellectualization: using reasoning to block out emotional stress and conflict
- ➢ Compensation: ignoring bad outcomes by thinking about one's successful activities.

> Sublimation: modifying the natural expression of an impulse or instinct (especially a sexual one) to one that is socially acceptable.
> Projection: attributing your own shortcomings and emotions to someone else.
> Regression: fleeing from reality by assuming a more infantile state.

In summary, defence mechanisms are unconscious processes that tend to reduce the anxiety associated with instinctive desires, bad memories, bad outcomes etc.

Behavioural psychology

The ancient Greeks classified people as having four temperament types: sanguine, choleric, phlegmatic, and melancholy.

Hans Eysenck classified people according to three the 'supertraits' or dimensions of psychoticism, extraversion/ introversion, and neuroticism (Gillespie, 2017).

This came to be known as the PEN model, it's characteristics including:

Extraverts are is less 'internally' excitable than introverts so they seek contact with others for stimulation. They tend to be optimistic and lively, and are sometimes unreliable risk takers who care little about how they are perceived.

Introverts are more 'internally' excitable and moody and this 'internal preoccupation' is mentally taxing so that they minimize social interaction. They worry more about life and tend to be pessimistic, and have low self-esteem.

Neurotic people are anxious and stressed, they over-react to stimuli and tend to be emotionally unstable. Neurotic introverts are worriers susceptible to phobias and panic attacks, whereas neurotic extraverts tend to repress their fears and concerns.

Psychotic people tend to be reckless and mentally unstable, in the extreme being an antisocial psychotic or sociopath/psychopath.

Type A and B personalities

US Cardiologists Friedman and Rosenman (1959) proposed that there were two basic personality types, Type A and Type B.

People with type A personalities are ambitious, competitive, industrious, goal-oriented, time conscious, impatient, highly motivated, energetic, easily annoyed, suspicious, verbally aggressive, and get angry when their efforts are frustrated.

Such people are often successful, but rarely satisfied, and tend to keep 'raising the bar' to make more money etc., often being impatient and easily irritated in the process.

People with Type B personalities tend to be the opposite of Type A, and are generally easy going, patient, calm, not overly ambitious, not highly competitive, in less of a hurry, and satisfied with their lives.

Friedman and Rosenman's research team interviewed each participant in their survey about their work and eating habits. During the 8.5 year study 7% of the participants had heart attacks, all of these with Type A personality, leading to the conclusion that Type A males were twice as likely to have a heart attack as Type B males.

Other studies on this issue gave mixed results, and other researchers suggested that only the higher levels of anger and hostility of Type A personality were significant risk factors for heart disease, and that hard-working people who enjoy their work are at no greater risk of heart disease than others.

Type C personality

Research has also indentified a Type C personality associated with an increased risk of cancer.

People with Type C personality tend to have a strong need to conform, be introverted, and be more submissive to the demands of others. They also tend to be pessimistic, avoid facing problems, and to be prone to depression.

In one research study, participants with Type C personality were found to be 16 times more likely to have developed cancer, whereas only 1% of those not of Type C personality developed cancer (Shaffer et al., 1987).

One explanation for this finding is that suppression of negative emotions such as anger and sadness is associated with suppression of immune system function (Eysenck, 1994).

Studies have shown that periods of intense or prolonged stress or depression do indeed impair functioning of the immune system, but other studies have failed to find a link between Type C personality and cancer.

The three A, B and C personality types do, however, provide a useful classification of human behaviours, as illustrated in Table 18.1 (Mamonov, 2001).

Table 18.1. Characteristics of personality types A, B and C.

Type A	Type B	Type C
Very competitive	Non-competitive	Passive
Quick to anger, easily irritated	Consciously controls anger	Suppresses anger
Copes via hostility and competitiveness	Expresses emotions appropriately	Tries to please others, doesn't show negative feelings
Focused on own needs	Capable of meeting own needs and of responding to others	Self-sacrificing, denies own needs
Always rushed	Never feels rushed, even under pressure	Lethargic
Wants a good job and to recognition	Prefers to satisfy self, no matter what others think	Tries to please others, avoids conflict
Impatient	Patient	Obedient, even when manipulated by others
Fast (eating, walking, speaking)	Normal speed	Slow in doing things
Hard-driving	Easygoing	Neutral
Struggling	Confident and content	Gives up easily
Few interests outside work	Many interests	Put interests of others above own
In control	Self-supportive	Sense of helplessness
Emphatic in speech (may pound desk)	Slow, deliberate speaker	Does not speak about own needs
Pursues opportunities the world offers	Moderately ambitious	Sense of hopelessness
Rejecting	Offering	Accepting

Conclusions

Freud's *id, ego,* and *superego* where, of course, an important early milestone in the early development of the science of psychology, and its competing components of basic needs, logical thought, and 'conscience' provide a still useful model of how the mind works.

Eysencks's four classifications of extraverts, introverts, neurotic and psychotic, on the other hand, combine aspects of personality (the first pair), and also mental health disorders (the second pair) such as depression and anxiety, and psychopathy.

Type A, B and C personality types do provide a simple classification of personalities and associated behaviours.

Comparable to these types, but somewhat simpler, 'Mohr's Morphology,' postulates three personality types based on a scale of aggressiveness (Mohr & Fear, 2015; Mohr et al., 2018d):

(a) Aggressive/assertive (the bossy types).
(b) Neutral (the OK guys).
(c) Placid (the meek).

The meek do not inherit the earth, as The Bible has it, for the bossy little Hitler types usually end up as boss. These bossy types typically have 'type A' behaviour associated with stress. Research has found that, contrary to popular belief enshrined in such terms as "executive stress," being boss involves less work stress and it is the slaves, of course, that really are stressed, and perhaps never more so than in today's consumer society.

Human history might not have been so catastrophic, in fact, had quieter, less aggressive, more intelligent, more honest, and harder working people been leading us.

Finally, whilst clearly much of our personality develops early in life by modeling, imitative and social learning, it is also important to note that there is some evidence that up to 50% of personality may be genetic (Galton, 2001).

☺ ☺ ☹ ☺ ☺ ☹ ☺ ☺ ☹ ☺ ☺ ☹ ☺ ☺ ☹

Chapter 18

THE PSYCHOLOGY OF DEPRESSION

*As an illness, depression exacts an enormously high cost
in both human and economic terms. At least one in every 10
Americans experiences a clinical depression or manic-depressive
episode in his or her lifetime. About 15 million people
(10 million women and 5 million men) in the United States at any given
time have major depression or some form of manic depression.
By comparison, about 6 million people suffer from coronary disease.*
J. Raymond DePaulo Jr, *Understanding Depression* (2002).

Introduction

Severe depression, as distinct from 'mild depression' is called clinical depression because it is debilitating. For some sufferers there is overwhelming sadness which may be accompanied by 'mental' numbness, dullness and apathy, whilst fatigue, lack of energy, and thoughts of suicide are also common. Often there is also a loss of self-esteem and feelings of hopelessness (Wolpert, 1999).

Marriage and other close relationships tend to protect against depression, but marital and other conflicts can, of course, increase depression.

Studies have confirmed that depressed people may also have a negative effect on others, sometimes putting a strain on relationships between people.

Depressives in a position of power tend to overuse that power and be uncooperative, whilst those low in a hierarchy tend to blame others (Wolpert, 1999).

Table 18.1. Main sources of disease burden in established market economies, 1990.

	Source of disease burden	Total DALYS* millions	% of total
1	Ischemic heart disease	8.9	9.0
2	Unipolar major depression	6.7	6.8
3	Cardiovascular disease	5.0	5.0
4	Alcohol use	4.7	4.7
5	Road traffic accidents	4.3	4.4
	All causes	98.7	
Disability-adjusted life year (DALY) = years of life lost by premature death or lived with a severe disability (U.S. Surgeon-General's Report on Mental Health, 2001).			

By 2020, depression is expected to be the second most debilitating disease worldwide, after ischemic heart disease, and one of the leading causes of death, as suicide takes more lives than traffic accidents, lung disease, or AIDS (DePaulo, 2002).

Table 18.1 shows the leading sources of 'disease burden' reported in the US in 2001, with unipolar major depression ranking second.

Psychological illnesses have become a good deal more prevalent since that time, with relatively new ones such as ADHD being common amongst young people.

With the world's human population becoming ever more excessive, and problems such as resource depletion, pollution, global warming, food shortages, and levels of unemployment etc. becoming more severe globally, the incidence of depression is, of course, set to increase further.

Most of those who commit suicide suffer from some form of depression, perhaps associated with other mental health problems.

A couple of decades ago there were 30,000 suicides annually in the US, two-thirds of them having some form of depressive illness, others having schizophrenia and thence delusions that lead to suicide.

Understanding depression

Depression is an episodic illness, and though episodes are usually brief, they can also last for weeks or even months, waxing and waning in intensity.

Being economically and socially deprived can, of course lead to depression, but depression also strikes many successful and wealth people who have many social outlets.

Divorce or death of a friend or relative can lead often leads to a period of bereavement, but this is normal and in itself not clinical depression. People who are genetically disposed to depression, however, may become depressed over relatively minor events such as losing a personal belonging, severe attacks of depression sometimes confining them to their beds for days or even weeks.

In summary depression is characterized by:

1. Feelings of sadness and/or despair which may be significantly 'deeper' and/or prolonged than normal.

2. Feeling mentally and physically drained and tired with reduced mental and physical vitality that may result in loss of muscle tone, changes in facial expression, and slowness of speech.

In extreme cases sufferers confine themselves to bed for long periods, whilst some fall into a stupor when depressed which may last for many hours.

3. Loss of self-esteem and self-confidence which may result in feelings of worthlessness.

4. Hallucinations or perceptions without a stimulus. These differ from illusions which are misinterpretations of a stimulus, for example seeing a cluster of stars in the sky and thinking it is a satellite or flying saucer, whereas hallucinations involve perceptions of 'something' when, in fact, there is nothing 'out there'.

5. Negative delusions: preoccupation with false ideas or judgments, for example false conviction that one has a certain disease, or that one's spouse is cheating on you.

Depression and anxiety

With both unipolar depression and bipolar or manic depression, sufferers often have a high level of anxiety, but, of course, anxiety disorders can also occur independently of depression and are another major type of mental illness.

Types of anxiety include:

1. Panic attacks involving rapid onset of symptoms including increased heart rate, sweating, tightness in the chest, lightheadedness, and shortness of breath.

2. Phobias, including agoraphobia (a morbid fear of open spaces), social phobias, fear of water, fear of heights, fear of driving, fear of speaking or eating, fear of being watched by others, etcetera.

Sufferers of panic attacks and phobias will typically try and avoid situations that have caused a previous attack.

3. Obsessive-compulsive behaviours, for example an obsession with shoes so that one hoards dozens, or even hundreds of pairs of shoes, and 'hoarders' are commonly found to have filled their houses with furniture, clothes, books etcetera to the point that it is difficult to access them.

Diagnosing depression

The American Psychiatric Association's Diagnostic and Statistical Manual fourth edition, DSM IV, defines four categories of 'mood' or affective disorders:

1. Major depressive disorder (unipolar disorder) involving changes in mood, vitality, and self-regard that tend to be episodic and may result in changes in sleeping and eating habits.

2. Dysthymia, or mild chronic depression, involving similar fewer symptoms to those for unipolar depression, but less in both number and severity.

3. Bipolar I disorder, which is discussed in the next chapter.

4. Bipolar 2 disorder, which is also discussed in the next chapter.

According to DSM IV, for a diagnosis of a major depressive episode at least five of the following symptoms should have been present for at least two weeks:

1. Depressed mood.
2. Diminished interest or pleasure in activities.
3. Significant appetite/weight loss or gain.
4. Insomnia or hypersomnia.
5. Feelings of worthlessness or excessive guilt.
6. Diminished ability to think or concentrate.
7. Recurrent thoughts of death or suicide.

and not be attributable to general medical condition, drugs, or bereavement.

For a diagnosis of mild chronic depression at least two of the following symptoms should have been present for at least two years (and not absent for more than 2 months in that time):

1. Poor appetite or overeating.
2. Insomnia or hypersomnia.
3. Low energy levels or fatigue.
4. Low self-esteem.
5. Poor concentration or difficulty making decisions.
6. Feelings of hopelessness.

These symptoms should have caused significant distress or impairment in important areas of functioning, not be better attributed to chronic depressive disorder or major depression in remission, and not be manic, hypomanic, due to schizophrenia, drugs (prescribed or abused), general medication condition.

People with major depression often feel abjectly hopeless and worthless, whereas those with mild depression feel 'a little' hopeless, but if it is chronic and persists for circa 2 years, it can affect the sufferer's life considerably, often without their family or friends noticing that they have depression.

According to Wolpert: *a useful and possibly fruitful way of thinking about depression is in terms of malignant sadness. Sadness is to depression what normal growth is to cancer* (Wolpert, 1999).

Causes of depression

Stressful events can often result in depression, for example losing one's job.

Repeated stress events and thence persistently elevated stress hormone levels can compromise brain cell function in critical regions of the brain linked to depressive illness.

To help prevent, or at least reduce the effects of stress, one should try to establish regular habits of eating, exercise, and sleep.

Then, of course, one should try to avoid stressful situations as far as possible, and learn to cope better with stressful situations that are unavoidable such as tight deadlines for completion of work assignments.

Seasonal and weather changes can, of course, result in mild depression, a phenomenon called *seasonal affective disorder* (SAD). For example, the peak levels of suicides and psychiatric hospitalizations occur with the onset of winter (DePaulo, 2002).

Genetic factors may play a role in depression, and siblings of offspring of people with major or manic depression have up to twice the likelihood of developing depression.

People with conditions causing chronic pain are much more likely to suffer from depression, and the newer non-narcotic pain treatments are also treatments for epilepsy, depression and manic depression.

Postnatal depression

Postnatal depression in women occurs soon after the birth of a child and has features in common with major depressive disorders. Often there are delusions concerning the new-born infant, for example, that the child is destined to have some terrible fate, and sometimes there may be thoughts of committing acts of violence to the child.

Women often feel guilty about such feelings, particularly because they occur at a time when they, and their family and friends, believe that they should be happy.

Hypochondriasis

Hypochondriasis, more commonly known as hypochondria, is a chronic and abnormal anxiety about imaginary symptoms and ailments. Sufferers show persistent concern about their health, and common sensations such as 'missed' heartbeats cause severe anxiety.

Such concerns are common in people suffering from depression and it is possible that hypochondriasis can simply be a symptom or 'somatisation' of depression.

Indeed, on study of 1,000 patients visiting a medical diagnostic clinic, no organic illness could be found in more than two thirds of them (Wolpert, 1999), suggesting that many of them had a psychosomatic disorder resulting from depression.

Heart attacks and depression

As might be expected, there is a link between depression and heart disease, and studies have shown that people who suffer episodes of depression are two to four times more likely to have a heart attack over a 13-year period then people who have never had depression.

In addition, people having heart attacks or strokes when they are depressed being from two to four times more likely to die from them (De Paulo, 2002).

Indeed, in one of the earliest studies the results suggested that the link between depression and the risk of heart attack was as strong as that between smoking and risk of heart attack.

There are three theories of this connection:

1. Depression causes the nerves that help regulate heart function to malfunction, causing arrhythmia.

2. Depression increases blood clotting mechanisms, resulting in blood clots that obstruct coronary arteries and thus cause a heart attack or stroke.

3. Depression increases adrenal gland production of the stress hormone cortisol, contracting coronary arteries and increasing blood pressure and likelihood of coronary artery obstruction and heart attack.

Conversely, studies have shown that heart attacks do not cause depression, but clearly hormones and pain are amongst the strongest influences on depression.

Treatment of depression

People suffering from depression to an 'abnormal' extent should discuss the problem with friends and relatives and begin planning to improve their mental health.

If professional help is sought this may involve a 'mental status examination' that includes:

- Appearance and general behavior.
- Speech and thought process.
- Mood, vitality, and self-attitude.
- Thought content, abnormal experiences, and beliefs.
- Accessibility and cognitive state.
- Insight and judgment.

Here the doctor will carefully scrutinize the patient's appearance, grooming, posture, and speed and agility of movement and speech. Anxious and manic patients, for example, may talk quickly and be difficult to interrupt. The patient may also be asked to describe how they feel, and compare this to how they felt before becoming depressed.

Assessment and diagnosis is also discussed in Chapter 21.

Once a diagnosis has been made, it is, of course, often well worthwhile getting a second opinion.

Treatment may then involve regular psychotherapy sessions and antidepressant medications such as Prozac, a selective serotonin reuptake inhibitor (SSRI), Nortriptyline, a tricyclic antidepressant (TCA), Trazodone, a serotonin antagonist reuptake inhibitor (SARI), and Buproprion, a norepinephrine reuptake blocker (NRI).

Cognitive Behavioural Therapy (CBT) and like techniques may be helpful, and these are discussed in Chapter 22.

Alternative treatments such as sleep therapy, light therapy and relaxation, meditation, and 'mindfulness' techniques may also prove helpful in some cases.

Conclusion

Episodes of unipolar major depression are relatively common, as indicated in Table 18.1, a high proportion of the population suffering from it at least once or twice in their lives, often as a result of bereavement, divorce, unemployment etcetera.

Chronic minor depression (dysthymia) is less common, but last for circa 2 years or more, and is often accompanied by bouts of major depression as well.

People with Attention Deficit Disorder (ADD) often have underlying depression as well, and in such case treatment focusing upon their depression, rather than their lack of attention, may be more appropriate.

More drastic treatments for depression include electro-convulsive therapy (ECT) and psychosurgery.

Manic depression or bipolar disorder and other treatments for depression are discussed in the following chapter.

Chapter 19

BIPOLAR DISORDERS

Like most illnesses,
bipolar disorder affects people from all walks of life;
it is free of prejudice and merciless in its execution.
But that's not to say that it cannot be managed successfully.
K. Eyers & G. Parker (eds), *Mastering Bipolar Disorder* (2008).

Introduction

Bipolar I disorder, once termed 'manic depressive illness', affects up to 1% of the population. Without treatment, it is a chronic and severe condition involving oscillating episodes of mania or 'highs', and depression, and during manic episode a person can become psychotic and experience hallucinations and delusions.

Bipolar II disorder is less severe and involves non-psychotic highs, or 'hypomania', that alternate with episodes of depression. It affects up to 5% of the population during their lifetime, but sufferers enjoy the mood elevation that comes with hypomania, and only seek help for the episodes of depression that often follow (Eyers & Parker, 2008).

The bipolar disorders are biologically-mediated conditions resulting from changes in brain neurotransmitters sometimes exacerbated by genetic factors.

Characteristic signs of bipolar disorder

During a bipolar 'high' people feel enhanced mood and energy: they have an adrenaline rush and feel creative, elated, and extremely confident, but may also feel irritable as well. They feel tireless and talk incessantly and sometimes loudly, are uninhibited in the choice of topics, and often sexually uninhibited.

The elevation, irritability, hyperactivity, excitability, and accelerated thinking and speaking, are usually accompanied by poor judgment.

As the elevated mood fades, depression often follows with low mood and energy, low self-esteem, loss of motivation, and a tendency to seek solitude.

For many people with manic depression the depressive phases come and go with changes in circumstances and hormonal balance. Both depression and mania disrupt appetite, sleep, and sexual drive.

Anxiety disorders may accompany both depression and manic depression.

With hypomania, a milder form of mania, people feel confident, or 'in the zone' in sporting terminology, and may make hasty and poor decisions, for example being careless with money, driving carelessly, or playing loud music.

They may also become irritable and critical of other people and things.

Diagnosing bipolar disorder

Bipolar I disorder typically involves both severe manias and major depressions, but mania is the defining element and people who have had mania but haven't had a depression are still called Bipolar 1. Hence Bipolar I disorder is defined by the presence of at least one full manic episode with or without a depressive episode.

Significant impairment in social and occupational functioning (perhaps requiring hospitalization) is indicative of mania.

Hallucinations or delusions occur in mania, not hypomania.

The American Psychiatric Association's DSMIV manual cites the following diagnostic criteria for a manic episode:

A. A distinct period of abnormally and persistently elevated expansive or irritable mood lasting at least one week of necessitating hospitalization – for hypomania lasting at least four days.

B. At least three of the following symptoms if mood is euphoric (four if mood is only irritable):
   1. Inflated self-esteem or grandiosity.
   2. Decreased need for sleep.
   3. More talkative than usual.
   4. Fight of ideas or subjective experience that thoughts are racing.
   5. Distractibility.
   6. Increased activity.
   7. Excessive involvement in pleasurable activities which have a high potential for painful consequences.

C. 1. For mania: symptoms sufficiently severe to cause marked impairment in function at work or in relationships or to necessitate hospitalization or psychotic symptoms are present.
   2. For hypomania: symptoms change from usual behavior noticeable by others but not sufficient to meet criteria for mania.

D. Not due to drugs or general medical condition.

E. (For mania only) Does not meet criteria for mixed episode.

Bipolar II disorder typically involves much less severe but still notable hypomanias (mild manias) associated with major depressive episodes. A DSMIV diagnosis of hypomania requires the presence of 3 or 4 of the manic symptoms shown above.

Bipolar II is defined in DSMIV as hypomania associated with one or more depressive episodes. In Bipolar II patients the depressions usually greatly outnumber and outlast the hypomanias. As well as major depressive episodes, Bipolar II may also involve long periods of 'low mood'.

Bipolar disorders may also involve 'mixed episodes'. The American Psychiatric Association's diagnostic criteria for a mixed episode are:

A. The criteria for both a manic episode and a major depressive episode (see Chapter 18), except for duration, are met nearly every day during at least a one-week period.
B. The mood disturbance is sufficiently severe to cause marked impairment in occupational functioning or in usual social activities or relationships with others, or to necessitate hospitalization to prevent harm to self or others, or there are psychotic features.
C. The symptoms are not due to the direct physiological effects of a substance (e.g., drug abuse, a medication or other treatment) or a general medical condition (e.g., hypothyroidism).

Suicide

Suicidal thoughts are common in depressed people and a disturbingly large number – circa one in ten severely depressed people – kill themselves, whilst for manic depressives the figure is between 10 and 20 percent (Wolpert, 1999).

Many writers and poets have written about their suicidal feelings, including Shelley and Tolstoy.

Poet Anne Sexton suffered from manic depression and committed suicide when 46, whilst Japanese writer Ryunosuke Akutagawa committed suicide at only 35.

The World Health Organization's 1994 data had suicide rates per 100,000 population as circa 40 for Latvia, Lithuania, Estonia and Russia; 30 for Finland; 25 for Austria, Denmark and Switzerland; 20 for Belgium and France; 15 for Germany and Sweden; and 10 for Ireland, Spain, the UK and USA.

Suicide rates are typically higher for males and older people, and for single people and those who have suffered bereavement, separation or social exclusion, whilst as many as 25% of drug and alcohol abusers eventually kill themselves.

Treatment of bipolar disorders

As discussed briefly in the preceding chapter, treatment of depressive disorders may involve seeking help and guidance from family and friends, professional counselling, and perhaps appropriate antidepressant medications.

Psychological assessment or diagnosis was briefly discussed in Chapter 18, and is also discussed in Chapter 21.

For manic states lithium is now widely used, along with new psychotropic medications including atypical neuroleptics (a type of tranquillizer) and anticonvulsants.

Cognitive Behavioural Therapy (CBT) and like techniques may be helpful, and these are discussed in Chapter 22.

Sufferers also identify 'triggers' that lead to highs, such as excessive stress, lack of sleep, excessive alcohol or caffeine etc., and also indentify early warning signs of a high developing to help avoid or at least minimize and perhaps control it.

Alternative treatments such as sleep therapy, light therapy, relaxation, meditation, and 'mindfulness' techniques may also prove helpful in some cases.

Conclusion

Clinical or major/severe depression, mild chronic depression, and bipolar disorder affect a substantial proportion of the population.

Indeed, we are all very likely to suffer from depression occasionally during our lives, but in most cases this will be transitory and relatively minor in scale.

When depression is persistent or recurrent, and relatively 'deep', however, sufferers should take action and perhaps get help to deal with it, perhaps using a combination of professional counseling, medication, relaxation and mindfulness techniques, improved diet, and regular exercise.

☺ ☺ ☹ ☺ ☺ ☹ ☺ ☺ ☹ ☺ ☺ ☹ ☺ ☺ ☹

Chapter 20

THE PSYCHOLOGY OF CONFLICT

There is no contradiction between saying (a) that contact tends to reduce the cultural differences among ethnic groups and (b) that contact also tends to stimulate efforts to preserve or increase these differences.
H. D. Forbes *Ethnic Conflict, Commerce, Culture, and the Contact Hypothesis* (1997).

Contact hypothesis

Forbes (1977) proposed that ethnocentricity of different ethnic groups tended to be increased by cultural differences and (presumed negative) contact between them, expressing the ethnocentrism within two groups A and B as

$$E_a = a_1 \, C_T \, D_T \qquad\qquad (20.1a)$$

$$E_b = b_1 \, C_T \, D_T \qquad\qquad (20.1b)$$

where a_1 and b_1 are assumed to be positive, and are measures of the latent tendency of each group to respond ethnocentrically to each other, C_T is the amount of contact between the two groups at time T and D_T is the magnitude of the cultural differences between the two groups at time T.

He further proposed that the amount of contact and the cultural differences between the groups depended upon their proximity, incentives for contact such as trade, and upon the ethnocentrism of the groups, expressing this as

$$C_{T+1} = C_T \, (1 + g)/(1 + a_2 E_a + b_2 E_b) \qquad\qquad (20.2)$$

$$D_{T+1} = D_T \, (1 + a_3 E_a + b_3 E_b)/(1 + h C_T) \qquad\qquad (20.3)$$

where g is a factor that represents the factors that determine growth or decline in contact other than the repulsive ethnocentrism and cultural differences of the two groups.

In equations 20.2 and 20.3 ethnocentricity decreases contact and increases cultural differences, as might be expected.

The denominator of the last equation ensures that cultural differences are reduced by contact so long as h is positive (the normal situation).

Contact theory has obvious application in marketing, PR and other activities involving persuasion, for example:

[1] It emphasizes that attitude changes with contact or, in general, information transfer.

If contact is 'positive', however, rather than negative as has generally been the case throughout man's sorry history, then equations 20.1 could be modified to reflect this by writing them in the form

$$E_{a,T+1} = E_{a,T} - a_1 C_T + a_4 D_T$$

where a_1 and a_4 are positive. Indeed, it might be hoped that the latter situation might be more likely in today's age of electronic communication and high speed travel. Moreover, it is in this situation that such equations might be applicable to advertising with E = 'resistance.'

[2] It reminds us that ethnic or 'local' considerations are important in international marketing of a product.

[3] It reminds us of the importance of targeting advertising towards an appropriate demographic for a product, and that cultural differences exist between teenagers and their parents and, more so, their grandparents.

An attitudinal model of conflict

Mohr proposed a simple 'first approximation' formula for assessing the potential for conflict between persons or groups. The basic formula is (Mohr, 2014a; Mohr et al. 2018c):

$$A^* = A + xB + yC + zD \qquad (20.4)$$

where A^* = current 'overall' attitude,
A = initial or 'basic' attitude (based on 'known history'),
B = attitudes towards behaviours of the second party,
C = contact history between the two parties,
D = degree of difference between the parties considered,
and x, y, z are scaling factors that indicate the relative importance of the terms and here these will be assumed unity for simplicity.

Equation 20.4 can, of course, be used to assess the attitude of both parties involved in the assessment.

Here attitude is assessed in the same way as attitude is measured by the information integration model of Equation 6.2 but for simplicity only scale values (but not weights) will be given to a small set of items in measuring A.

Similarly, only scale values are used in assessing B, C and D. These extra terms add a great deal to the 'basic' A assessment to give a 'picture' of the 'overall' attitude.

Example application

As an example of application of the simple model of Equation 20.4 the attitude of a typical individual towards a hypothetical terrorist organization 'HTO' is considered.

To assess this only five items are assessed by simple questions for the initial attitude, behavioural, contact and difference terms in Equation 20.4. Assessment is similar to that used for the 'five-factor' model of personality (Larsen & Buss, 2002) and uses five possible scores:
+2 = strongly like/very similar etc.
+1 = like/similar etc.
0 = neutral
-1 = dislike/different etc.
-2 = strongly dislike/very different etc.

Table 20.1. Person's hypothetical attitude towards 'HTO'.

SCORE:	-2	-1	0	1	2
A, initial/basic attitude	Dislike/Like				
The people			0		
Their government(s)		-1			
How they look		-1			
What they say	-2				
What they do	-2				
B, group behaviour	Dislike/Like				
Sectarian conflict		-1			
Negative rhetoric		-1			
'Pushing' their religion	-2				
Threats	-2				
Terrorism	-2				
C, contact history	Uncomfortable/Comfortable				
See on TV			0		
See on street			0		
Close to		-1			
Talk to		-1			
Socialize	-2				
D, differences	Different/Similar				
Language		-1			
Economic				1	
Culture		-1			
Religion	-2				
History		-1			
TOTAL SCORE, A*:	-22				

Table 20.1 gives an example assessment for a hypothetical individual. Here total scores less than -30 are 'very negative', -10 to -20 'negative', -10 to +10 are moderate, +10 to +20 'positive', and more than +20 'very positive'.

Thus the results of Table 20.1 are mostly 'negative', the total of -22 indicating a considerable degree of disapproval. It is only very negative scores of less than -30 that might be a cause for concern if they were obtained for a significant percentage of a population.

Weighting factors can be assigned to items in Table 20.1 to reflect differing importance associated with them, for example the 9th and 10th items might have weights >1.

Effect of Societal views

The effect of the views of society on individuals and groups can be included in Equation 20.4 by adding an extra term to account for the affect of social norms on attitude formation:

$$A** = A* + fS = A + xB + yC + zD + fS$$

where f is a scaling factor here assumed = 1 for simplicity, and the factors x, y, z are also assumed =1 so that:

$$A** = A + B + C + D + S \tag{20.5}$$

and S is the person or group's assessment of the attitude or 'position' of society, society here including the media, politicians, religious leaders, the public, friends and family.

Then measurement of S is done in the same way as for A, B, C and D in Table 20.1.

Table 20.2. Person's assessment of society's attitude.

SCORE:	-2	-1	0	1	2
S, perceived society view	Negative/Positive				
TV/radio/papers		-1			
Politicians			0		
Religious leaders		-1			
The public		-1			
Friends & family		-1			
TOTAL SCORE:			-4		

For the views of a typical person regarding society's attitude towards 'HTO' the result might be that shown in Table 20.2. Adding this result to that of Table 20.1 the aggregate score is -26, a 'negative' overall result.

A 'very negative' score would be less than -30, so the combined result of Tables 20.1 and 20.2 (i.e. -26) for an individual or a group is not of concern but worth taking some notice of.

Responses to conflict

When the group, attitudes towards which are sought, is in some form of dispute or conflict, whether this be economic, concerning mistreatment of a few people, or armed conflict on any scale, the attitudes concerning what measures should be taken against the group can also be measured in like fashion to Table 20.1.

Table 20.3. Attitudes towards measures against group.

SCORE:	0	1	2	3	4
	Level of support for action				
Government condemns					4
Cut diplomatic ties				3	
Trade embargo			2		
Public demonstrations				3	
UN sanctions		1			
War	0				-
TOTAL SCORE:	13				

Table 20.3 shows an example of such an assessment for a hypothetical individual concerning his or her views towards HTO's terrorism around the world. The total score is $R = 13$ out of a possible 24, perhaps a 'fail' mark by way of assessment of the group in question, but not an extremely bad score.

Total scores of close to 20, on the other hand, would indicate very strong feelings of which, perhaps, considerable notice should be taken should they be found to apply to a significant number of people.

The results of Tables 20.1 – 20.3 can be combined as:

$$A^{***} = A + B + C + D + S - (R - 12)$$

with the last term adjusted to allow for its different scale of measurement, giving $A^{***} = -27$ for the present example case.

Other factors affecting attitudes & conflict

[1] Hierarchical influences.

These include the influence of strongly hierarchical organizations that have very great influence on society and its individual people, some of these being:

(a) Governments of any type, whether they be monarchies or dictatorships have considerable influence on the populace by way of propaganda and enforceable laws, for example those of conscription.

(b) Political parties. Even when they are not in government, supporters of political parties are often considerably influenced by their views.

(c) Religions. These, of course, have had great influence throughout history but have less influence in the West now, whilst in contrast Muslim sects still have great influence on many of the world's 1.5 billion Muslims.

(d) TV, radio and print media also tend to come from 'on high' and also have considerable influence.

[2] Social norms.

Social norms have a great influence on the thinking of individuals and groups within any society, for example the wearing of scarves, veils and burkas by Muslim women is still very widely practiced.

The structure of society has also been an important factor. Fairly soon after the Agricultural Revolution and the formation of man's first permanent towns and farms the first small armies would have been formed to defend them, at first only temporarily.

Indeed, with the diversification of occupations that the Agricultural Revolution brought, permanent armies were one eventual result, notably in Rome and its empire, for example. Then, of course, given the availability of armies, there has always been a tendency to use them sooner or later, most obviously as the 'external police force' to deal with external problems, albeit a very large force all too often in history.

[3] Economic factors.

Economic considerations have often been the cause of human conflict, for example competition for resources, a good historical example being the Spanish Empire's enthusiastic search for gold in the Americas.

Man has always been inventing new tools and weapons, particularly since the Industrial Revolution. Now the arms industries have become massive and are able to considerably influence government policy in many countries whose economies have suffered a steep decline in their manufacturing industries in recent decades (Sampson, 1977; Thomas, 2006).

An example of the absurdity of it all, the CIA knew that chemical weapons were pouring into Iraq from Chile and South Africa in the 1980s. Cardoen industries in Santiago, for example, sent its chemical weapons, and the German-made artillery 'cups' or shells to contain them, to Iraq (Ben-Menashe, 1992). Then, the US later condemned Iraq for using these weapons on the Kurds and used this as an excuse for their first invasion of Iraq early in 1991.

[4] Growing populations.
Even as far back as early man's troglodyte days it is not hard to imagine an extended family group growing to the point at which a second cave was needed.

Similarly, when man had towns and then cities these too grew in size, needing ever more space and, more importantly, resources, particularly food.

This, coupled with man's habit of exploration, which no doubt dates back to his hunter-gatherer days and thence the hunt for food, has led man to engage in conflict with neighbouring populations.

Conflicts may have arisen simply out of the suspicion that the sight of strangers aroused when they suddenly appeared. Perhaps, for example, a spear might be thrown to scare them away. Then, of course, there might be retaliation and thus conflict.

As man's population continued to increase, of course, the tendency for migration and thence conflict must have increased, for example people leaving crowded and disease-ridden cities in Europe to colonize the 'New World' from the 16th to 19th centuries.

[5] Proximity.
Proximity also affects people's attitudes as does contact which, of course, is facilitated by proximity, the more 'negative' the contact the more negative the attitude formed.

Thus for tribal man, as with his chimpanzee relatives, proximity was a key factor in regular tribal conflicts.

Indeed, until only about two thousand years ago, human conflicts were only between neighbouring cities, regions, or countries. With the building of ships capable of sailing hundreds of miles, however, came the ability to explore more widely, and human conflict began to occur over greater distances and on a greater scale.

[6] Competitiveness.

In the Roman Empire, for example, there was a competitiveness in its governments, an obvious drive that made it wish to become 'bigger and grander' and go out and conquer other lands to achieve that end.

This obsession with competition runs all through the history and cultures of Homo sapiens, an example being our obsession with sport, or any kind of competition even if it is called a 'game.' It seems fundamentally related to the alpha-male behaviour of several other animal species.

Man, however, takes the alpha-male issue to absurd lengths, for example the original Olympic Games in Ancient Greece being conducted in the nude and, indeed, it seems to be returning slowly towards that situation now.

Equally, man has often indulged in war without good reason, usually because some loony leader and his acolytes want to 'beat' some other foe.

Conclusions

Very relevant to attitude also is the vexatious question of ethnic conflict and, indeed, the equations of Forbes' contact hypothesis do emphasize that, over time, attitudes change. Moreover, models like that of contact hypothesis could be applied to the effects of advertising.

The simple formula of Equation 20.4 combines the measurement techniques of attitudinal psychology with the concepts of the contact hypothesis to assess the attitudes of individuals and groups of people to other groups of people. The point of this exercise is that, when the attitude of one group to another is very negative, then conflict between the groups is, of course, more likely.

The attitudes of leaders are of particular importance, as it is these that may lead to conflict and war. The attitudes of leaders will, of course, be influenced by many of the same factors and stimuli that affect the public.

There are many other factors that affect modern human conflict. For example, particularly in modern times, alliances between nations have played a part in many wars, World War 1 and World War 2 being notable examples.

One difficulty is that, if two groups of 4 nations are allied, then a single nation attacking some part of another may quickly result in 8 nations being at war. In other words, the larger the parties involved, the bigger the conflict.

One fear for the future, therefore, is the increasing power of such huge nations as China and India, and also of the 1.5 billion Muslims around the world, so many of whom become involved in Islamic jihad all around the world, and to the extent that many believe that we have been in the midst of *World War 3* for some time (Mohr & Fear, 2015b).

The numbers involved here are an order of magnitude greater than those involved in the two world wars of the last century and war between any of these three entities and another of perhaps similar size could well be the war to end all wars.

Mankind's disastrous history of conflict seems unlikely to end and we face other threats as a result of overpopulation, resource depletion, climate change etcetera. The authors HOPES we can solve some of these problems, however, and thus increase our chances of avoiding the extinction forecast for many animal species, including ourselves (Mohr, 2012a).

To improve our prospects we should push for *real democracy,* as outlined in *The Doomsday Calculation* (Mohr, 2012a) and *The Population Explosion* (Mohr et al., 2018b), rather than the highly oligarchical and antiquated Westminster system that still governs much of the Western world today, and only then, perhaps, might there be any real chance of avoiding increasing global catastrophes and perhaps extinction.

At a personal level conflict with family, friends or fellow-workers will, like bereavement, tend to cause depression, and thus should be avoided as far as possible.

☺☻☹☺☻☹☺☻☹☺☻☹☺☻☹

Chapter 21

PSYCHOLOGICAL ASSESSMENT

> *We have lost the art of living; and in the most important science of all, the science of daily life, the science of behaviour, we are complete ignoramuses. We have psychology instead.*
> D. H. Lawrence, *Etruscan Places*, ch. 4 (1932).

Introduction

Chapter 16 discussed some of the early history of psychiatry, then discussing a range of common mental illnesses.

The present chapter briefly discusses some of the main methods by which psychological problems are diagnosed.

Mental illness

Mental health professionals use the term *mental health problem* when a person experiences difficulties that are mild, temporary, and able to be treated in a relatively short term.

The term *mental illness* is then used when a person's problems are more serious and likely to persist for a relatively long time, and thus require long-term treatment.

Mental illness can be defined as a psychological dysfunction involving distress, difficulty in coping with everyday life, and inappropriate behaviours.

Psychological dysfunction involves a breakdown of cognitive, emotional and/or behavioural functioning during which thoughts, feelings or behavior differ from those normal for the person in question, and the situation involved.

A key characteristic of mental illness is *atypical* thoughts, feelings, and behavior.

If, for example, a person usually friendly, but becomes withdrawn and uncommunicative for extended periods such behavior would be deemed atypical.

In contrast, a person whose behavior is normally eccentric, would not be deemed to be mentally ill because their eccentric behavior would not be atypical for them.

If a person's thoughts, feelings, or behavior appear abnormal, but are, in fact, 'normal' in the society or culture to which they belong, they too would not be considered mentally ill by that society. If they were members of the Islamic State terrorist group, for example, with that organization they would be considered normal, but in the world at large they would be considered criminal, and their behaviors might be deemed to involve mental illness.

Homosexuality is perhaps a good example, for in Western societies it was deemed by many to be an aberrant behavior requiring psychiatric treatment, but is now widely accepted.

Similarly, ADHD or Attention Deficit Hyperactivity Disorder, is relatively new in the annals of psychology, but now a great many young children are diagnosed with it and given prescription medications for long periods.

Mental health professionals use a variety of methods of assessing a person's mental health, including clinical interviews, behavioural observations, and various kinds of tests such as personality tests to develop a *clinical profile* of the thoughts, feelings, and behaviours of a person, and the factors and life experiences that may have contributed to their current mental health status.

Clinical interviews

These are usually the first step in assessing a person's mental health, and involve a *mental status exam* which records the results of observations and questions about five aspects of a person (Grivas & Carter, 2005):

1. *Appearance and behavior,* including grooming and cleanliness, hunched or upright posture, smiling or sad facial expressions, slow or lethargic body movements, downcast eyes. Then, for example, downcast eyes, a sad expression, and hunched posture might be indicative of depression.

2. *Thought processes* as indicated by a how a person talks. For example, fast, disjointed speech about unrealistic experiences suggest a distorted sense of reality, perhaps indicating schizophrenia.

3. *Mood and affect. Mood* is a person's current emotional state, for example, 'down' or 'highly excitable'. *Affect* here refers to responses. For example, our affect is 'appropriate' if we laugh at something funny, but 'inappropriate' if we laugh about the death of a friend or relative. If, on the other hand, we show no feeling at all about a highly emotional situation, our affect may be recorded as 'flat'.

4. *Intellectual functioning* and aspects of intelligence, such as vocabulary, and response to questions requiring problem-solving and decision-making ability. Sometimes a formal IQ test is done.

5. *Sensorium* or general awareness of one's surroundings, for example does the person know who they are, where they are, the day, date, time, place etcetera. People with some types of brain damage, or psychological dysfunction as a result of substance abuse, may be unable to answer some such questions.

This mental status exam enables the mental health professional to initially assess which aspects of a person's thoughts, feelings, and behaviours require more detailed assessment using a psychological test designed to diagnose a specific mental illness.

Psychological testing

One of the most widely used *diagnostic tests* is the Minnesota Multiphase Personality Inventory (MMPI) which focuses on the 10 aspects of personality called *clinical scales* shown in Table 21.1 (Kassin, 2004).

Table 21.1. Clinical scales of the MMPI.

	Clinical scale	Description
1	**Hypochondriasis**	Chronic and abnormal anxiety about imaginary symptoms and ailments
2	**Depression**	Sad feelings of gloom and inadequacy, low morale, pessimistic, hopelessness, unhappy, sluggish.
3	**Hysteria**	Attention-seeking emotional outbreaks
4	**Psychopathic deviation**	Impulsive, selfish, unreliable disregard of social rules and authority
5	**Masculinity-femininity**	Identification with masculine and/or feminine sex roles
6	**Paranoia**	Feelings of persecution &/or grandeur, suspiciousness, overly sensitive
7	**Psychasthenia**	Fears, self-doubt, guilt, obsessions and compulsions
8	**Schizophrenia**	Social isolation, confusion, disorientation, bizarre perceptions
9	**Mania**	Hyperactivity and impulsiveness
10	**Social introversion**	Shyness, social withdrawal, inhibited

The 'inventory' has 567 questions presented in random order, each related to one of the 10 clinical scales, to which the respondent answers 'true', 'false' or 'cannot say'.

The scores for each clinical scale range from 0 to 120, a score of 50 being considered average, and two-thirds of the population score between 40 and 60 on each scale.

A score above 65 on a particular scale may be deemed 'clinically significant' or abnormal.

Validity and reliability of tests

Psychological tests for a specific mental illness should have (Grivas & Carter, 2005):

1. *Construct validity*, for example, a test for depression should differentiate the characteristics of depression from those of other categories of mental illness such as anxiety disorders.

2. *Concurrent validity* or results consistent with those from another test for the specific mental illness in question known to be valid for that illness.

3. *Reliability* which can be assessed by giving repeating the test on the same individuals on a later occasion, and then checking to see if the results are consistent. A problem here is that people may remember the answers they gave the first time, and simply repeat them, and to help reduce this problem another version of the same test can be used the second time.

Classification of mental illnesses

The most widely used system for identifying and classifying mental illnesses is the Diagnostic and Statistical Manual of Mental Disorders (DSM), which was first developed in by the American Psychiatric Association in 1952. The 2000 "text revision" of the fourth edition, the DSM-IV-TR, uses the following five 'axes' to classify mental disorders:

1. Clinical disorders: symptoms causing distress or impairing occupational or social functioning such as anxiety disorders.

2. Personality disorders and mental retardation: chronic disorders impairing occupational and social functioning.

3. General medical condition: physical disorders that may contribute to a psychological disorder.

4. Psychosocial and environmental problems: contributing negative life events and personal relationship problems.

5. Global assessment of functioning: overall level of functioning in occupational, social and leisure activities.

Axis 1 comprises 400 mental disorders in 16 categories, these including (Grivas & Carter, 2005):

➢ Disorders usually diagnosed in infancy, childhood, and adolescence, including autism, ADHD and separation anxiety disorder (anxiety etc. when separated from home or family).

➢ Mood disorders involving inappropriate and extreme highs and lows for extended periods, including bipolarity (manic depressive disorder).

➢ Eating disorders including anorexia nervosa and bulimia.

➢ Substance-related disorders involving substances that affect the central nervous system, including alcohol, opioid, amphetamine, cocaine and hallucinogen use disorders.

➢ Anxiety disorders, including generalized anxiety disorder, phobias, panic disorder, obsessive-compulsive disorder (OCD), acute stress disorder, and post-traumatic stress disorder (PTSD).

➢ Impulse-control disorders including pathological gambling, kleptomania, and pyromania.

➢ Sleep disorders including insomnia, hypersomnia, sleep terror disorder, and sleepwalking.

➢ Somatoform disorders involving physical symptoms mainly caused by psychological factors, including conversion disorder (mental conflict causing paralysis or anaesthesia) and hypochondriasis.

➢ Schizophrenia and other psychotic disorders involving a loss of contact with reality.

➢ Cognitive disorders such as delirium, dementia, and amnestic disorders, including Alzheimer's disease and Huntington's disease.

Axis 2 disorders, for example mental retardation, are less common but usually continue for the rest of a person's life and are thus part of a person's personality.

Axes 3 and 4 provide mental health professional with additional information that may be relevant to diagnosis and treatment, for example heart disease (axis 3) or problems with family or at work (axis 4).

Axis 5 involves assessment of how well a person copes with everyday life and this is done using the Global Assessment of Functioning (GAF) scale and extract of which is shown in Table 21.2 (Grivas & Carter, 2005):

Table 21.2. Example scores from GAF scale.

Score	
91-100	Superior functioning with no symptoms.
81-90	Good functioning with minimal symptoms such as anxiety.
51-60	Some difficulty with work, friends etc. and occasional moderate anxiety etc.
21-30	Serious impairment of function and communication, for example no job, home or friends.
11-20	Some risk of hurting self or others through self-harm, violence, or carelessness, poor hygiene etc.
1-10	Serious risk of " " " " "

One research study on the reliability of the DSM-IV-TR as an assessment tool found 70% agreement of classifications of mental disorders by mental health professionals (DiNardo et al., 1993).

Labelling and high rate of misdiagnoses

'Labelling' a person with some mental disorder can, of course, have a negative effect upon that person, also influencing how they are viewed by others.

A classic study had eight normal people present at psychiatric hospitals as 'pseudo-patients' saying they had been hearing voices. All were diagnosed as having schizophrenia and admitted. Their stays ranged from 7 to 52 days, and all were released as being "in remission", leading to the conclusion that psychologists could not recognize 'normal behaviour'.

In a follow-up study staff at one hospital were warned of pseudo-patients appearing in the next three months, and staff were asked to identify which of their patients were pseudo-patients. No pseudo-patients were actually sent, but one staff member identified 41 out of 193 patients as pseudo-patients.

Such results emphasize that accurate diagnosis of mental health issues is often difficult, for example because much reliance is placed upon patient interviews, but some patients may not provide accurate or honest answers to key question, not wanting, of course, to admit to weaknesses and faults.

Conclusions

Mental illness involves, of course, psychological dysfunction and thence difficulty in coping with life that may involve, for example, excessive anxiety.

Diagnosis of mental illness involves clinical interviews and psychological tests and relies heavily upon the patient's performance and the tester 'reading between the lines' at times to interpret this.

Testing of attitudes, which was discussed in Chapters 6 and 20, might also be helpful in diagnosing mental illnesses.

Many of the most common mental illnesses were discussed in Chapter 16, and Table 21.1 summarizes some of these.

The most common clinical disorders were summarized in a preceding section, ranging from autism and ADHS in childhood to Alzheimer's disease in the elderly.

Table 21.2 shows example scores in the Global Assessment of Functioning scale for assessment of a how well a person is coping with life in general, this being Axis 5 of the Diagnostic and Statistical Manual of Mental Disorders.

Psychopathy is the largest category of abnormal psychological behaviours and was briefly discussed in Chapter 16, whilst the Hare checklist for diagnosing psychopaths was given and briefly discussed in Chapter 12 (see Table 12.1).

Chapter 22

TREATMENT OF MENTAL DISORDERS

> *Yet today's practitioners too easily forget their debt*
> *to Freud's original "talking cure" of listening to and analyzing*
> *the content of a patient's mind, and his insight that*
> *a person can simply be sabotaged by the irrational within.*
> Tom Butler-Bowdon, *50 Psychology Classics* (2017).

Introduction

Chapter 16 discussed the early history of psychiatry, a wide variety of psychological ailments, and treatment for some of these was briefly discussed.

In the following section various broad classifications of psychological traits are discussed.

According to Gillespie (2017), everyone experiences some sort of behavioural disorder at some time in their lives, and low 'scores' or assessments of psychological traits are relatively normal. High scores, especially for prolonged periods, however, may indicate a need for treatment and several types of treatment for psychological problems are discussed in the remainder of this chapter.

Behavioural psychology

According to Gillespie (2017), psychological behaviours these fall into three categories:

1. **Schizophrenic:**
    (a) Paranoid – irrational suspicion and mistrust.
    (b) Schizoid – detached from social relationships.
    (c) Schizotypal – extreme discomfort with social
          interaction.

2. Dramatic:
  (a) Antisocial – disregard for others, lack of empathy and manipulative behaviour.
  (b) Borderline – unstable self-image and relationships.
  (c) Histrionic – attention-seeking behaviour.
  (d) Narcissistic – needing admiration; lack of empathy.

3. Anxious:
  (a) Avoidant – feeling inadequate and very sensitive.
  (b) Dependent – needing care from others.
  (c) Obsessive-compulsive – perfectionism: rigid conformity to rule and procedures.

Treatment of psychiatric disorders

Psychiatrists and psychologists use interviewing techniques and tests to diagnose mental illnesses.

Treatments for psychological problems may include:

➢ Regular appointments for 'talk therapy'.

➢ Cognitive therapies are now the most widely used procedures used by psychologists and are discussed in the following section.

➢ Hypnosis in which patients are told to relax, clear their minds, close their eyes etcetera, eventually being coaxed into a hypnotic or semi-conscious state in which their minds are supposed to be open to suggestion, for example that they don't really need to smoke and should not want to when they awake.

➢ Prescription drugs, for example, lithium salts for manic depression, Valium for anxiety disorders, and several new drugs for ADHD.

➢ Group therapy, for example monthly meetings of AA (Alcoholics Anonymous) or groups of people with OCD, the latter usually being chaired by a psychologist.

➢ Mindfulness meditation groups chaired by a practitioner in which quiet music is played and patients are told to clear their minds, relax, breathe slowly, close their eyes, and picture some beautiful scenery in their minds.

In extreme cases, of course, patients are confined to 'mental hospitals', usually for short periods in cases where patients are having bouts of severe depression accompanied with thoughts of suicide, for example, but for periods of several years or more in extreme cases of schizophrenia in which patients begin to lose all contact with reality and are unable to care for themselves.

In a few extreme cases ECT (Electroconvulsive shock therapy) is sometimes used. ECT was once regarded as causing significant permanent damage to the brain. Now, thanks to modern anaesthesia, it is much safer with a morality rate 1/10th that of childbirth. ECT is used to treat extreme depression and schizophrenia (Lillienfeld et al., 2010).

Cognitive behavior therapy (CBT)

Cognitive therapies in which patients talk about their mental issues, sometimes in groups, are now the most widely used procedures used by psychologists (Grivas & Carter, 2005).

Cognitive behavior therapy (CBT) assumes that emotional or behavioural problems are caused by unrealistic or irrational thinking about oneself, others and situations, resulting in 'mentally unhealthy' thoughts and behaviours.

A student who gets a low mark on an exam, for example, may begin to lose hope of coping with the subject satisfactorily and, to some extent at least, give up trying to do so.

According to the principles of CBT one can think more positively and optimistically and plan to work harder to obtain better results in the near future.

CBT is often used to treat anxiety and depression, with the patients being taught to identify irrational negative thoughts and replace them with more realistic, more optimistic ones. For example, a student fearful of bad marks in exams, may be encouraged to think along the lines: *Relax. If the exam is hard, it will be hard for everyone else too.*

Thus, cognitive therapy's "revolutionary idea" is that depression isn't an emotional disorder, and the bad feelings of depression stem from negative thoughts which can be replaced with positive thoughts (Burns, 1980).

Issues concerning psychiatric treatment

It was Freud who pioneered hypnosis as a means of psychotherapy, later discarding it in favour of "free association" in which a patient was encouraged to reveal repressed memories responsible for hysterical symptoms that Freud thought were always of a sexual nature, a view which many other psychiatrists felt incorrect, if not obsessive (Krapp, 2005).

A modern medical scandal is the way in which such drugs as Valium are prescribed for the long term to people. Such drugs are bound to be addictive and when patients forget to take their daily dose there will inevitably be withdrawal symptoms.

Such drugs, like the brain stimulant tobacco or the depressant and tranquilizer alcohol, alter pulse rate and blood pressure. Smoking two or three strong cigarettes in an hour, for example, will increase pulse rate significantly. The discomfort we feel when the next 'dose' of the drug is missed is known as 'withdrawal', in the case of alcohol overdose the symptoms being an increase in blood pressure and pulse rate.

Unless absolutely necessary, therefore, it seems madness to addict people to pharmaceutical drugs when they might only be briefly affected by some stressful event in their lives.

In an article entitled *Medication*, the *Weekend Australian* magazine of 10/9/2016 reported that: "Children are being over diagnosed as having ADHD – and now even 'daydreaming'." They are then put on drugs for the long-term and left feeling that they will suffer this really nonexistent disease for life, when in fact the problem will usually be one of poor study habits and motivation, often exacerbated by lack of a home environment that encourages good study habits, and the much too long and drawn out education system.

All this is good for the 'pysch. professions' as they can much increase the size of their practices with the many visits children will have to make for further prescriptions.

It is also good for the pharmaceutical industry which sometimes rewards doctors financially or with holidays and other perks to encourage them to prescribe their drugs.

New treatments

Examples of new treatments for psychological problems include:

> - Many people with depression, for example, suffer from social isolation, and regular social 'chat groups run at local council centres are a simple low-cost alternative to psychotherapy. AA have long had good results with comparable groups for several decades, whilst groups mediated by a counsellor are also used for people with OCD.
> - "Motivational Interviewing" in which patients are motivated to think positively etc. (Arkowitz et al., 2015).
> - Just a few sessions with a psychologist in which the patient writes down their bad memory/experience and reads it out aloud 'as though it happened to someone else' can help reduce PTSD. Good results have been had in conjunction with the drug propanol (Miller, 2017), but no doubt good results could also be had using such 'thought transference' without this drug.
> - Comparable to the latter, patients suffering many psychological problems can be helped by being told to 'couple' their negative feelings with positive ones.

Support organizations

There are several organizations that help people with mental health problems, including:

> - Lifeline – a free phone chat service to help people with mental health crises such as suicidal thoughts.
> - Beyond Blue – free phone chat service to help people with mental health issues such as depression.
> - Organizations such as Rainbows, "the world's largest grief support organization for children and young people" (Marta, 2004).
> - Anxiety Disorders Association of Victoria.
> - SANE Australia.
> - Anxiety Treatment Australia.

Conclusion

It should also be noted that recent studies in which one group of depressed patients were given a healthy Mediterranean-style diet, and a second just regular 'consultations' with a counsellor, found that the healthier diet option significantly reduced levels of depression.

Notably, the 'Mediterranean diet' usually includes a couple of glasses of red wine daily for 'relaxational purposes', the procyanidins and other antioxidants in red wine being particularly helpful in reducing cardiovascular disease, and in this context it should be noted that brain function, and thence such ailments as Alzheimer's disease, are affected by poor diets that increase atherosclerosis. Thus 'natural therapies' involving healthy diet, including plenty of appropriate dietary vitamin and other supplements, and plenty of exercise, relaxation and sleep, improve both physical and mental health (Mohr, 2012c, 2013a, 2015, 2018a, 2018b).

The author therefore recommends improved diet and lifestyle, including occasional contact with supportive and helpful friends and neighbours, as a means of improving mental health, perhaps in conjunction with professional counselling if need be, though in most cases the latter should only be required for the short term, for example to help deal with a particular event such as a death in the family, divorce etcetera.

In the case of marriage problems, of course, marriage guidance counsellors have traditionally been used by many people, whilst some Christian church groups now run more general counselling services in offices run at sites not connected/adjacent to a church.

In choosing a counsellor one might, for example, be wary of those overly obsessed with sexual issues or dreams as being the root of many problems, as the author believes Sigmund Freud and Carl Jung were.

When professional 'talk therapy' is used, however, the patient should take care to choose a counsellor intelligent enough to quickly work out what memories etc. are affecting them and suggest sensible and effective ideas to deal with any 'mental problems', and using pharmaceutical drugs only when clearly necessary, and then only for the short or medium term.

In dealing with psychological problems in children, of course, teachers should also be involved as soon as possible to help children cope. As with adults, involving children with sports or other activity or 'interest' groups can provide social connections that may reduce such issues as depression, and autism, and ADHD.

Optimism and hope, of course, can greatly improve mental health, and life outcomes, as discussed in the recent books *The Psychology of Hope* (Mohr et al, 2018), *The Psychology of Success* (Mohr et al., 2018f), and *The Psychology of Life* (Mohr, 2018f)

Viktor Frankl's *logotherapy*, which encourages one to believe that each individual's life has a meaning, and is not just a product of one's environment, is perhaps also worth note in the context of optimism etc. (Frankl, 1969).

Carl Rogers' view that the main problem most of his patients had was that they approached life with "'false roles" or "masks" and were usually worried about what other people thought of them and expected them to do, and that they needed to become their "real selves" is also perhaps worth note (Rogers, 1961).

Finally, note that, in emergency situations people in psychological crisis should establish phone contact with organizations such as Lifeline and Beyond Blue.

22. TREATMENT OF MENTAL DISORDERS

PART V
CONCLUSIONS

Chapter 23

IMPROVING LIFE

There are many paths to the top of the mountain,
but the view is always the same.
Chinese Proverb

If A is a success in life, then A equals x plus y plus z. Work is x;
y is play; and z is keeping your mouth shut.
Albert Einstein, quoted in: Observer, London, 15 Jan. 1950.

Introduction

When one undertakes a self-assessment such as that of Table 10.1 and finds one or two aspect of one's life need improvement, it is best to begin thinking about how to improve those aspects as soon as possible, taking any advice and offers from friends etc. along the way.

Being 'less than happy' and underpaid etc. in your current job, for example, is a major issue that will probably affect most other aspects of your life, including health and wealth, happiness, quality of family life etcetera. If that is the case producing a half-way good CV and beginning the search for another job, or perhaps giving though to starting one's own business, perhaps with some financial help from extended family.

Alternatively, one might have been living in the same place for several years and want to move, perhaps to live closer to work to make life easier for yourself, and perhaps the rest of the family.

Whatever the life improvement you seek, it is best to for it as well as possible, and following sections make a few suggestions that might be helpful to some readers.

Life assessment

One can assess the quality of a particular aspect of one's life using the Expectation-Value and Information Integration methods of attitude assessment.

To assess the quality of several key aspects of one's life the simplest and most widely used method is Likert Scaling.

Table 23.1 shows an example assessment for an adult person, scoring being done simply by using a printed copy of this table and circling the scores/ratings given to each of the items listed in the first column.

An 'average' rating of 3 on all 20 items gives, of course, a total score of 60. More important, perhaps, ratings of 1/poor for such important items as the first two (job and pay) might motivate one to try and improve these important life factors.

Similarly, a low rating for some of the health items might spur one into taking action to improve one's health.

In the wide range of items in Table 23.1 some items are much more important than others. Generally recreation and social life, for example, are not as important as one's job, and some jobs, of course, involve long hours 6 or 7 days a week, allowing little time for social life in any case.

Thus an evaluation such as that of Table 23.1 could be extended to include weights for each factor, as in the Information Integration method of attitude assessment discussed earlier, and this is done for the 'work' items of Table 23.1 in the following section.

Table 23.1. Life quality questionnaire using Likert scaling.

Aspect of life: Circle the appropriate number	Very good	Good	Aver -age	Fair	Poor
Your work:					
1. Your job	5	4	3	2	1
2. Your pay	5	4	3	2	1
3. Relationship with boss	5	4	3	2	1
4. Workplace conditions	5	4	3	2	1
5. Relations with workmates	5	4	3	2	1
Your home life:					
6. Your financial situation	5	4	3	2	1
7. Your home	5	4	3	2	1
8. Your parent(s) or partner	5	4	3	2	1
9. Your siblings or children	5	4	3	2	1
10. Your health	5	4	3	2	1
Recreation and social life:					
11. Evening activities	5	4	3	2	1
12. Weekend activities	5	4	3	2	1
13. Friends	5	4	3	2	1
14. Regular outings	5	4	3	2	1
15. Social, sport etc. groups	5	4	3	2	1
Your health:					
16. General health	5	4	3	2	1
17. Fitness	5	4	3	2	1
18. Diet	5	4	3	2	1
19. Weight	5	4	3	2	1
20. Mental health	5	4	3	2	1
Add the numbers you circled:	Score/100:				

Assessing a key aspect of life

One can assess the quality of a particular aspect of one's life using the Expectation-Value and Information Integration methods of attitude assessment discussed earlier.

As an example, we shall now assess the five 'work' items of Table 23.1 for a 'typical' person using the Information Integration method, giving the following result with weights and scores 1-10.

Attribute 1 (job): $w_1 = 5$, $s_1 = 5/10$ (i.e. 'halfway' values)

Attribute 2 (pay): $w_2 = 8/10$, $s_2 = 3/10$

Attribute 3 (relationship with boss): $w_3 = 7/10$, $s_3 = 4/10$

Attribute 4 (workplace conditions): $w_4 = 5/10$, $s_4 = 5/10$

Attribute 5 (relations with workmates): $w_5 = 4/10$, $s_5 = 5/10$

giving a total score

$$= 5 \times 5 + 8 \times 3 + 7 \times 4 + 5 \times 5 + 4 \times 5$$
$$= 25 + 24 + 28 + 25 + 20 = 122$$

whereas a 'middling evaluation score' with 5/10 for both the weights and scale values for all five items would give a total score of 125, so that the situation is perhaps 'satisfactory', for the present at least, but the low score of 3/10 for 'pay' is deserving of some attention sooner rather than later.

Dealing with problems at work

If you are having problems at work, whether these be boredom with the job, finding it too hard, or finding being too low in the hierarchy too hard, then using a simple table like that of Table 23.2 might be a good start in dealing with the issue.

Table 23.2 illustrates an action plan to improve the work situation with one or two actions suggested for each of the five work items, including an approximate timing for each action.

Perhaps the key item is 1, where the plan is the cautious and sensible one of staying for a couple of years, but beginning to look for another job immediately – sensible because it can take a long time to find a job, and even longer to find a good one.

Most important, however, is that a simple plan such as this is far wiser than, for example, impatiently barging into the boss's office and abusing him about being underpaid, not an entirely unheard of situation.

Table 23.2. Action plan re. job.

Item		Actions	Timing
1	Job	Stay	1-2 years
		Look for another job	Now
2	Pay	Ask for a pay rise	Now
3	Boss	Talk to boss	Next week
		Make complaint	In 3 months
4	Conditions	Talk to union	Next month
		Talk to boss	In 3 months
5	Workmates	Meeting to raise issues	Next month

Furthermore, having a sensible plan gives one hope for the immediate and medium term, as well as time to come up with other ideas to improve one's work situation, and to obtain help and advice from others on it.

Job searching

When searching for a job it is, of course, important to have a good Curriculum Vitae (CV).

This might have the following sections:

> ➤ A short summary section of about 10 lines.
> ➤ A table summarizing you professional experience with column 1 = type of experience , column 2 = details of this, entries in this being, for example, management, sales etcetera.
> ➤ A table summarizing your work experience with column 1 = years (e.g. 2012-2018), column 2 = company you worked for, and a line or two on what work you did. This might include, for example, any voluntary work, work you did privately to help friends or relatives, or writing work you did at home.
> ➤ For an academic, for example, a list of courses given, and perhaps another on publications in journals etc.
> ➤ A list of any organizations you belong to: for example the local branch of a political party, a charitable organization etc.
> ➤ A list of any special achievements.

- ➢ A list of any awards you have received.
- ➢ A list or table of any good comments you have received throughout life.
- ➢ The contact details of 3 referees, including at least one of your last bosses, if you are young one of your school teachers or University, TAFE etc. lecturers, and perhaps a 'personal referee' to attest to your good character etc.

At least once in life, it might be well worth paying a professional CV writer such as those who advertise in the local newspapers, and some of these will often also give advice on how to get a job, interview well etcetera.

Referees and job references

In choosing who to nominate as referees one should be careful to consider several factors, including:

- ➢ Preferably one should be 'relevant' in some way to the job in question.
- ➢ They should be people you trust.
- ➢ Always ask for an 'upfront' referee statement to be given to you, and take it to the interview and quote the best lines from it.
- ➢ Often the organization offering the job will get a 'confidential' referee statement from a past boss, either over the phone or by email. Always ask at interview for a copy of (or what was said if verbal) these references. If they differ significantly from the upfront statement you got then this proves that ex boss is dishonest/a liar.
- ➢ When you have references from two past bosses, point out that the best reference should be that considered.
- ➢ Get past colleagues to give you a 'statement' about any past boss you use as referee. If this is weak or somewhat negative, that will help overcome any negativity that he might have said about you in confidence.

For personal referees, who are usually friends etc., the latter step should not be necessary.

Improving family life

Improvements in family life might include:

- ➤ Moving house so that you or your wife live closer to work.

- ➤ Moving house so your children are closer to school.

- ➤ Changing school for your children, perhaps so they are close to home which has many advantages.

- ➤ Improving family health with improved diet, exercise, and lifestyle routines.

- ➤ Improving family recreation options to healthier and perhaps cheaper ones close to home.

- ➤ Improving the family's social life.

Conclusion

Getting a suitable job, of course, one of the keys to a more successful and happier life and the foregoing discussion of aspects of that important task will hopefully prove useful to some readers. Note also Table 24.1, which illustrates the sort of process by which a pool of job applicants is assessed, and an understanding of this process should help improve one's prospects of making successful job applications.

There are many other things one can do to improve life, and thereby perhaps make life happier and more successful, and only a few examples have been considered in the preceding chapter.

Many others were given in preceding chapters, however, and a couple more are given in the following chapter.

☺ ☹ ☹ ☺ ☺ ☹ ☺ ☺ ☹ ☺ ☺ ☹ ☺ ☺ ☹

Chapter 24

PLANNING FOR SUCCESS

> *Planning is as natural to the process of success
> as its absence is to the process of failure.*
> Robin Seiger, *Natural Born Winners* (1999).

Introduction

All too many of us go through life without sufficient planning, in part because we grow up with our lives largely controlled by parents and educators. Even at a young age, however, we should acquire the habit of planning our lives, at least in part, for example planning weekend activities with friends, and joining in planning of family activities.

In adult life, of course, planning is very important, for example planning personal and family activities and finances. We should also plan our working lives as far as possible, including in such plans our goals and aspirations, for example for better pay or a better job.

The following chapter gives examples of some of the common tools that can be used for planning, beginning with creative thinking to come up with ideas and goals for which we can then make plans.

Creative thinking

Divergent thinking involves considering a number of alternatives, some of which may be new and/or impractical, rather than seeking a single logical solution.

Creative thinking involves finding novel but practical solutions to a problem or task using divergent thinking and may occur in three stages (Morgan et al., 1979):

[1] Preparation: define the facts and materials needed for the new solution.

[2] Incubation: acquire further information, think about, and 'sleep on' the problem.

{3] Assembly: combine information to find the solution.

Creativity may be enhanced by 'undirected' or *autistic thinking*, as occurs in dreams, in which one's own 'personal' and unique concepts are freely associated. This is accomplished by *brainstorming* in which the mind is allowed to roam freely through as many ideas as possible.

Creative people enjoy creating things, are assertive, have a risk taking approach, tend to be impulsive, dislike constraints, like a little complexity, are objective about their efforts (i.e., able to critically examine them), and accept feedback from others.

Among other characteristics, creative people may also be intuitive, perceptive, ingenious, industrious, persistent, independent, unconventional, courageous, uninhibited, moody, self-centred and eccentric.

In conclusion: "- - *creativity is central to a rich, meaningful life"* (Butler-Bowdon, 2017). More important, it is a key component of *real IQ* (Mohr, Sinclair & Fear, 2017).

Sometimes *brainstorming* helps solve a problem, and group brainstorming has been found effective because:

[1] People tend to have twice as many ideas in the group situation because of the more stimulating environment, 'cross fertilization' of ideas and arousal of competitive spirit.

[2] Alternation of individual and group thinking improves results.

[3] As more ideas are produced they tend to improve.

[4] Second sessions a few days later improve results because of the 'incubation' process so important in creative thinking.

[5] The group uses *critical thinking* to evaluate the ideas.

Problem solving

Problems can be attacked in three stages:

[1] Defining the problem

At first this might involve realizing that a problem exists.

Then we need to determine:

(a) What is the initial situation, i.e., what is known about the problem?

(b) What is the goal?

(c) What are the restrictions or *constraints*?

(d) What moves or *operations* are required to reach the goal?

[2] Generating possible solutions

Solutions to a problem can be obtained by such *strategies* as:

(a) In the case of mathematics problems, for example, *algorithms* can be used to try large numbers of solutions on a computer.

(b) Use an existing *heuristic rule* or 'rule of thumb.'

(c) Redefine the problem, for example by breaking it down into stages and seeking a 'solution' for each stage. Such *means-end analysis* is sometimes more successful if the problem is examined by working backwards through these stages.

(d) Use a new arrangement of existing techniques or materials.

(e) Invent new techniques or materials, i.e., use *insight learning*. This requires *creative thinking* which, as described earlier, often involves *incubation* periods.

Creative thinking can be inhibited by:

(i) *Functional fixedness,* the difficulty of imagining new uses for materials or devices.

(ii) *Mental set,* the difficulty in finding new strategies for approaching a problem. Mental set can be induced by recent experiences or old habits.

[3] Testing and evaluating the solutions

Alternative solutions are tested to see how well they work in relation to predetermined criteria.

Sometimes problems can be solved by *trial and error* so that trial solutions are repetitively adjusted until satisfactory.

Selection of the best solution from a number of alternatives should be done with a quantitative basis.

Lateral thinking

Edward de Bono proposed lateral thinking as an alternative to logical or *vertical* thinking. Some of the features of lateral thinking are:

➢ Steps can be jumped (and 'filled' later).

➢ Steps need not be 'correct' so long as the conclusion is correct and may be made in order to *generate* a new direction or branch.

➢ Interpretation of task criteria and alternative solution properties can be changed and the process is not *finite,* that is it need not reach a conclusion in any given time.

➢ It is *probabilistic* so that less obvious solutions are considered so that the best solution is obtained (if a valid solution exists).

De Bono (1982) recommends use of the word PO:

"PO is the laxative of language"

as an alternative to the words 'yes' and 'no' to emphasize that lateral thinking is not quick to say no to less obvious solutions and, rather than stop at obstacles to a solution, one should *go around* them by such means as those summarized above.

Whilst 'po' seems a somewhat trivial, if not absurd, idea, it may have some merit for many of us do indeed have a tendency to persist trying to solve some problems rather than 'go around' them.

Selecting the best candidate for a job is a good example. If this is done with lateral thinking:

[1] Some criteria might be ignored or downgraded in importance so that more candidates will be considered.

[2] Those that do not satisfy some criteria might remain under consideration.

[3] Candidates not at the top of the list are re-evaluated.

Lateral thinking is better understood with reference to the decision trees described in a later section. In these lateral thinking might encourage us to consider branches that have lower probabilities of success.

The bottom line, however, is that lateral thinking simply involves considering more than one possible solution to a problem or task.

In this context the first author uses the term 'bilemma' when one has difficulty deciding between two alternatives, and then the term 'trilemma' when there are three alternatives, viewing the latter as the preferred situation as he feels it fairly easy to knock out one of three alternatives.

As in 'Mohr's Law of Politics', deciding between two almost equal alternatives is harder. In the farcical and outdated Westminster system, for example, the 2 main parties are relatively similar in policies, incompetence etcetera, so many a voter makes up their mind on which side of the political fence to place their vote only at the last minute.

Mohr's laws of decisions

Essentially, the major problem of the human race is the habit of making bad decisions.

Some of us, at least, are very good at creative thinking to produce new ideas and products, and others are good at making the things we most need such as food, clothing and shelter.

As a result of the devastatingly accurate Peter Principle, all too many of our leaders and managers are, more often than not, guilty of bad decisions, if not corruption.

If a leader commits us to an unjustified war then, just as architects do, he praises his mistake. If a worker makes a small error or two he is dismissed.

Self-evident as they may be, Mohr's Laws of Decision (Mohr, 2014b) are some help:

1) Don't rush.

2) Don't take the first offer or run with the first idea.

3) Look for alternative ideas and build an ideas/options list.

4) List the requirements or inputs for each option.

5) List the results or outputs for each option.

6) Calculate the ratio of the outputs to inputs for each option.

7) Double check the accuracy of 4 - 6.

8) Select the option with the highest output/input ratio.

9) Ask at least a second opinion.

10) Sleep on it.

The analysis of steps 4 - 6 corresponds to *cost-benefit* analysis, a simple technique widely used in economic studies of infrastructure and other plans to decide on the best program of work.

Many a housewife probably uses a somewhat similar decision making approach but the usually moronic politicians who run countries find such stuff hard going and have to employ thousands of economists and statisticians to perform these rudimentary analyses.

Needless to say they usually get it wrong, often when somebody's palm is greased, for example by a construction company seeking the contract for a major government project.

Decision tables

A good example is the following table of the performance of three categories of stocks and shares under boom, steady and slump market conditions.

	Boom (a)	Steady (b)	Slump (c)
Gilt edged (x)	5 %	5	5
Speculative (y)	20	0	-10
Unit trusts (z)	10	5	0

What then is the best mix of shares to buy?

The *deterministic solution* is as follows. For a 10 year cycle time in business conditions assume $a = 1$, $b = 6$ and $c = 3$ years. Then the profit (%) from each of the three share types is:

$$x: \; 5 + 30 + 15 = 50$$
$$y: \; 20 - 30 = -10$$
$$z: \; 10 + 30 = 40$$

so that one should buy x or z but not y (unless boom conditions are assured for a known period).

Selection of the best solution from a number of alternatives should be done with a quantitative basis, preferably using a process of summing *weighted attributes.*

A good example is the task of selecting the 'best' of three candidates Tom, Dick and Harry, for a job using the *decision table* of Table 24.1.

Here five attributes: qualifications, experience (relevant), age (or total experience), impression made at interview and strength of recommendations made by referees, are used and each of these is given a weight in the second column.

Then the three candidates are given a score out of ten for each attribute by each member of the selection panel and the results averaged (to the nearest round number for simplicity here), giving the results shown in columns 3,4,5.

Table 24.1.
Job candidate selection using weighted attribute scores.

Attribute	Weight	Score			Weighted score		
		Tom	Dick	Harry	Tom	Dick	Harry
Qualific-ations	2	8	5	3	16	10	6
Experience	3	5	7	6	15	21	18
Age	1	5	5	8	5	5	8
Interview	2	3	5	8	6	10	16
Referees	1	5	5	5	5	5	5
Total					46	51	53

Finally, these scores are multiplied by the weights, giving the results of columns 6, 7, 8 and these figures are summed to give the totals shown.

The final result indicates Harry as the best candidate.

In practice, however, it is best to include other considerations such as:

[1] Who top scored in the most important attributes?

[2] If the candidate is an existing employee (in another position) has there been any bias?

In this sort of analysis the choice of attributes is crucial, as is their weighting, so that such factors can also be reviewed before making a final decision.

Job seekers would do well, of course, to be aware of the decision-making process illustrated in Table 24.1, for example making a special effort to emphasize their previous work experience, especially *relevant* work experience, and also such factors as the *breadth,* 'quality' and *duration* of their work history, putting more emphasis on 'quality rather than quantity' of their qualifications and experience if they are younger applicants.

Decision trees

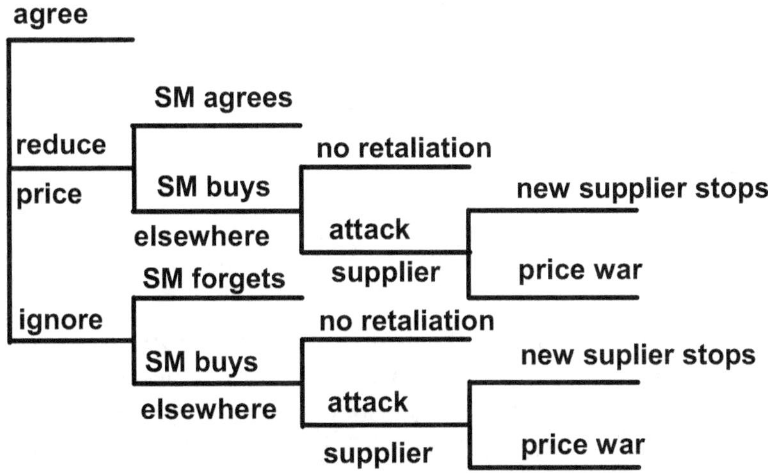

Figure 24.1. Example of a decision tree.

Decision trees are a useful way of depicting business strategies. A simple example is that of a manufacturer asked by a supermarket chain to make a 'home brand' version of its product, a decision tree for which is shown in Figure 24.1.

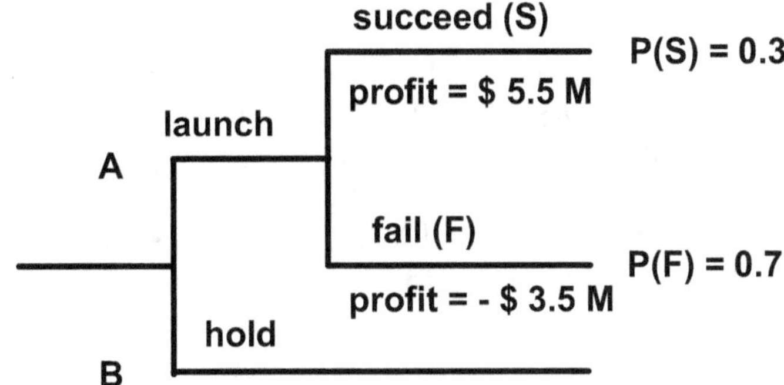

Figure 24.2. Decision tree with probabilities and financial outcomes.

As another example Figure 24.2 considers the problem of deciding whether to launch a rocket at a certain time or not, attaching probabilities and profit figures to the decision tree.

Then the Expected Monetary Value (EMV) of a launch is 0.3(5.5) - 0.7(3.5) = - \$0.8M so we should decide to hold.

With more optimistic figures, for example $P(S) = 0.7$ and $P(F) = 0.3$, the EMV of **A** is \$2.85M and the launch decision is much more favourable, though perhaps still not certain.

Conclusion

The decision making processes discussed in the foregoing chapter can improve one's chances of a more successful and happier life.

Decision trees, especially if they have probabilities and costs attached, are useful tools in the decision making process. Decision tables are also useful, especially if they have weighted quantities to enable a total score to be given to the alternatives under consideration.

Mohr's Laws of Decisions are for the most part rudimentary, but nonetheless worth note. 'Don't rush', for example is very important and the basis of the cliché: *Err in haste, repent at leisure,* people regretting serious mistakes often, of course, suffering from depression as a result.

Similarly, getting a second (if not more) opinion and 'sleeping on it' are, of course, important.

In dealing with enthusiastic and 'pushy' sales persons, for example, one must be very careful, and trying to sell or buy a house can be a nightmare for 'ordinary' people. Auctions, in particular, cruelly force first home buyers to compete with experienced investors in a ridiculously hasty 'sidewalk show', often pressuring them into paying too high a price.

In such situations, of course, they need to have planned carefully in what area they want to live, how much they can afford to pay, what is a fair price they can limit themselves to paying, of course getting as much advice from friends or independent professional advisors as possible.

☺☹☺☺☺☺☹☺☺☺☹☺☺☺☹☺☺☹

Chapter 25

CONCLUSIONS

He who does not hope to win has already lost.
José Juaquin Olmedo, (1780-1847), attrib.

True hope is swift, and flies with swallows' wings.
William Shakespeare, *Richard III,* act 5, sc. 2, 1.23 (1592-3).

Mental health

Mental illness can be caused by events that can occur in any person's life, for example:

- ➢ Stress-related conditions.
- ➢ Unemployment.
- ➢ Retirement.
- ➢ Bereavement.
- ➢ Child abuse.
- ➢ Marriage breakdown.
- ➢ Alcoholism or drug addiction.

Being diagnosed with a mental illness such as depression can have negative affects upon a person both:
Externally: withdrawal of friends, relatives, neighbours and employers.
Internally: feelings of rejection, loneliness and depression.

People suffering from mental illness, therefore, should be encouraged to take a optimistic view that envisages them overcoming their problems and leading healthy, successful life.

Positivity to improve life

Taking a more positive, optimistic outlook is one of the keys to success, whereas negative-minded people tend to say: "It won't work" etcetera to most propositions and ideas.

The following table gives some examples of how to turn negative thinking into positive thinking, including examples suggested by Kemp (2014).

Table 25.1. Turning negativity into positivity

Negative self-talk	Positive self-talk
I've never done it before.	It's a chance to learn something.
It's too hard.	I'll try and make it easier.
I don't have the time.	I'll try and fit it into my plans.
I'm too tired.	I'll try and make the effort.
It won't work.	Let's try anyway.
It's too radical a change.	So much the better
Nobody talks to me.	I'll keep trying.

The bottom line here is that it is often best 'to give it a try' when it comes to things that might improves one's life at home or in the workplace.

Optimism improves health

A team of psychologists, having done preliminary experiments with rats that showed the 'helplessness' weakened the body, studied 120 men who had had a first heart attack (Kemp, 2014).

The interviewed the men extensively to rate their optimism, counting the "because" statements they used to explain events in their lives. They found that none of the usual risk factors such as blood pressure, cholesterol levels, or how extensive the damage from the first heart attack was, predicted death, but that "only the men's level of optimism eight and a half years earlier predicted a second heart attack."

Of the 16 most pessimistic men, 15 died, whereas of the 16 most optimistic men, only 5 died.

The results of this a study of 999 people aged from 65 to 85 which began in 1991 in the Netherlands.

The meta-study "Optimism and Physical Health" analyzed 83 separate studies of the relationship between optimism and physical health, 18 of which involved 2,858 patients and their cancer history. The results gave "robust" support to the notion that more optimistic people had better cancer outcomes (Kemp, 2014).

A recent German study that 'priming' of people to increase their confidence resulted in a 35% better chance of their succeeding (ABC2 TV news report, ^PM, 16/6/2018).

The bottom line here, of course, is that not only will optimism improve quality of life, and the likelihood of success in life, but it also improves both mental and physical health.

Slow down, don't overstress

Cheryl Richardson suggest that often we should "slow down to succeed", allowing ourselves regular 'downtime' because we "all need a holiday from thinking too much", and try to lessen the impact of things in life that we find stressful and worrying (Richardson, 1998).

The Yerkes-Dodson law of arousal suggests that there is an optimum stress level at which we perform best, and to be *in the zone* for a purely intellectual activity such as reading a book we need only a low stress level, to be in the zone for activities that combine physical and intellectual performance a medium stress level is needed, whilst purely physical activities may involve higher stress levels, if they are very competitive *fight or flight* hormones sometimes having negative effects such as shrinking the hippocampus, reducing self-control, memory function, and emotional regulation.

Perseverance needed for success

Angela Duckworth, believing that talent was overrated as the main factor for success, proposed that one should be both talented and hardworking for best results, summarizing this as (Duckworth, 2016):

1. Talent x *effort* = skill
2. Skill x *effort* = achievement

Becoming a leader

In his book *On Becoming a Leader* Warren Bennis says that becoming a leader involves (Bennis, 1989):

- Curiosity and continuous learning.
- A compelling vision.
- The ability to communicate that vision.
- Being prepared to take a risk.
- Personal integrity: maturity, open to criticism etc.
- Allowing time to think and plan.
- Seeking success in small increments, not one 'big rush'.

One also requires, of course, some of the other key attributes discussed in the present book, including optimism, perseverance, patience and wisdom (Gracian, 1647).

Money and wealth

Mohr's Law of Capitalism was discussed in Chapter 12, being of a hierarchical nature and thus leading to an exponential result, explaining how in capitalism the rich get richer, and the poor get poorer, which has been the case throughout most of the world for most of history, and certainly in the last decade or more also.

The pigs in Orwell's *Animal Farm* are the fat capitalists, of course, but in the 2017 book *Success: The Psychology of Achievement,* it is claimed that whilst US gross GNP tripled from between 1947 to 1998, life satisfaction remained approximately constant, in line with clichés such as *money isn't everything.*

Self-assessment

Table 25.2. Daily record of progress etc.

Item	Results	Action needed
Progress	What achieved?	New goals?
Affect on others	Positive?	Any regrets?
Reputation	Increase?	Anything needing fix?
Support	Who supported me?	Who else might?
Supporting others	People I helped.	Who should I help?
Time	Did I waste time?	Avoid next time
Problems solved	What fixed?	What needs fixing?
Skills, connections etc.	Increased?	What needs increase?
Personal life	OK?	New goals?

Accurate self-assessment is, of course, very important in helping pinpoint problems, and in solving them, and Tables 10.1 and 23.1 are examples of such self-assessment, whilst the expectancy-value and information integration methods of attitude evaluation may also be useful in this context.

The 2017 book *Success: The Psychology of Achievement* gives a "daily diary" which includes such items as those shown in Table 25.2 [this need only be done weekly or monthly] shown on the following page.

In assessing just about anything, and any aspect of life, Mohr's Metrology, which is the 10th law of Mohronism, and which is briefly outlined in the following section, is also useful (Mohr & Fear, 2015; Mohr et al., 2018d).

Mohr's Metrology

This requires a little elaboration. It asserts that all human traits can be measured. Madness, for example, is not a black and white thing, and we should be given a score, though this may vary a little according to such factors as the weather and countless others that hardly need mention.

For this law one can use the **Mohr Scale**, noting that a score of 10 is not possible as perfect madness, for example, would surely be rapidly terminal. Furthermore a score of zero is not possible as perfect sanity would surely constitute insanity.

In the case of general health, or how much alive one is, 0 would be dead (not a valid health score), whilst 10 would be too good to be true (also not a valid health score).

Hence the Mohr Scale is 1 - 9, and the median score is the sum of the possible scores divided by the number of possible scores, that is 45/9 = 5. This is the median score with four possible scores above and below it. With this score you don't pass or fail but are borderline.

The Mohr scale is also useful in the study of *ethics* where the questions of what is 'right' or 'good' are put, quickly followed by the question: "how good?" For this purpose the Mohr scale provides a set of ordinal numbers where, for example, 9 is the maximum goodness (10 would be too good to be true).

For those suffering from depression it is important to realize that depression is a normal part of life and can be expected to occur as a result of accidents, injury, financial loss, or bereavement. It is also important for those who suffer from major, chronic or manic depression to realize, perhaps with the help from relatives and friends, that their depression is excessive and that advice, help and treatment should be considered.

Drugs for depression

The two-part UK TV program *The Doctor Who Took Kids Off Drugs* pointed out that in the UK the number of prescriptions of anti-depressant drugs for children increased from 30,000 in 2005 to 58,000 in 2015, but that an Oxford study had found that only one of 14 anti-depressant drugs (the SSRI Prozac) was more effective than a placebo sugar pill.

The presenter introduced a 15-year-old girl who suffered from depression and anxiety, finding it difficult to cope with crowded classrooms at school, and whose anti-depressant dosage had been increased from 50 mg daily to 100 mg, and then to 125 mg daily.

As an alternative therapy he introduced her to 'wilderness therapy' in which groups of young people were led on expeditions through the countryside, this having become an "accepted therapy" for young people in the US.

A University study found that 85% of young people who had undertaken wilderness therapy had progressed in their education and then into the workplace.

After 3 days, however, the girl attempted suicide, but nevertheless wanted to continue with wilderness therapy and, after another 3 weeks of it began to overcome her fear of crowds when taken shopping in a large shopping centre.

Another 16 year-old girl discussed had had a severe reaction to Prozac involving shaking and then a suicide attempt.

Nine months later she was given Sentraline, a drug prescribed to 40% of young people with depression in the UK, and after 11 days she committed suicide.

Another popular drug, Seroxat, which the raw data of trials had suggested to be effective, was found by a further study to be of doubtful effectiveness and to be unsafe, involving a significant risk of suicide. All trials of the drug showed that, overall, it was less effective than placebo and did more harm than good. It was therefore banned from prescription to people less than 18, and the manufacturer fined 3 billion dollars.

The bottom line here, of course, that we should be wary of the great growth in the use of prescription drugs for depression, anxiety and like issues, and consider alternative treatments such as relaxation, meditation, group therapy etc. to at least reduce, if not eliminate, dependence on psychiatric drugs.

Conclusions

There are many things one can do to improve mental health and wellbeing, including:
  - Sound diet.
  - Regular exercise.
  - Getting plenty of sleep.
  - Allowing plenty of quite time for relaxation.
  - Spending time with friends and family.
  - Sharing feelings with others.
  - Discussing problems with others.
  - Having regular and enjoyable recreational activities.
  - Volunteering and helping others.
  - Working hard to eliminate any bad habits.

For best results one must, of course, tackle life and its occasional problems with the inter-related personal characteristics and behaviours:

- ➢ Self-esteem.
- ➢ Self-confidence.
- ➢ Self-reliance.
- ➢ Self-belief.
- ➢ Self-regulation or control.
- ➢ Self-assessment in similar fashion to the Expectation-Value and Information Integration models of attitude formation and assessment.
- ➢ Realistic goal-setting.
- ➢ Support from friends etc. with problems, and in achieving one's goals.

Then, if one has self-confidence, achievable goals etc., one is much more likely to have a more successful and happier life.

One bottom line, trivial as it may seem, is that, as Macy emphasizes (Macy, 2015):

Never quit . . . except when you should quit.

When professional help is needed, for example, after an extreme episode of anxiety or depression, then prescription drugs should only be used for as short a term as practical.

Then, in addition one should tackle any 'mental issues' with determination and thought, enlisting help from family and friends, and considering alternative treatments such as relaxation therapies, meditation techniques, and group therapies involving talk sessions and/or exercise.

Appendix A

THE MOHR PSYCHOLOGICAL INVENTORY

> *Considered in its entirety, psychoanalysis won't do.*
> *It's an end product, moreover, like a dinosaur or a zeppelin;*
> *no better theory can ever be erected on its ruins,*
> *which will remain forever one of the saddest and strangest*
> *of all landmarks in the history of twentieth-century thought.*
> Sir Peter Medawar, *The Hope of Progress*,
> "Further Comments on Psychoanalysis" (1972).

Introduction

The Science of psychology is still relatively new, in broad historical terms, and still in a relatively primitive state.

Freud's division of personality into just three basic components, the id, ego, and superego, for example, is somewhat simplistic. In addition, his obsession with sex many people find questionable, if not somewhat psychotic.

Similarly, Jung's obsession with dreams, seems somewhat psychotic, as dreams generally are somewhat random in nature and thus of little importance. Nightmares, more common in young children, may sometimes have some real meaning in terms of fears etc. that they may have, for example, of ghosts etc. that they have heard of in 'fairy tales'. Generally, however, dreams are a minor issue in relation to the totality of the human psyche.

Eysenck's classification of people as extroverts, introverts, neurotic, and psychotic is of some use, but limited in scope, as there must in reality be far more 'types' of human personality.

The type A, B and C personality classification has, however, proved popular, type A corresponding approximately to psychopath.

In contrast, Frankl's "logotherapy" is an absurdly overly simplistic idea in contrast the complexity of the human psyche.

Herewith therefore, is the 'Mohr Psychological Inventory' (MPI), which seeks to give a modestly detailed view of the contents and workings of a person's mind (Mohr, 2018f).

The Mohr Psychological Inventory

The Mohr Psychological Inventory (MPI) divides the human mind and its workings into circa 20 categories, some of which can be evaluated and given a score for a particular individual, scores with negative connotations in some categories perhaps being indicative of mental health problems.

In a somewhat logical order, these categories are:

1. *Basic animal instincts.*
These include basic needs for survival such as for food, and shelter, basic hormonal 'urges' such as those for sex, and 'fight or flight', and basic 'societal' practices such as pairing for breeding purposes and thereafter, and living in groups (tribalism).

2. *Basic identity.*
One's age, sex (M or F), skin colour (B or W etc.), other key physical characteristics such as height, weight, hair colour, 'figure', baldness etc. Also, where one was born (town, country etc.), and key characteristics of one's family (size, wealth etc.).

3. *Childhood and education.*
Place in family one grew up in (e.g. youngest child), childhood hobbies etc., education and training: schools etc. attended, marks obtained in exams, qualifications obtained.

4. *Life history.*

Childhood (as in 3) + past jobs, old friends, old hobbies and pastimes, past beliefs and religions etc.

5. *Present life role.*

Job/occupation (work, unemployed, disabled, retired etc.), rank or 'status' (manager, front line worker etc.), family (wife, children etc.), home and key possessions such as car(s) etc.

6. *Memories.*

(a) Positive memories: good marks in exams, praise, prizes, winning at sports etc., good friends, good experiences such as happy holidays.

(b) Negative memories: illnesses, accidents, injuries, bad marks in exams, disputes/fights/arguments, losses (money, deaths in family etc.)

7. *Personality.*

Extraverted or introverted, happy or depressed, neurotic or psychotic etc. + self-perceived effect of past on personality [noting that up to 50% of personality may be genetic (Galton, 2001), and much of the rest from imitative and social learning].

8. *Beliefs.*

Religious, political, and 'societal' beliefs of what is 'right or wrong' etc., these beliefs constituting our 'conscience' or moral and ethical principles.

9. *Likes and dislikes* (including prejudices).

(a) Likes, e.g. dogs or cats, fast food such as pizza, certain types of music etc.

(b) Dislikes, e.g. people of a certain religion, ethnicity or sexual persuasion/inclination, certain foods (for example sausages or 'mystery bags') etc.

10. *Habits.*

Sleep, diet, and exercise routines. Hobbies and routine recreational activities, including TV, music, reading etc. Consumption of 'fast food', alcohol, prescribed drugs, and 'recreational' drugs.

11. *Social life.*
Friends and family one meets regularly, active membership of sporting clubs and other organizations (religious, political, etc.), restaurants or pubs/clubs attended regularly etc.

12. *Goals.*
Things one hopes to achieve in life, for example promotion, more money, better house, better health, lose weight etc.

13. *Worries.*
Things one is worried about, e.g. unhappy with job and pay, losing job, cost of living, paying off a mortgage, health etc.

14. *Fears.*
Real and imagined things that scare one, e.g. spiders, heights, ghosts etc.

15. *Behaviour.*
Bossy, controlling, argumentative etc., shy/retiring, sexual habits, e.g. sexual identity & preferences, or sexual promiscuity.

16. *Appearance.*
e.g. unkempt, unclean, sad looking, hunched body, fidgeting etc.

17. *Mood.*
e.g. short-tempered and impatient, excitable, easily angered, disagreeable, depressed etc.

18. *Awareness.*
Accuracy of perception of surroundings, current events etc.

19. *Communication.*
Comprehension, ability to communicate effectively etc.

20. *Thinking skills and IQ.*
Responses to ideas and suggestions, e.g. responding with good alternative ideas quickly is suggestive of intelligence (a formal IQ test can, of course, also be used).

21. *Inner thoughts.*
Inner thoughts kept private, such as dislike, hatred or envy of certain people, or thoughts of self-harm or suicide.

22. *Health.*

(a) Physical: e.g. any physical problems/ailments that may affect mental health such as chronic heart disease.

(b) Mental: neural system ailments such as Alzheimer's disease, mental retardation etc.

(c) Psychological: anxiety, high levels of psychopathy (bossiness, dishonesty etc.) etc.

Category 22 is largely of a summary nature and issues in this category may be evident from examination of some of the other categories.

High levels of undesirable traits in one or more of these inventory categories may be indicative of a mental health problem, for example (see also Chapter 21 & Table 21.1 etc.):

> ➢ Traumatic memories of bad experiences in 6(b) may be suggestive of *PTSD*.
> ➢ High levels of *depression* in 7 are, of course, suggestive of mental illness.
> ➢ High levels of concern about a wide range of issues in 13 and/or 14 are suggestive of an *anxiety* disorder.
> ➢ High levels of ambition in 12 and bossiness and shortness of temper in 17 are suggestive of *psychopathy*.
> ➢ Low levels of response and 19 and 20 are suggestive of *low intelligence*, or in extreme cases *mental retardation*.
> ➢ Thoughts of *suicide* in 21, especially if frequent, may be indicative of a need for supportive counselling etc.

Conclusion

The MPI can be used as a guide to examining a person's psyche, and perhaps identifying any psychological issues and problems that may be indicative of a mental health problem or illness. Then one should follow Mohr's Metrology and give the issue a score from 0 to 9 to prevent people assuming the person is a 'full blown' case of it, and to encourage them to work towards reducing this score. For simplicity, however, most people would probably prefer to score such issues as anxiety from 0 to 10, one would hope realizing that some degree of anxiety is normal and required for survival.

A smaller animal crossing an empty field, for example, would need to be a little anxious and look hither and thither to see if any larger animals of prey such as lions etc. might be around and thus a potential threat.

Similarly, whilst introversion is viewed negatively, people who talk and gossip too much should be viewed more negatively, suggesting a scale for introversion/extroversion.

As noted in the penultimate section of Chapter 21, entitled *Labelling and high rate of misdiagnoses*, some studies find incorrect diagnosis of mental illness is all too frequent, and the success rate in diagnosis of just 'some sort of mental illness', and not which particular mental illnesses the person has, is quite poor.

A 2-episode program on Australia's SBS1 TV channel aired from 8.30 to 9.30 PM on the 11th and 18th of October 2018 had 3 very experienced psychologists assess 10 people, 5 of whom had suffered from, and been diagnosed with, a mental illness several years earlier. The 'experts' only identified one of the 5 people with mental illness, getting it wrong with the other 9 people of the study, i.e., they got only 1/10, so we should all be wary of psych. diagnoses these days, driven as they are by ignorance, the relatively primitive state of the science of psychology and the practice of psychiatry, and the greed of 'Big Pharma' which, for example only, has resulted in far too many young children being unfairly diagnosed with ADHD and put on drugs for years, if not life.

Mental health issues, however, do seem to be a growing problem. In recent decades asylums were greatly reduced in number to 'deinstitutionalise' mental health systems in the West. Now, however, "more than 600 Victorians die annually from suicide. They don't have terminal illnesses and their deaths are therefore preventable" (Patrick McGorry, *Our mental breakdown,* The Age, Thursday, October 25, 2018).

☺☻☹☺☻☹☺☻☹☺☻☹☺☺☻☹

Appendix B

CASE STUDIES

*The psychological observer ought to be more agile
than the tightrope dancer in order to insinuate himself
under the skin of other people,* Soren Kierkegaard,
The Concept of Dread, 1844 (tr. W. Lowrie, 1957).

Lewis Wolpert

In Lewis Wolpert's book *Malignant Sadness* (Wolpert, 1999) the Introduction begins with:

It was the worst experience of my life. More terrible even than watching my wife die of cancer. I am ashamed to admit that my depression felt worse than her death but it is true. I was in a state that bears no resemblance to anything I had experienced before. I was not just feeling very low, depressed in the commonly used sense of the word. I was seriously ill. I was totally self-involved, negative and thought about suicide most of the time. I could not think properly, let alone work, and wanted to remain curled up in bed all day.

He then adds that his skin felt like it was "on fire" and he developed "uncontrollable twitches". He suffered extreme anxiety, needed sleeping pills to sleep for just a few hours, and had a "strong fear" that he would go mad.

Previously when he had occasional mild depressions he would just go jogging, but this time he sought the help of a psychiatrist and was hospitalized. There he says his room had a large window which he felt like smashing with a chair and jumping from the seventh floor, but realized he would be too scared to jump.

At home he hoarded his sleeping pills and heart pills but was not sure they would work. He also imagined running across the room and crashing his head through the pane glass in the door and thus cutting his throat.

Fortunately, his wife was able to discourage his suicidal thoughts by pointing out the "intolerable" effect it would have on her and their children.

Wolpert makes the important point that:

Memory plays an important role in depression and there is preferential access to memories of negative events.

He also notes that:

Early adverse experiences are linked to a current negative evaluation of one's self.

To emphasize how serious depression can be, and how important it is to treat it, he quotes Elizabeth Wurtzel (Wurtzel, 1994):

But you won't even notice it coming on, thinking that it is somehow normal, something about getting older, about turning eight or turning twelve or turning fifteen, and then one day you realize that your entire life is just awful, not worth living, a horror and a black blot on the white terrain of human existence. One morning you wake up afraid you are going to live . . .

That's the one thing I want to make clear about depression: it's got nothing at all to do with life. In the course of life, there is sadness and pain and sorrow, all of which, in their right time and season, are normal – unpleasant, but normal. Depression is in an altogether different zone because it involves a complete absence: absence of affect, absence of feeling, absence of response, absence of interest. The pain you feel in the course of a major clinical depression is an attempt on nature's part (nature, after all, abhors a vacuum) to fill up an empty space. But for all intents and purposes, the deeply depressed are just the walking, waking dead.

Todd Latarette

In early November 2018 BBC's international radio news played an interview with American actor Todd Latarette.

Todd, who had had bit parts in movies, had shown early signs of mental health issues at only 19.

At age 31 he was diagnosed with full-blown bipolar disorder after a suicide attempt, and hospitalized for two weeks.

In hypomanic episodes he experienced elevated moods and would do "unhealthy" but not life-threatening things.

His mood swings involved "cycling" on an hourly or daily basis. During his "upswings" he felt he didn't need his medications, the side-effects of which he wished to avoid.

One day, having stopped taking his medications when in a 'high', he took a large knife and severed both his hands by plunging them into the path of a circular saw. When he was taken to hospital one hand had to be amputated, along with a part of his forearm.

He said that he had planned this self-inflicted harm "meticulously" for two days while having a "mixed psychotic episode".

Since that time, and now aged 48, he still has flashbacks of this terrible episode daily, also suffering 'phantom pains' in the missing hand and forearm, these being exacerbated by one of his part-time jobs as a carpenter. His medications, however, help him cope with such episodes.

Geoff

On 8th November 2018 ABC News Radio discussed Todd Latarette's case, inviting callers to discuss their cases (of bipolar disorder). One caller, Geoff, said that he had wanted to commit suicide and had attempted it once. He said his medications were a "bummer" and slowed him down, but that if he didn't take them he had difficulty sleeping. He said that he had had two jobs, but now couldn't work.

Anonymous (name not provided)

The book *Mastering Bipolar Disorder* (Eyers & Parker, 2008) in Chapter 8 gives the following account:

In March last year, aged thirty-six, my life seemed to have hit rock bottom when I became psychotic for the first time in my life. It took two brief hospital admissions in two months to reach a proper diagnosis of Bipolar I Disorder. Luckily, the psychosis only lasted a few days. At first there was the initial shock of 'having' and 'accepting' the mental condition, but I was truly 'relieved' to finally understand what was going on with me and that 'bipolar is treatable'.

A psychiatrist prescribed 500 mg sodium valproate twice daily to manage the patient's highs. Side-effects including slight hair loss and weight gain, but with dosage reduction weight was normalized and the patient began exercising regularly.

After a year off work the sufferer was able to begin some casual work, showing some prospect of returning to normal life eventually, reflecting:

There were moments I spent in a state of mania that were quite blissful where I felt so connected with the earth and evolved and knowledgeable, and not really needing to be in a human form. The only problem was – it took a miserable three or four days of not being able to sleep, nightmares, stress, despair, exhaustion and suicidal depression to get me there! I can remember times of mania when I'd talked to my friends with such loud conviction and confidence that after a while my brain just physically hurt! Hence, I believe from my experience that creative surges from elevation do ultimately lead to burn-out. It isn't any wonder why people who are manic, and untreated, self-medicate with alcohol or any drug to avoid the burn-out feeling. It's just too taxing on the body!

People suffering anxiety

As noted in Chapter 18, people suffering from depression often suffer from anxiety as well.

Australia's SBS TV Channel 3's regular program *Insight* on the 6th of November 2018 had several people who suffered from anxiety in its live audience.

They described some anxiety and panic attacks as "crippling", "feeling like a heart attack", being "like a tsunami", making them "unable to concentrate" on their work, involving "weird feelings" and "bad thoughts", one person saying of one attack: *I didn't think I would get through it.*

One person noted that "triggers" for a panic attack included unfamiliar situations, saying that: *anxiety never goes away for an anxiety sufferer.*

In one case, the person had boarded a plane ready to take off, but after sudden panic attack they left the aircraft and went home, then not wanting to leave the house, despite having previously been "sociable" person.

One person had had to take several weeks off work and seek professional help after a panic attack. Then, only two days after returning to work, they another panic attack.

Most reported that they had found medication helpful.

Two said that they had found CBT (Cognitive Behaviour Therapy – see Chapter 22) helpful, three others saying that they had found "Acceptance Behaviour Therapy" (ACT) helpful, one saying that ACT belong to the "family of CBT".

One person noted that CBT involved 'pausing' to think and deal "realistically" with any anxiety-based concerns.

Another, who suffered from Generalized Anxiety Disorder involving various levels of anxiety, said that she had found that ACT helped "immensely" by focusing on positives and not negatives and worries.

One had found 'mindfulness' techniques helpful, but another had not found mindfulness and meditation techniques helpful.

☺ ☺ ☹ ☹ ☺ ☺ ☹ ☺ ☺ ☺ ☹ ☺ ☺ ☺ ☹ ☺ ☺ ☹

REFERENCES

Anthony, R (Dr), *The Ultimate Secrets of Total Self-Confidence, Master the Simple Step-by-step principles and change your life,* John Blake, London (2010).

American Psychiatric Association, *American Psychiatric Association Diagnostic and Statistic Manual of Mental Disorders,* 4th ed., Washington D.C. (1994).

Arkowitz H, Miller WR, Rollnick S, *Motivational Interviewing in The Treatment of Psychological Problems,* The Guilford Press, New York (2015).

Atkinson RC, Shiffrin RM, Human memory: A proposed system and its control processes. RW Spence, JT Spence (eds), *The Psychology of Learning and Motivation, Vol. 2,* Academic Press, New York (1968).

Atrens D, Curthoys I, *The Neurosciences and Behaviour: An Introduction,* 2nd edn, Academic Press, Sydney (1982).

Ben-Menashe A, *Profits of War: The Sensational Story of the World-Wide Arms Conspiracy,* Allen & Unwin, Sydney (1992).

Bennis, Warren, *On Becoming a Leader* (1989).

Blanchard, Kenneth; Johnson, Spencer, *The One Minute Manager* (1981).

Burns, David D, *Feeling Good: The New Mood Therapy* (1980).

Butler-Bowden, Tom, *50 Psychology Classics,* 2nd edition, Nicholas Brealey Publishing, London (2017).

Butler-Bowden, Tom, *50 Success Classics,* 2nd edition, Nicholas Brealey Publishing, London (2017b).

References

Cantwell A, *The Cancer Microbe,* Aries Rising Press, LA (1990).

Carter P, *IQ and Psychometric Tests* 2nd edn, Kogan Page, London (2007).

Collins AM, Quillian MR, Retrieval time from semantic memory, *Journal of Verbal Learning and Verbal Behaviour,* 8 (1969) 240-247.

Cozolino L, *The Neuroscience of Psychotherapy, Building and Rebuilding the Human Brain,* W.W. Norton & Co., NY (2002).

Craughwell, Thomas J, *How Smart Are You?, Test Your IQ,* Black Dog & Leventhal, New York NY (2012).

Davies B, *An Introduction to Clinical Psychiatry,* Melbourne University Press, Melbourne (1971).

Delgado JMR, *Physical Control of the Mind: Towards a Psychocivilized Society,* Colophon Books (Harper & Row), New York (1971).

DePaulo Jr, J. Raymon, *Understanding Depression: What We Know and What You Can Do About It,* John Wiley & Sons, New York (2002).

Duckworth, Angela, *Grit: The Power of Passion and Perseverance* (2016).

Dweck, Carol, *Mindset: The New Psychology of Success* (2006).

Eagly AH, Chaiken S, *The Psychology of Attitudes,* Harcourt Brace Jovanovich, Orlando FA (1993).

Egerton Eastwick RW (ed.), *The Oracle Encyclopaedia,* George Newnes, London (1896).

Eyers, Kerrie & Parker, Gordon, *Mastering Bipolar Disorder: An insider's guide to managing mood swings and finding balance,* Allen & Unwin, Crows Nest, NSW (2008).

Eysenck HJ, Cancer, personality and stress: Prediction and prevention, *Advances in Behaviour Research and Therapy,* 16, 167 – 215 (1994).

Firshein R, *The Neutraceutical Revolution,* Riverhead Books, New York (1998).

Forbes HD, *Ethnic Conflict: Commerce, Culture, and the Contact Hypothesis,* Yale University Press, New Haven (1997).

Foss DJ, Hakes DT, *Psycholinguistics: An Introduction to the Psychology of Language,* Prentice-Hall, Englewood Cliffs NJ (1978).

Frankl, Viktor, *The Will to Meaning: Foundations and Applications of Logotherapy* (1969).

Friedman M, Rosenman RH, *Association of specific overt behaviour pattern with blood cardiovascular findings, Journal of the American Medical Assocation,* 169, 1286 (1959).

Galton D, *In Our Own Image, Eugenics and the Genetic Modification of People*, Little Brown & Co, London (2001).

Gillespie, David, *Taming Toxic People, The science of identifying & dealing with psychopaths at work & at home,* Pan MacMillan Australia, Sydney (2017).

Gladwell, Malcolm, *Outliers: The Story of Success* (2008).

Goodall (van Lawick-Goodall) J, *In the Shadow of Man,* Houghton-Mifflin, Boston (1971).

Govoni N, Eng R, Morton G, *Promotional Management: Issues and Perspectives,* Prentice-Hall, Englewood Cliffs NJ (1988).

Gracian, Baltasar, *The Art of Worldly Wisdom* (1647).

Grivas, John, and Carter, Linda, *Psychology for the VCE Student: Units 1 and 2*, 4th edn, Jacaranda Press/John Wiley & Sons, Milton QLD (2005).

Holford C, *New Optimum Nutrition For The Mind,* Basic Health, Laguna Beach CA (2009).

Holford C, Colson D, *Optimum Nutrition For Your Child,* Piatkus, London (2008).

Insight vol. 7, part 91, Marshall Cavendish, London (1982).

Jencks C, Smith M, Acland H, Bane MJ, Cohen D, Gintis H, Heyns B, Michelson S, *Inequality: A Reassessment of the Effect of Family and Schooling in America,* Penguin, Harmondsworth (1975).

Jonas G, Into the brain, *New Yorker,* July 1, 1974, p 57.

Kassin S, *Psychology,* 4th edn, Prentice-Hall, Upper Saddle River, New Jersey (2004).

Kemp, Jurrian, *The Intelligent Optimist's Guide to Life: How to Find Health and Success in a World That's a Better Place Than You Think,* Berret-Koehler Publishers Inc., San Francisco (2014).

Krapp K, editor, *Psychologists & Their Theories for Students,* vol. 1: A-K, Thomson Gale, Farmington Hills, MI (2005).

Larsen RJ, Buss DM, *Personality Psychology, Domains of Knowledge About Human Nature,* McGraw-Hill, NY (2002).

Lieberman JA, *Shrinks, The Untold Story of Psychiatry,* Little Brown & Co, NY (2015).

Likert R, *New Patterns of Management,* McGraw-Hill, New York (1961).

Lindzey G, Hall CS, Thompson RF, *Psychology,* 2nd edn, Worth, New York (1978).

Lopez, Shane J, *Making Hope Happen, Create The Future You Want for Yourself and Others,* Atria, New York (2013).

Lynch G, Granger R, *Big Brain, The Origins and Future of Human Intelligence,* Palgrave Macmillan, Houndmills, Basingstoke (2008).

Mackintosh NJ, *IQ and Human Intelligence,* 2nd ed., Oxford University Press, Oxford (2011).

Macy, Travis, *The Ultra Mindset: An Endurance Champion's 8 Core Principles for Success in Business, Sports, and Life,* De Capo Press, Philadelphia PA (2015).

Mamonov V, *Control for life extension: A personalized holistic approach* (2001).

Marta, Suzy Yehl, *Healing the Hurt, Restoring the Hope*, Rodale, London (2004).

McGuire WJ, A syllogistic analysis of cognitive relationships, in *Attitude Organization And Change*, CI Hovland & MJ Rosenberg (eds.), Yale University Press, New Haven (1960).

Meadows DH, Meadows DL, Randers J, Behrens WW, *The Limits to Growth*, Pan, London (1974).

Miller, Nick, 'New hope of escaping the dark', *The Age*, 26 August, 2017.

Mohr GA, *The Finite Element Method for Solids, Fluids, and Optimization*, OUP Oxford (1992).

Mohr GA, *The Doomsday Calculation: The End of the Human Race*, Xlibris, Sydney (2012a).

Mohr GA, *The War of the Sexes: Women Are Getting On Top*, Xlibris, Sydney (2012b).

Mohr GA, *Curing Cancer & Heart Disease: Proven Ways to Combat Aging, Atherosclerosis & Cancer*, Xlibris, Sydney (2012c).

Mohr GA, *Heart Disease, Cancer & Aging: Proven Neutraceutical and Lifestyle Solutions*, Horizon Publishing Group, Sydney (2013a).

Mohr GA, *The Pretentious Persuaders: A Brief History & Science of Mass Persuasion*, 2nd edn, Horizon Publishing Group, Sydney (2013b).

Mohr GA, *The History & Psychology of Human Conflicts*, Horizon Publishing Group, Sydney (2014a).

Mohr GA, *Elementary Thinking for the 21st Century*, Xlibris, Sydney (2014b).

Mohr GA, Sinclair R, Fear E, *The Evolving Universe: Relativity, Redshift and Life From Space*, Xlibris, Sydney (2014).

Mohr GA, *The 8-Week+ Program to Reverse Cardiovascular Disease*, Book Venture, Ishpeming MI (2015).

Mohr GA, Fear E, *World Religions: The History, Psychology, Issues & Truth,* Xlibris, Sydney (2015).

Mohr GA, Fear E, Sinclair R, *World War 3: When & How Will It End?,* Inspiring Publishers, Canberra (2015b).

Mohr GA, Fear E, *The Brainwashed: From Consumer Zombies to Islamism and Jihad,* Inspiring Publishers, Canberra (2016).

Mohr GA, *The Scientific MBA,* 5th edn, *Balboa Press,* Bloomington IN (2017).

Mohr GA, Sinclair R, Fear R, *Human Intelligence, Learning & Behavior,* Inspiring Publishers, Canberra (2017).

Mohr GA, *The DIY Cardiovascular Cure: A Comprehensive Program to Reverse Atherosclerosis,* Amazon-Kindle (2018a).

Mohr GA, *Combating Cancer: Proven Neutraceutical & Lifestyle Solutions,* Amazon-Kindle (2018b).

Mohr GA, *The War of the Sexes: The Problems & the Solutions,* Amazon-Kindle (2018c).

Mohr GA, *Elementary Thinking for Modern Management,* Amazon-Kindle (2018d).

Mohr GA, *Mohr's Law of Hierarchies, and many other Mohr's Laws,* Amazon-Kindle (2018e).

Mohr GA, *The Psychology of Life: A practical introduction to psychology,* Amazon-Kindle (2018f).

Mohr GA, Mohr RS, Mohr PE, *The Psychology of Hope,* Balboa Press, Bloomington IN (2018).

Mohr GA, Mohr RS, Mohr PE, *New Theories of the Universe, Evolution and Relativity,* Amazon-Kindle (2018a).

Mohr GA, Mohr PE, Mohr RS, *The Population Explosion,* Amazon-Kindle (2018b).

Mohr GA, Mohr RS, Mohr PE, *Human Conflict: An Attitudinal Psychology Model,* Amazon-Kindle (2018c).

REFERENCES

Mohr GA, Mohr PE, Mohr RS, *World Religions: From Animism to Mohronism,* Amazon-Kindle (2018d).

Mohr GA, Mohr PE, Mohr RS, *Brainwashed Zombies: Religious, Political & Consumer Persuasion,* Amazon-Kindle (2018e).

Mohr GA, Mohr PE, Mohr RS, *The Psychology of Success: Keys to a successful and happier life,* Amazon-Kindle (2018f).

Morgan CT, King RA, Robinson NM, *Introduction to Psychology,* 6th edn, McGraw-Hill, Tokyo (1979).

Newcomb TM, Persistence and regression of changed attitudes, Journal of Sociological Issues 19 (1963) 3-14.

O'Guinn TC, Allen CT, Semenik RJ, *Advertising and Integrated Brand Promotion.* Thomson South-Western, Mason OH (2006).

Ostrander S, Schroeder L, *Superlearning,* Delacorte Press/Confucian Press, New York (1979).

Packard V, *The Waste Makers,* Pelican, Harmondsworth, London (1963).

Packard V, *The People Shapers,* Nelson, Melbourne (1978).

Penn, *Microtrends, The Small Forces Behind Today's Big Changes,* Allen Lane, London (2007).

Peter LJ, Hull R, *The Peter Principle,* Souvenir Press, London (1969).

Richardson, Cheryl, *Take Time for Your Life: A Seven-Step Program for Creating the Life You Want* (1998).

Ripps LJ, Schoben EJ, Smith EE, Semantic distance and the verification of semantic relations, *Journal of Verbal Learning and Verbal Behaviour,* 12 (1973) 203-210.

Robertson I, *Sociology,* 2nd edn, Worth, New York (1981).

Rogers, Carl, *On Becoming a Person: A Therapist's View of Psychotherapy* (1961).

Sampson A, *The Arms Bazaar,* Coronet Books, London (1977).

REFERENCES

Sargent M, *Drinking and Alcoholism in Australia: A Power Relations Theory,* Longman Cheshire, Melbourne (1979).

Schmidt-Nielsen K, *Animal Physiology: Adaptation and Environment,* 2nd edn, Cambridge University Press, Cambridge (1979),

Shaffer JW, Graves PL, Swank RT, Pearson TA, Clustering personality traits in youth and subsequent development of cancer among physicians, *Journal of Behavioural Medicine,* 10, 441-447 (1987).

Shealy CN (editor), *The Complete Illustrated Encyclopedia of Alternative Healing Therapies,* Element, Shaftesbury, Dorset (1999).

Solomon MR, *Consumer Behaviour: Buying, Having and Being,* Allyn and Bacon, Boston (1992).

Snyder, CR, *The Psychology of Hope, You Can Get Here From There,* Simon & Schuster, New York, NY (1994).

Sternberg RJ, *In Search of the Human Mind,* 2nd edn, Harcourt Brace College Publishers, Orlando FL (1998).

Sweeney MS, *Brain, The Complete Mind: How it Develops, How it Works, and How to Keep it Sharp,* National Geographic, Washington D.C. (2009).

Thomas, Keith (ed.), *The Oxford Book of Work,* Oxford University Press, Oxford (1999).

Thomas M, *As Used on the Famous Nelson Mandela, Underground Adventures in the Arms and Torture Trade,* Ebury Press, London (2006).

Thomas J, Hughes T, *You Don't Have to be Famous to Have Manic Depression: The Insider's Guide to Mental Health,* Michael Joseph, London (2006).

Trump, Donald, *The Way to the Top, The Best Business Advice I Ever Received,* Crown Business, New York, NY (2004).

Ungar G, Desidero DM, Parr W, Isolation, identification and synthesis of a specific behaviour inducing brain peptide, *Nature* 238 (1972) 198-202.

Vander AJ, Sherman JH, Luciano DS, *Human Physiology, The Mechanisms of Body Function,* 6th edn, McGraw-Hill, New York (1994).

van Lawick-Goodall, Jane, *In the Shadow of Man*, Houghton Mifflin, Boston (1971).

Vernon, PE, *Intelligence and Attainment Tests,* University of London Press, London (1960).

Walther DS, *Applied Kinesiology, Synopsis*, Systems DC, Pueblo CO (1988).

Weiss ML, Mann AE, *Human Biology and Behaviour, An Anthropological Perspective*, 2nd edn, Little Brown, Boston MA (1978).

Wolpert, Lewis, *Malignant Sadness: The Anatomy of Depression,* Faber & Faber, London (1999).

Wurtzel, Elizabeth, *Prozac Nation,* Riverhead, New York (1994).

Youngson RM, Schott I, *Medical Blunders,* Robinson, London (1996).

Zajonc RB, Attitudinal effects of mere exposure, *Journal of Personality and Social Psychology,* 9 (2, Pt. 2), 1-17 (1968).

☺ ☻ ☹ ☺ ☻ ☹ ☺ ☻ ☹ ☺ ☻ ☹ ☺ ☻ ☹

THE PSYCHOLOGY OF DEPRESSION

The book discusses depression and how it affects our lives:

- ➢ The human brain, memory, language and learning.
- ➢ Imitative and social learning, education, and *Real IQ*.
- ➢ The psychology of attitude formation and measurement.
- ➢ The psychology of habits.
- ➢ The importance of self-confidence, optimism and hope.
- ➢ The psychology of the workplace and hierarchical organizations.
- ➢ Home life and social life. Retirement and old age.
- ➢ Psychology and psychiatry. Personality.
- ➢ The psychology of depression. Bipolar disorders.
- ➢ The psychology of Conflict.
- ➢ Psychological assessment and treatment.
- ➢ Improving life. The Mohr Psychological Inventory (MPI).

G. A. Mohr did his PhD at Churchill College, Cambridge. He published circa 60 papers for 20 international journals and more than 30 books, including:

A Microcomputer Introduction to the Finite Element Method
Finite Elements for Solids, Fluids, and Optimization
The Pretentious Persuaders, A Brief History & Science of Mass Persuasion
Curing Cancer & Heart Disease
The Variant Virus, Introducing Secret Agent Simon Sinclair
The Doomsday Calculation: The End Of The Human Race
Heart Disease, Cancer, & Ageing: Proven Neutraceutical & Lifestyle Solutions
2045: A Remote Town Survives Global Holocaust
The History & Psychology of Human Conflict;   The War of the Sexes
Elementary Thinking for the 21st Century;   Mohr's Law of Hierarchies
The 8-Week+ Program to Reverse Cardiovascular Disease
The DIY Cardiovascular Cure;   Combating Cancer
Elementary Thinking for Modern Management;   The Scientific MBA
The Psychology of Life

Also with R.S. Mohr/Richard Sinclair & P.E. Mohr/Edwin Fear:

The Evolving Universe: Relativity, Redshift and Life from Space
World Religions: The History, Psychology, Issues & Truth
World War 3, When & How Will It End?
The Brainwashed, From Consumer Zombies to Islamic Jihad
Human Intelligence, Learning & Behaviour
New Theories of The Universe, Evolution, and Relativity
The Psychology of Hope;   The Population Explosion
Brainwashed Zombies: Religious, Political & Consumer Persuasion
Human Conflict: An Attitudinal Psychology Model
World Religions: From Animism to Mohronism;   The Psychology of Success

www.ingramcontent.com/pod-product-compliance
Lightning Source LLC
Chambersburg PA
CBHW061747250726
48657CB00001B/40